THE CASE FOR PARENTAL CHOICE

CATHOLIC SCHOOLS AND THE COMMON GOOD

Ernest Morrell and Nicole Garnett, *series editors*

Catholic Schools and the Common Good, a collaboration between Notre Dame's Institute for Educational Initiatives and the University of Notre Dame Press, is the first book series devoted to researching the largest private school system in the world. Volumes in this series provide both original research on Catholic schools specifically and comparative research on the effects of Catholic vs. other schooling sectors. The books in the series will focus on the the K–12 educational system, examining a wide variety of topics in order to understand trends and establish best practices in Catholic education in the United States and globally. Intended to provide practical advice and theoretical underpinnings, books in the series will provide useful information and ideas for Catholic educators and administrators.

THE CASE FOR
PARENTAL
CHOICE

God, Family, and Educational Liberty

JOHN E. COONS

Edited by
Nicole Stelle Garnett, Richard W. Garnett, and Ernest Morrell

University of Notre Dame Press
Notre Dame, Indiana

University of Notre Dame Press
Notre Dame, Indiana 46556
undpress.nd.edu

Copyright © 2023 by John E. Coons

Published in the United States of America

Library of Congress Control Number: 2022950295

ISBN: 978-0-268-20484-6 (Hardback)
ISBN: 978-0-268-20496-9 (WebPDF)
ISBN: 978-0-268-20483-9 (Epub)

CONTENTS

In June 2020, the U.S. Supreme Court held that the First Amendment's free exercise clause prohibits the government from excluding religious schools from school choice programs. The decision, *Espinoza v. Montana*, is momentous. Supporters of parental choice in education, including Jack Coons for more than half of a century, have long fought for the principle endorsed by Chief Justice John Roberts's majority opinion: preventing schools from accessing public resources *because they are religious* is unjust, born of bigotry, and ought to end. Their arguments have, at long last, prevailed. Countless children who would be best served by faith-based schools will benefit from the Court's decision, which clears away major legal and political hurdles to the expansion of parental choice.

Few voices have been as influential, for as long, in debates about American education policy as Jack Coons's. His steadfast, unrelenting, and clarion call for parental choice, reflected in these pages, and many, many more, is finally bearing fruit. The vast majority of American schoolchildren continue to attend public schools, but momentum for parental choice has accelerated exponentially in recent years. Today, thirty-one states, the District of Columbia, and Puerto Rico have publicly funded private-school-choice programs. These programs enable more than six-hundred thousand children to attend private and faith-based schools. And, forty-four states authorize public charter schools, which enroll more than 3.4 million children, or 7.2 percent of all public-school students. This dramatic expansion in the educational options available to families, especially disadvantaged ones, is the result of a complex array of political and legal factors. But no single factor has been more important than proponents' embrace of the argument that parental choice is, at its core, about opportunity, equality, and dignity rather than efficiency and competition. As Terry Moe has observed, "The modern arguments for vouchers have less to do with free markets than with . . . the commonsense notion that disadvantaged kids should never be forced to attend failing schools and that they should be given as many attractive options as possible."[1]

Jack Coons not only anticipated, but in many ways originated, that crucial shift in focus. Many of the essays republished here were written decades ago. Yet they presciently outlined, anticipated, and advocated policy reforms, including private-school choice and charter schools (see chapter 2's proposal for New Public Schools) years before these policies became a reality anywhere in the United States. Jack has been more than an advocate for parental choice, he has been its prophet. Throughout his long and distinguished career, Coons has argued that education policies, and especially parental choice policies, ought to focus on empowering the disadvantaged and marginalized, rather than on increasing standardized test scores. As he wrote in a seminal article reproduced here, "school choice is simple justice." It gives voice to the voiceless and power to the powerless. Jack's words echo today in the halls of state legislatures debating parental-choice programs, they are reflected on the faces of parents who gather at rallies demanding more for their children that our education system has given them to date, and they are now enshrined in the Supreme Court's First Amendment jurisprudence. They are powerful words, as the essays reproduced in this volume remind us all.

We are grateful to Jack Coons for his powerful words on behalf of families, especially those who are most vulnerable, and for the opportunity to publish his essays in this volume. We are also grateful to the University of Notre Dame's Institute for Educational Initiatives and the Notre Dame Law School for supporting our work on this project and for the editing assistance of Alicia Cummins and Notre Dame Law School students Timothy Borgerson, Mitchell Koppinger, Paige Lommerin, Ross D'Entremont, and Carter Wietecha.

FOREWORD

Jesse Choper

It has been my distinct pleasure to have known the pioneer of school choice, John (Jack) Coons, for the better part of fifty years, both as a distinguished colleague at UC Berkeley and as a civil rights advocate. Since the 1960s, Jack has continually vocalized the debate over education choices in our school system and the deeply fundamental rights of children within that "system." He has articulated his beliefs throughout his teaching, publications, books, speeches, and even blogs. In our society that has ever-increasingly removed any discussion of God from the topic of education, Jack does not fail to pose the ethical and religious components of educational choice as an inalienable right of children.

We may differ on some of our beliefs, but I am confident that through Jack's thorough explanations and reasoning I have become better equipped to understand exactly what is at stake when considering the evolution of the education system in the United States. Jack's extreme intelligence along with his gentle humor are salves on an otherwise overwhelmingly confusing topic. His humility would prevent his agreement with my compliments, but everyone who has been fortunate enough to spend time with Jack has become more informed and enlightened on their view of the current state of educational choice and personal freedoms.

Given our ever-changing politics, school choice in education is once again rising to the forefront of debates. Whether or not the child's rights extend to religious schools is also on the line. Without a doubt, Jack will continue to share his wealth of knowledge, experience, and insight with all who are interested.

PREFACE

John E. Coons

Why, in so many cases, does the state appoint professional strangers—the "public" school—to conscript the children of our poor and working-class families to serve 180 days a year for 13 years in government-operated schools that parents would shun, if only they had the resources either to better their residence or to pay private tuition? Why does U.S. law—unlike most of Europe—impose what we mislabel a "public" school upon such families when, instead, the state could deploy these same resources to honor family preferences about their children's schools?

This observer has grown old and boring striving to answer this question. I have on occasion promoted parental choice politically, but primarily by writing books (with the admirable Stephen Sugarman) and essays of the kind in this collection. I am deeply grateful for University of Notre Dame Press for making this volume possible.

Many are the justifications I have heard offered for our government school system, one that musters the child of the poor like a draftee but gives choice only to those of sufficient resources, according to their parents' preferences. I will try to suggest the diverse nature of these apologies. Some are devices of special interests, such as the educational bureaucracy and the teachers unions, who strive to maximize clientele. There are also unspoken but evident convictions among some educators and residents in high-income districts that there are profound civic and social differences in poor urban families that make their separation necessary. I suppose this too is a form of special interest. In any case, none of these seem like legitimate "justifications" in any moral sense—they are merely empirical-political explanations for the systemic frustration of parental choice for the disadvantaged.

There are other defenses of the system that are morally more plausible, and that deserve to be addressed. Some are sotto voce. There are honest and generous folk who believe that poor parents are simply unready to choose a school for their own children; that permitting them to do so would do damage to both the child and the civil order. Montaigne complained that some governments leave the child's case and education "to the mercy of parents, let them be as foolish and ill-conditioned as they may, without any manner of discretion."[1] All right, suppose this is plausible. The next question then is this: Would not, if given the power to choose, the experience of exercising the responsibility of choosing help parents become better choosers? Would not choice contribute to the general capacity of the parent-citizen? And next, if so, can society abide the effects of inevitable parental mistakes while awaiting this presumed civic payoff?

Another legitimate concern: perhaps our historical conscription of the disadvantaged child by the professional stranger is expected to maximize intelligence as reflected by test scores. There is much ado about this question. So far, the evidence suggests the opposite. Parental choice seems to help (at least a bit) in promoting the measurable academic growth of the child. It is a better device than the systematic randomness of coercive assignment by home address. Or does compulsory assignment to a state school best enhances the ultimate civility of the graduate—more than choice does by pauperized mothers? Essays that follow will suggest the opposite.

Still another plausible justification: compulsory assignment of the poor promotes racial integration. Are assigned schools in fact, then, less racially segregated than those freely chosen by the parent? The supporting evidence for this claim is thin and getting thinner. My own experience as an attorney seeking integration in a large urban district under court order was disheartening: private schools of various faith traditions (and none) formally offered thousands of integrating spaces for parental choice. The district (Kansas City, Missouri) refused the invitation. School districts that survive by conscription seem today to be resegregating.

Is choice for the nonrich too costly in dollars, as opponents often claim? The evidence seems strongly the other way. Charter schools, tax credits, and voucher programs can be designed either to increase or decrease the net cost to the taxpayers. This is a complex and technical question, and much would depend upon the design of a system. But, choice is compatible with fiscal responsibility, and often promotes it.

Last and most profound: Is financial compulsion of the poor parent and child to enroll in PS 99 justified by assuming that these children thereby are exposed to core ideas of the society about the True and the Good, ideas that schools of choice cannot be trusted to embrace and to teach? In the United States, there is a widely shared, if fuzzy, belief in a real human good, both of truth and of behavior, and it is understood that this same insight should be invested in the minds of all children. However, except for the securing of the technical competence of the graduate, the identity of these core values and their actual presence in our public curricula are quite unsettled. Competence in reading, writing, and arithmetic plus science may be widely shared universal goals, but there are many conflicts over values concerning behavior and aspiration, and about their ultimate source. Ancient and profound differences persist respecting the identity and origin of these disputed goods and of how, if at all, they should be transmitted in a professional context. God and his will for humankind—as variously understood—have played feature roles in many of these conflicts over the specifics of the good life. For some, God is a necessary element, but for other curriculum critics, his expulsion from public school discourse in the last century was good and necessary. Either way, God plays a role in the national conversation and will do so in the essays to follow.

Objections to the pro-divinity attitude and content in state schools were few and feeble in the nineteenth and early twentieth centuries. Taxpayers expected and received reverence for the divine in the classroom and were unfazed by a broad deference to and subtle reliance upon the deity and the occasional literature that gave him a favorable role, so long as the story remained nondenominational. This attitude suited well the general Protestant ambience of society at the time. And, in fact, the system was partly designed in the hope of luring the minds of immigrant Catholic children from impoverished families—as Parliament had done for Irish Catholics two centuries earlier (see chapter 8, "Magna Charter"). In the American setting, one unintended effect was the creation and flourishing of Catholic schools as an escape for many immigrants.

This deliberate but subtle God-consciousness of the state's classroom was to cease with the Supreme Court's belated discovery circa 1950 that such deference constituted an establishment of religion of the

sort forbidden by the First Amendment. Gradually, public schools ac-
commodated the judiciary with secularism and the censorship of God-
talk. This purification of the classroom was much assisted by the general
drift toward agnosticism in the society as a whole and, most evidently,
in the university and its education schools. They were the quickest to
honor the Court's decision. The teaching of religion had played but
a small role in their curriculum, and it was happily dispatched in
most cases.

The public schools themselves were and remain another matter.
Curricula in the United States are officially silent about things transcendental. But what happens in class rarely escapes the four walls of
the classroom, and few besides the students and their teacher know
their lived day-to-day experiences in government schools. What does
seem evident is the heterogeneity and conflict of moral propositions offered to the students, whether about sex, politics, or the nature of the
good itself (or if even there be such a thing). Until our current jungle
of gnostic brawls, the most public of such squabbles has arisen around
the introduction of Darwin, who has—quite properly I think—made
it to most high schools in the United States. His empirical findings are
worth knowing, even if his basic inference seems quaintly circular. If
survival equals fitness, it is, indeed, the fittest who survive. Evangelical
Christians vainly strove to keep him from the curriculum. To them, his
findings seem to challenge and replace the biblical calendar for creation.
And, of course in the end, Darwin himself fell to atheism. I wonder
whether his opponents might have fared better in the courts had they
simply insisted on the teacher's right and duty to pose for children the
neutral question: How did all this stuff—everything physical—come
to be in the first place? Would that Socratic moment violate the establishment clause?

If this American struggle for choice by all parents interests you,
read the essays. You may prefer to start with the batch of short blog en-
tries that follows as an appendix; these were prepared from 2013 to 2018
for the blog *reimaginED* (redefinedonline.org).

Three of my immediate family members have had substantial experience as teachers—two in public schools, one in Catholic. Our five
children did sixty-five semesters as students in each domain. Steve, our
third son, is currently a public high school principal. The dinner table
is frequently a place for discussion on parental choice of schools, and I

here thank my children and my late wife of sixty-two years, Marylyn, a former public school teacher.

I refer often to the late great Stephen Sugarman, the best student in my twelve happy years at Northwestern University and, for over half a century since, my colleague at UC Berkeley; he and my equally best student, Professor William Clune of the University of Wisconsin, were classmates (1964–67). In 1970, we three published *Private Wealth and Public Education* (Harvard University Press). I have then and thereafter relied on them; Steve and I coauthored four books on school choice plus an oral history project (and printed volume) from the Berkeley Campus Library (2016). This project, I believe, was originally prompted by Berkeley professor of U.S. history Mark Brilliant and law professor Steven Solomon, to whom I extend robust thanks. The resulting volumes were expertly monitored and executed by the director of the Oral History Department, Martin Meeker. Professors Brilliant and Solomon have themselves written insightfully of our tales of victory and frustration. Look for their work over the years to come.

A close friend of fifty years and our fair critic, Dean Emeritus Jesse Choper, has written a second foreword to this book. He is a disarmingly encouraging reader. I am most grateful.

William Loughman—trial attorney, instructor in law, armchair political economist, philosopher, and my old friend—is a special case. Bill saw what I was doing here and approved. He monitored my new writings for this collection and enriched the bibliography with relevant authors and ideas that I had overlooked or misunderstood. It was good fun working together. His generosity has my gratitude and admiration.

Notre Dame law professors Nicole and Rick Garnett and Ernest Morrell deserve my special gratitude for their foreword, which makes this collection seem all that its author could wish.

John Witte and his associate Amy Wheeler manage the remarkable Program in Law and Religion at the Emory University School of Law. Out of sheer generosity, they made efforts to ensure that these essays achieved a form proper to publication. Thanks and blessings to both. The editors of this volume brought these efforts to fruition.

Marylyn, my love for sixty-two years, deserves the final observation that without her patience and inspiration, there would have been little worth collecting. I look forward to our reunion.

John E. Coons
Berkeley, 2022

PART ONE

Religion, Liberty, and Education

CHAPTER ONE

Intellectual Liberty and the Schools

The U.S. constitutional order has sheltered a wide range of conflicting policies. Its primary symbols are spacious and accommodate a variety of interpretations. Still, the temptation persists to probe for a central animating theme. A case sometimes is made for equality as the core, and another for individual liberty. There are also religious constructions: the Pilgrims saw America as the hope for a new Jerusalem, and eschatology remains a national addiction, even when it assumes the form of a civil religion that no pilgrim would recognize. In contrast, skeptics can plausibly hold that any apparent drift is merely a vector of interest group purposes—that there is neither soul nor center but only conflicting parts; a version of this thesis would interpret our organic law as a medium for the quick, the clever, and the rich. And those who think in terms of class view the whole structure as a club to beat the workers.[1]

It would be naive to suppose that any of our major institutions could be adequately explained by a single popular value. Nevertheless, it might be an instructive exercise to pretend so, and this is not beyond the imaginative capacity. Without absurdity, one could suppose the existence of an implicit consensus that has crystallized around some particular ideal, such as equality or material progress, which is conceived to explain our major institutions. To be sure, the number of values available for such an exercise is severely limited, for to be instructive they must be empirically plausible; theocracy and pacifism might

Originally published: *Notre Dame Journal of Law, Ethics & Public Policy* 1, no. 4 (1985), 495–533. Republished in "Symposium on Education," *Notre Dame Journal of Law, Ethics & Public Policy* (2014).

not qualify. But, with that qualification, the comparison of a particular focused ideal with bureaucratic structures and social practice may teach us something about the ideal, the institutions, and even ourselves. To measure the church, work, childhood, business, or the army against a single explanatory value is to parallel, at least weakly, the scientific method. One observes the data to see whether the particular hypothesis "saves the appearances." For example, an economist tries to squeeze what is known about the family into a paradigm of economic rationality; eventually he may come to modify either the model or the data, but so much the better for his understanding and ours.[2]

This brief essay applies that familiar tactic of analysis to the schools. In an informal and selective manner, it looks at the American system of education in the light of one assumed version of the national purpose, asking to what extent that purpose and this institution could be reconciled. A more ambitious and systematic evaluation of education would replicate the process, setting the schools successively against competing teleologies; it would describe a plausible working model of schools and then ask, in order: Could such an institution be sensibly viewed as a conspiracy of the bourgeoisie? as a transmitter of WASP culture and religion? as the wedge for a national dream of equality? as the incubator of a rationalistic, scientific utopia? And such questions as these.

The device is limited in its uses. By its nature it cannot demonstrate that an institution is in every respect in harmony with some ideal. Since the data can never be exhausted, the positive hypothesis is beyond proof. It is not, however, beyond disproof. Sometimes it can be shown that an institution is in some major respect incompatible with a particular value. And the more instances of disharmony—and the greater their individual moment—the more difficult will it be to maintain an interpretation of that institution as salvific, egalitarian, progressive, hedonistic, or what have you. Depending upon one's own values and purposes, that negative insight may be advantageous, and, in any case, it is clarifying.

Autonomy as the Core

Here the school system will be set against an assumed civic commitment to individual liberty. The justification for this focus is the plausible priority of liberty in the American polity and the settled habit of educational spokesmen and the Supreme Court to associate the public school with that value.

In this society, liberty has competition as an explanatory value, nevertheless it enjoys at least the degree of priority required for the exercise here projected. It is "constitutional" in the broad English sense of fundamental institutions and understandings as well as in the narrower included domain of judicial review under the specific guarantees of our written constitution. In both senses, the American idea embodies a more or less coherent conception of the central place of individual rights. An argument for a single dominating value—liberty or any other—could begin with the observation that, for a system so complex, dynamic, and political, it has maintained a remarkable consistency. The relevant opinions of the Supreme Court seldom surprise, and the normative symbols they invoke are generally common to majority and dissent. Indeed, whether in court or legislature, and amidst the sharpest conflict, most arguments seem cut from the same basic cloth.

Broadly speaking, that cloth is the ideal of personal autonomy. The centerpiece of domestic human rights is the presumption, often explicit, that each of us can choose for him- or herself. Individual freedom to forge an identity is one main theme of our common purpose, whether it be expressed in terms of speech, privacy, association, mobility, or (even) property. Under protection of law, men and women may travel at will and choose their religion and associations; they may read, see, or say basically what they choose for themselves. This commitment suffuses the full range of our governmental structures and informs the content of law far beyond the perimeter of the relatively few enumerated and court-declared rights. This was so from the beginning. The major institutions of American political life were fashioned as insurance for dissenters. What Madison preached concerning the self-canceling effect of private faction was embedded in the foundation. The mutual balancing of the powers of the national government as well as the structure of federalism were instruments to protect the individual will, and they continue to serve that end, if imperfectly.[3]

True, the autonomy theme has never been accepted in the libertarian sense that less government always is better government; as the history of economic and social regulation attests, at no point has the Watchman State approached constitutional status or consensus. Nonetheless, even the vexing legal constraints of modern life can be interpreted less as a limit upon autonomy than as its intended instrument. Every reformer hopes to "liberate" the individual, whether in the role of consumer, voter, worker, woman, minority, or student. From the FCC to OSHA to affirmative action there continually reemerges the theme that the maximizing of liberty entails not the elimination but the artful tailoring of constraints. However one may assess the actual effect of all this law, the promotion of autonomy has been regulation's most prominent rationale. Such efforts to legislate liberty may in many cases be self-defeating, but this does not necessarily alter the centrality or sincerity of the objective.

This has been true even of the Supreme Court in its occasional interventions on behalf of oppressed groups. When it patches a rent in the social safety net, as in *Plyler v. Doe* (1982), the Court no doubt is moved by many concerns, not least of which is the simple samaritan impulse to help the underdog. And, of course, the Court may represent a multitude of other values more or less distinct from liberty, including federalism, efficiency, liberal guilt, and judicial restraint. But, at a deeper level, it seeks the larger end of a "free society." Each of the other aims, though explicitly normative, is, in its relation to liberty, instrumental. The teleology of judicial review remains the preservation and extension of a system of individual autonomy. When the Court opens the schoolhouse door to undocumented children, it expresses a conviction that, for some, the safety net in its various forms is necessary to the practical exercise of individual choice. Even the health, education, and welfare structure, including its constitutional aspects, can be pictured as an instrument of liberty.[4]

It is their sharing in this ideology that makes John Rawls, Milton Friedman, Ronald Dworkin, and Ronald Reagan intellectual cousins. Their mutual wars are intense, as befits relatives, but it really is all in the family. For their difference is only about the proper means to deliver liberty and responsibility to the individual. They can all claim to represent the genus *liberal*. Even Dworkin's most energetic invocations of equality often reduce to instrumental judgments about the minimum conditions of autonomy. And although most comment on Rawls concerns itself with the "difference principle," the primary maxim in his lexical scheme is grounded in liberty. It is not clear how much credit should go to eighteenth- and nineteenth-century ideologies for the present content of the ideal. The moral premise that most nearly unites and typifies them is J. S. Mills's imperative: no description of the good may claim priority; value must remain in a matter of personal preference. For contemporaries such as Dworkin, this continues to be expressed as an absolute. There is, to be sure, a problem here. Driven to its logical boundaries, dogmatic relativism may conflict with its own common ideal of tolerance. A radical equality of values cannot without contradiction give special place to anything—including liberty.[5]

Thus, it can be argued that our substantial liberty and its supporting structures persist not so much because of, but in spite of, an allegiance to moral neutrality. The primacy of the individual could rather be an inheritance from competing creeds holding that some choices are better than others. Some have always supposed on religious or philosophical grounds that the fully human life consists in the free exercise of a capacity to choose or to refuse some identifiable good, and it is on this premise that they would support the liberal state. Such an ethic demands opportunities suited to that capacity; the conditions of moral choice become the foundation for tolerance. If virtue by its nature requires the discretion to sin, a substantial liberty is its indispensable instrument.[6]

In any event, such contests over the intellectual pedigree of liberty really only confirm a curiously stable agreement among very diverse minds that—whatever in the end life may be about—our government and society are about the provision of the structural and material support for autonomy. Or—for the last time—so it may plausibly be argued. Liberty, then, is worth testing as the explanatory value of our institutions, including the schools.

The Special Problem of Children's Liberty

A major difficulty in this enterprise is the meaning of liberty in the context of childhood. In school, as in virtually all aspects of life, children remain subject to adult rule to a fairly advanced age, generally eighteen. This does not deny that the child at an early age has a will—and often a reason—as distinct and effective as that of an adult. Most adults agree that children lead a moral life that is significant even if relatively narrow in scope. And, as the child advances in competence and understanding, the justification for limiting his choices becomes progressively problematic. Nevertheless, a general subordination to parents and/or bureaucrats endures. What is its rationale? Confusion and ambivalence on this issue are evident both in the literature of childhood and in judicial opinions deciding whether to support the will of the child, the state, or the parent regarding such matters as obscenity, curfews, arm bands in the classroom, cosmetic surgery, abortion, and the selection of school library books. Why is the autonomy principle so murky in its application even to relatively mature children?[7]

One possible answer is that self-determination for children is necessarily in conflict with the autonomy of supervising adults. It is unlikely that father and junior can both know best, but it is certain that they cannot both rule. Yet, though this is technically correct, it could mislead. In spite of formal subordination, it may be that the child's autonomy can in practice be consistent with the rule of adults; indeed, extending the point, it will be argued here that without an adult regime, the younger child's liberty can scarcely be imagined. If the experience of autonomy is to be available to a child, adult authority must be its instrument, for a child's freedom to choose at all depends upon protections and limits.[8]

Analysis here can start with the political reality that children will be formally subject to the discretion of some particular adult or set of adults. This adult regime will be arranged in the name of child protection, children's liberty, parental liberty, or the interests of third persons—or all four. A parent or a public bureaucracy, or some combination of both, will hold the legal authority to direct his comings and goings until some age. If eighteen is the wrong age, make it fifteen—or twenty-one. The principle remains the same. Universal liberation for children in the sense of formal legal autonomy is a nonstarter. The only real question here is by what rationale and under what structures should legal authority over the child be parceled out between parent, state, and the child himself if liberty—as opposed to other possible values—is to remain primary?

This inescapable limit on children's freedom is not merely an artifact of politics. It is a fact of nature. Even if one held liberty to be the sole concern, there would remain a practical, insuperable, and permanent obstacle to liberation. Children are small, weak, and inexperienced; adults are big, strong, and initiated. One may liberate children from the law of man, but the law of nature is beyond repeal. There is no way to send an eight-year-old out of the sovereignty of the family and into a world of liberty. For he will there be introduced to a new sovereignty of one kind or another. It may be a regime of want, ignorance, and general oppression; it may be one of delightful gratification. The ringmaster could be Fagin or Mary Poppins. Whatever the reality, it will be created by people with more power. Children—at least small children—will not be liberated: they will be dominated. And none of this can be altered by providing "open schools" and permissive child-rearing. These are merely indulgences granted by and within the dominion of adults who meanwhile stand ready forcibly to rescue the child, even against his will, from nature, hostile adults, and the child's own mistakes.

This is true even of mature teenagers who might have a ripened capacity for autonomy or at least for autonomy in regard to specific activities, such as driving. Until formal emancipation, these persons will be subject to general-purpose adult regimes either of the state, the family, or both. And even though particular rights of a child to drive, travel, or choose a religion could theoretically be recognized by law, the overall adult regime will retain very significant reins through its control of the purse and its other general powers. The state might decide to allow every child of fifteen to choose his or her own school; nevertheless, so long as parents can retaliate by withholding the car, the allowance, new clothes, and other privileges, the child's so-called right loses much of its substance. But consider the other side. Despite this inevitability of adult dominion, a de facto liberty for children is not a self-contradiction. The child's strong and important interest in liberty can indeed be a favored object of policy. It can be pursued precisely by securing his legal subordination to the particular adult regime that most respects that interest. A child subject to adult authority will in practice be allowed his own choice in varying doses; these will depend upon what the particular authority thinks appropriate. The relevant question then becomes this: Which regime is the likelier source of such practical autonomy? There are two candidates. On the one hand stands the parent or parent substitute; on the other, some agency of the state. And, of course, authority may be parceled between them in countless ways. This is an oversimplification, but it is a place to start.

Now let us raise slightly the level of complexity. Obviously the child has not merely a liberty interest but what can fairly be labeled a "welfare" interest; this is composed of physical safety, growth, affection, education, and the like. His or her liberty interest—our special focus here—is related to but quite different from the welfare interest. Its core is the religious-philosophic premise that children, like adults, have wills and make choices. In this capacity for choice lies the child's claim to be part of the moral community. Ideally, the choices of a child display an advancing rationality and virtue, but, in any case, choice has an absolute value for the child just as it has for adults. However, unlike adults, in the case of children the liberty interest often must be subordinated to the welfare interest; otherwise little Lucy will not survive—or at least not develop sufficiently—so as to exercise her full potential for autonomy. Children can make choices that society deems too costly both to the child's welfare interest and to his or her expanding capacity for choice. We want the adult free to decide whether to stay up late, hence we curfew the child.

Insofar as one wished to maximize children's liberty, the trick would be to find that special adult regime that would make the daily selections between yea and nay with sensitivity to the child's interest in choice here and now but with equal concern for his growing capacity for self-determination. Employing these criteria, an ideal regime would decide when self-direction by the child is desirable and when it is not. It may be beneficial or baneful today for Lucy to be allowed to choose for herself whether to read or go to the movies; it may be wise or foolish to give her the choice to attend either School A or School B. In which adult shall we lodge the authority to decide whether Lucy may decide for herself? And in those cases where choice is to be denied her, who shall then decide the substantive issue?

This last question is not exclusively about liberty, for it does not arise until it has already been determined that the child shall not make the decision. It could be decided, for example, that ten-year-olds shall not be free to consent to surgery, but which adult shall then consent or refuse, the state or the parent or both in some combination? The focus here seems to be welfare. Nevertheless, the question remains at least partly about the child's liberty. For, though the child's own preference in the matter cannot be decisive, it may be relevant to the correctness of the decision judged in terms either of liberty or welfare. Thus which regime has the most effective access to his or her views and can give them proper weight is often an important liberty issue. In truth, decisions about a child's welfare implicate the child's interest in autonomy to the extent that there would be something eccentric about any theory that simply divorced the two. Nevertheless, the primary concern in this essay justifies a somewhat lopsided emphasis upon liberty.

It is now necessary to consider some criteria by which to evaluate the two adult regimes that compete for authority. The questions are these: Who shall determine whether the child is to choose or be chosen for? And, if the latter, who shall decide? On the one hand stands the state operating through its professionalized agencies; on the other stands the family composed ambiguously of at least two, and usually more, human wills. Would there be a preferred way to approach the allocation of authority over these issues, if the object were to enhance liberty?

Parental Representation of the Child's Liberty Interest

Let us begin with a reservation. Since the child's welfare interest must be respected (even in the name of liberty), it is silly to suppose that the state should simply remain inert in the face of grave risk to the child. When the chips are down, few would abandon the child to a sadistic or wholly neglectful parent. The state may not be much good at setting minimum standards of protection, but it is all we have, unless we are to invite vigilante enforcement of child protection. Throughout I shall assume that such a need for minimum protection would apply to formal education. One can respect those who oppose compulsory education, but it is not clear that liberty is advanced by allowing families to leave their offspring in ignorance. In any case, to concede the necessity for some minimum standard of educational protection hardly settles the important questions about what form education should take or what content it should have. It would only bring us to the question of who best should decide how the minimum in education (as in anything else) is to be satisfied and what should happen beyond the minimum.

Intuitively, one may be inclined to assume that in education or any other matter, an adult who knows the individual child will be the best judge both of the child's readiness for autonomy in any particular matter and—where rejecting autonomy—of the "correct" answer to be imposed. If this intuition is sound, it is a reason to lodge primary control in the parents through legal presumptions in their favor. But it could be wrong and surely would be wrong in individual instances. At best it wants justification as a general proposition.

There are at least four reasons to expect parental primacy to be in general the most effective agent of liberty. Three concern promotion of the child's own liberty and will be described briefly in this subsection. The fourth, discussed in the following subsection, is grounded in the liberty of the parent. At the risk of being tiresome, I shall state now and repeat that these speculations and assertions are based principally upon my personal observations through my own experiences of watching schools and families and raising more than my quota of the world's progeny. There is no social science bearing directly on this issue.[9]

Regarding the liberty of the child, it should be observed, for the first reason, that the normal parent has a selfish interest in the child becoming independent. Few adults want their children to be permanent moral and economic burdens. Parents suffer when the child's autonomy suffers; what is good for the child's liberty tends to be good for parents, and vice versa. This conclusion, of course, is not a logical necessity, nor could it be proved by experiment; without self-contradiction one could imagine that most parents prefer that their offspring remain moral puppets and economic parasites. Doubtless some do want just that for reasons that, long before Freud, the mass of mankind recognized as pathetic and pathological. It is the stuff of sad novels about the high bourgeoisie.

But that is the point: such motivation is not a normality. Emphatically it is not the stuff of ordinary families where adults work for a living and expect their children to do likewise. For them such an attitude constitutes moral and economic insanity. Quite evidently most parents feel that they prosper by making decisions that enhance their child's autonomy, and they suffer from those that create dependency.

Professionally, bureaucrats may also in most instances work for the child's autonomy. If so, this is to their credit, for often they have a strong objective interest in maintaining dominance over the child and family; the less the child advances, the more the professional is needed. One can admire professional restraint where it occurs, but the question nonetheless would remain whether the best strategy is to entrust the fostering of the child's liberty to the altruism of experts. Of course, the danger to liberty from professional domination arises chiefly in situations where the client is captive; when, by contrast, the family is free to "exit," economic incentives can help to unite the self-interest of the professional to that of the child. Later we shall have to assess the degree of liberty typical of the relation between professional and client in the schools.[10]

Accountability for decisions may increase the adult decider's interest in the child's advancement to autonomy, but it does not follow necessarily that the accountable adult is the decider. Conceivably, he or she could be accountable but ineffective. On that issue, one has nothing, again, but experience and sense as a guide. Mine suggest that having a stake in the outcome provides a healthy discipline for the decider. Furthermore, if I am deceived — if the best decider is disinterested — we will have introduced a grave difficulty. Applied to adults, the same conclusion would disable anyone from deciding for himself, for in the adult, the two roles of subject and decision-maker merge, producing the ultimate in accountability for mistakes. A preference for the disinterested decider would become a premise for universal dependency.

The second reason for parental choice is that parents care most about the child and that caring promotes decisions that advance the child's autonomy. Caring is cousin to accountability, but there is a real difference. The distinction is one of altruism or, more properly, love. Caring denotes not self-interest but disinterest coupled with an affection focused upon a particular child. Such a focus is normal to the family and uncharacteristic, or even improper, to the professions.

There will no doubt be instances in which accountability and caring will conflict. The support of and special care for a disabled child, for example, is seldom in an adult's self-interest; this is especially true when the exhausted parent is offered the opportunity to lodge their child in an institution. Love, of course, may persist where interest fails, and heroism is common in the parental role. But whether or not love prevails over interest, it must in every case be accounted a benefit to the child in the decision process. And the normal case in which both love and self-interest are allied in the deciding parent must be accounted the ideal.[11]

Still, there remains the question whether parental love seeks autonomy as a specific good. To the extent that parental love is conceived as a kind of narcissism, one could be led to expect conflict and ambivalence regarding the child's autonomy. On this issue, one consults his encounters with people who are parents and with the central traditions of our culture. At least the latter—and for me the former too—hold that generally the relation is not only profoundly unselfish but provides the principal, if imperfect, model of selflessness. For to love selflessly is by definition to love one who is distinctly other; perhaps, indeed, the more distinct the other becomes, the richer the possibility for loving him or her. It may take Albert Schweitzer to love all of humankind, but a mere mother could love Lucy. And the more the child becomes Lucy, the more her mother loves her.[12]

But let us lean over backward. The very intensity of the relation could be thought problematic. Parental fervor could get in the way of good judgment about the proper means to secure autonomy. This too seems plausible and is confirmed intermittently, especially in medical decision-making. On rare occasions, parents seem misled by their very concern into neurotic and bizarre decisions. Surely, however, these are the exceptions proving the rule that parental caring, on the whole, supports autonomy. Equally important, these aberrations are precisely the kind of behavior that minimum standards of protection are designed to prevent.

The third reason is simply that the parent's knowledge of what will nourish autonomy will in general be superior to that of the bureaucratic decision-maker, at least for purposes of reaching decisions in difficult cases. This is probable for two reasons. The first is that the parent has special access to the child's own view of things. For obvious reasons, the child's voice is difficult to hear in large institutions; indeed, outside the home, many youngsters respond to crises in their school or daycare experience with a silent passivity that masks the problem and discourages adult inquiry. By contrast, the intimacy of the family maximizes the child's own power to move adults to do his or her will. In the normal family, even the silence of a child is a strong form of communication. Whatever the family is, it is a debating society, and the child's voice is difficult to exclude.

The parents' knowledge is thereby enhanced in ways closed to an alien professional. Doubtless, the professionals' own knowledge is in certain dimensions wholly superior. He "knows" about children in general—the pathologies that sometimes bind them and the therapies that can loose them. There are unfortunately narrow limits to this kind of science and a striking dissensus among the professionals. Still, no one doubts its potential importance. Insofar as this kind of knowledge is reliable, however, its conclusion can usually be shared effectively with parents in various ways during the decision-making process, whether the subject be medicine, discipline, or education. The parents' knowledge, by contrast, is less subject to communication — it is too immediate, too immanent. It is often literally unspeakable. It follows, curiously, that in an important sense parents can be the more knowledgeable deciders, for they can combine the conclusions of the professional with their own incommunicable insights. This, of course, assumes a relation in which parents not only control the final decision but have access to professionals (of varying opinions).

The import of these first three reasons for parental primacy — self-interest, caring, and knowledge — is that the family (almost without regard to its lifestyle) tends to be the right environment for the child's gradual transition from a dependent and dominated infancy to an adolescence marked by an ever-increasing practical liberty bestowed by parents. In the run of families, the child achieves formal autonomy at eighteen almost without a ripple. Granted, the pilgrimage through adolescence is seldom negotiated without pain; the family, nevertheless, represents the best odds for "breaking away" with one's soul intact. Were it a most miserable institution, the family might in relative terms represent the efficient medium of liberty.[13]

Again, the parental primacy is limited. It cannot preempt the duty of the state, where necessary, to intervene to protect the child's health and safety and, thereby, indirectly, to support his or her liberty. To that end, the state imposes its minimum standards, but their application is triggered only by demonstrated and basic family failure. To justify intervention, government historically has been required to overcome a strong presumption favoring parental authority. Quite plausibly this policy may rest on the conviction that constant or unpredictable intrusion into the family would poison the source of the very liberty of the child that the state is trying to protect.

Parental Liberty

The fourth reason for parental primacy is the parent's own liberty interest. Presumably, it is equal in political dignity to the liberty interest of the child. In terms of autonomy, there is a great deal at stake here for the parent. The right to form families and to determine the scope of their children's practical liberty is for most men and women the primary occasion for choice and responsibility. One does not have to be rich or well placed to experience the family. The opportunity over a span of fifteen or twenty years to attempt the transmission of one's own deepest values to a beloved child provides a unique arena for the creative impulse. Here is the communication of ideas in its most elemental mode. Parental expression, for all its invisibility to the media, is an activity with profound First Amendment implications. Nor, of course, is parental expression lacking in legal protection. Indeed, fathers and mothers may be the only speakers with an enforceable claim to an audience. At the same time, the intimacy of the family ensures that the child enjoys a reciprocal advantage in the practical if not in the legal order; in matters that concern children, they can expect a hearing for their own view.[14]

The implications of all this remain to be captured in First Amendment doctrine. For understandable reasons, political and legal theories of free expression have been preoccupied with public expression. But it is no exaggeration to say that intellectual liberty has a primary locus in the family and that the heart of the forum is the home.

Indeed, even as we view parental primacy in its traditional forms, it emerges as a source of intellectual, social, and political liberty for both child and parent. It is in the name of liberty that the legal system blesses child-rearing practices that range far from the norm. Parents can allow children to make dangerous air trips, stay up late, drink wine, work at various employments otherwise forbidden, and pursue exotic religious and political beliefs. So long as parents feed and clothe their children and keep them in school and out of the hospital, the U.S. Constitution generally protects parental judgment, even where it is manifested in a broad permissiveness.[15]

There are exceptions. *Prince v. Massachusetts* (1944) allowed the state to limit the dispensing authority of parents whose children wished to join them in selling religious tracts on the street. But, *Prince* is aging and lonesome. The authority of its 5–4 majority is enfeebled by the variety of recent opinions legitimating very marginal parenting practices and also by a general reform of custody law that has narrowed the state's capacity to interfere with the family. Of course, the picture is complicated by countercurrents, such as separate age-based standards for purchase of sexually explicit materials, and by statutes directed at the child pornography industry. The latter statutes upheld in *New York v. Ferber* (1982) are clearly a (sensible) restraint upon the liberty of both parent and child. The state's purpose was wholly to eliminate practices it deemed to constitute child abuse. They were below the "minimum" level of proper protection, and even parents cannot allow them.[16]

On the other hand, superficially similar laws regulating purchase by children of certain reading material suggest a rather different kind of legislative purpose, one consistent with one version of parental liberty. Statutes barring the sale of sexually explicit materials to younger children are a good example; in *Ginsberg v. New York* (1968) these were upheld against First Amendment attack. But although *Ginsberg* does limit the child's right to secure these materials on his or her own, it suggests no limit upon the parental liberty to decide whether they shall nonetheless be made available to the child. Indeed, *Ginsberg* can be interpreted as a legislative effort to support parental discretion against the invasion of external forces of the media that would frustrate the parents' will in the practical order. Given a parental authority to license the child's reading of particular books—or to bestow upon him full discretion—it is hard to paint cases such as *Ginsberg* simply as a restraint. In any case, the central point remains: parental liberty weighs in the accounting.[17]

It would be fair to observe that, in declaring parental primacy and their authority over children to be a form of liberty, I have defined every legal constraint upon parents (including compulsory education) as a liberty lost; the same is true for every legal autonomy bestowed upon children, such as a right to contraceptives. In a polity devoted exclusively to parental liberty, this line of thought would lead inexorably to the paterfamilias. Had that been my intention, I should not have emphasized the contribution of parental primacy to children's liberty. Still, the many conflicts between the liberty of parent and the liberty of the child are inevitable and obvious, and there is no reason that all of them be resolved in favor of the adults. More to the point, they are not to be resolved at all in the sense that there is some decisive calculus of net liberty. No division of power will ever be authoritative. For sanity in policymaking, it is enough that society appreciate both the ordinary harmony and the respective importance of the distinctive liberty interests of parent and child. This harmony is quite sufficient to explain most of the traditional law of childhood in terms that are consistent with liberty. However—and we come at last to the point—it is no assistance in explaining the American system of education.[18]

THE EDUCATIONAL EXCEPTION TO PARENTAL LIBERTY

Since *Meyer v. Nebraska* (1923) and *Pierce v. Society of Sisters* (1925), it has commonly been supposed that, above some reasonable minimum set by the state, the parent's liberty interest in the education of the child is secure. The reality is more complex and constraining. The congeries of structures legislated to deliver education forces most children into state schools whatever their wishes or their parents'. To put it briefly: schooling is compulsory, a state-operated school is available at no tuition, content and method in such schools are settled by majoritarian politics, and assignments are made on impersonal grounds by agents of the state. In such a regime, those with means buy their liberty by residing in their preferred attendance zone or by paying tuition to attend a private school. For the rest, the school is selected by compulsion.[19]

This embarrassment to liberty in the "public" schools can be accounted for in historical and even pseudo-libertarian terms. It derives from basic attitudes of the patrician founders of the system. Even today their outlook appears essentially benign. Granted, they paternalized the ordinary family in ways that now would seem offensive. They nevertheless viewed themselves as pursuing liberty in ways that may have seemed plausible in the nineteenth century. They imagined that education would in due course become a science, that there was "one best way," that it would be found, and that any rational person would freely choose it. Compulsion was necessary pro tempore only for the barbarian fringe of society. Further, they felt honestly—if paradoxically—that imposition of mainline Yankee culture was the best assurance of a free society. In applying these assumptions, the schools were often abetted by their wards. Many immigrants were content to be paternalized in the sense of being assimilated to the mainstream culture. Having their children forced to learn English was seldom perceived as oppression. No doubt the teaching of majoritarian religion in the public schools was another matter, being in many cases odious to dissenters, but various compromises on this issue kept the bondage tolerable.[20]

Both justifications have long since evaporated. Only computer salesmen can still believe that education will become a science like physics or even like economics. The competing medicines for the learning disease are too many to sustain the view that professionals can tell which style and which school is best for the individual child — except in very unusual cases. And as for cultural unity, Americans have long since concluded that there are many models of the good life. David Bridges puts it well:

> It is precisely because individuals and factions in society differ in their views about what is in the interests of children individually and collectively that the question of political rights of determination becomes significant. Nor is the "liberal" or "neutral" alternative, of presenting the alternative conceptions of the good life to children so that they can choose, an entirely satisfactory answer to the problem. For this is precisely one of the versions of what is good for children which may be and indeed is in practice fiercely challenged. . . . In short, the division of opinion among the adult community as to what is in fact good for children undermines their claims to paternalistic intervention in children's liberty in the name of such good.[21]

The short of it is that the original justifications for a monopoly school system in a free society have become wholly discredited. This leaves the system standing as a great puzzle — at best an anachronism — in a constitutional order that values liberty. From top to bottom, its structure effectively frustrates the choices of parent and child that the law protects in every other realm of life. Parents choose shoes, food, games, hours, and every other important feature of a child's life. In education, this liberty is not only opposed but squelched. Ordinary families with all their rich variety in culture and values are forced to accept the form, content, and ideology of a politically dictated education. Public schools, as currently organized, chill the traffic in ideas that is generated by free family choices in every other area of life. Though they vest in the mantle of freedom and diversity, they in fact flout this deepest purpose of the First Amendment.[22]

The process of ideological inculcation for the nonrich begins at the textbook publisher's house. Large school systems can and do compel millions of children to come and to read what has been chosen for them by strangers. It is the understandable desire of publishers to please such decision-makers. Upon close examination, these turn out to be not only elective and appointed boards at various levels but a whirling circle of intellectual lobbyists. As Mike Bowler reports:

> The publishers cannot survive if their books are not chosen. . . . The pressures appear to be more intense than they ever were, and they come from any number of sources on both the "left" and the "right." There are NOW and the Creationists, whose interests are 180 degrees in opposition. . . . There are the unions and the right-to-work people, those who would rid the books of racial stereotypes, those who would give Indians, Chicanos and Arabs . . . their rightful place. There are the farmers and the meatpackers. There are the urbanists and the ruralists, both opposed to the white picket fences of Dick and Jane. There are the overlapping "back-to-basics" folks promoting pure phonics and the old math, and there are those who see the federal government as the only hope for bringing imaginative and effective curriculum to American children. . . . [T]he industry, already a conservative one, is becoming even more conservative.[23]

The pressures are not exclusively of this informal sort. Many state codes mandate that the curriculum emphasize the contributions of various interest groups—minority and otherwise. Some states have distributed to all teachers prescriptive statements of the content and method for teaching morals. The effect of such official grunts in the classroom may be problematic, but majority sentiment expressed in school board elections and in organized or disorganized protest often do have consequences. Likewise, teachers unions strongly influence the character of the institutions. Much can still depend upon the private preferences and behavior of the assigned teacher, but tenure and credentialing systems tend even further to homogenize the teaching corps. The drift overall is unmistakable—the system is tuned to keep the message mellow. The vectored pressures of interest politics crush the sharp edges of ideas and work to make school the instrument of a smoothly textured ideology. There are exceptions. One occurs where like-minded ideologues capture a school board and dictate the school's mission. Another arises where the school board and administration are indifferent, for in that event the individual teacher can effectively become the master of the students in his or her hands. But these would hardly be exceptions that would enhance the liberty of parents and children—certainly not of those who cannot afford to move or pay tuition.[24]

The decisions about style and content thus are made and imposed by strangers. Any hope for redress at the school board elections is reserved for those enjoying leisure time; in larger cities, such as New York or Los Angeles, that hope is fatuous. In any event, if you wind up in the minority, you lose. Of course, no one can specify the precise effects of monopoly. Maybe some children learn better under a fully coercive regime. And, no doubt, some ill-considered decisions by parents are avoided. In this respect, the system—despite its anomic pattern—has some of the advantages of any intellectual paternalism. It is, however, hard to defend as a contribution to liberty.

The Deliverance Defense

That defense nevertheless is sometimes attempted in terms that have yet to be considered in this essay. The argument I have in mind must be treated with respect, for it is made with sincerity by intelligent persons. It commences with faith in the possibility of a "neutral" education that would help to produce adults of a sturdy independence of mind and spirit. This education is thought to represent the child's best chance for deliverance from the prejudice of family and for an introduction to the sunlight of an adult autonomy. There are many variations of this professional vision. Among schoolmen, it has the properties almost of a folk legend that is passed across generations. In his criticism of the opinion in the 1968 armband case, Robert Burt expresses the core of the tradition:

> The *Tinker* Court erred not in its result, but in its failure to acknowledge the potential educational and constitutional relevance of the facts in the case suggesting that the children's armbands reflected more their parents' convictions than theirs. The Court ignored the possibility that school officials might exclude parental political views from school in order to free children to think

through these questions themselves. As noted, that motivation was implausible on the face of the *Tinker* record, but it is not an implausible educational goal, nor should that goal be prohibited by the Constitution. The *Tinker* Court should have acknowledged that the constitutional question would have changed complexion if the school officials had convincingly argued that they were acting not to impose their political views on students, but rather on behalf of the root values of the First Amendment—tolerance, diversity of thought, individual autonomy—against parental impositions on children.[25]

Here are the public schools in the role of liberator, a role fully alternative and candidly competitive to the claims I have made for parents. In the deliverance legend, the public system becomes the quintessential hope for a place where "parental impositions" are excluded and children "think for themselves," developing thereby a commitment to First Amendment ideals.

The theme is developed at greater length in the dialogues of Bruce Ackerman, *Social Justice in the Liberal State*, who in his chapter titled "Liberal Education" explains the view that, in the name of the liberal vision, parents should be stopped from taking unfair advantage of teenage minds. It may be necessary to allow parents to push their eccentricities on young children, but high school is the place where the liberal state must compel (as it were) a free dialogue. The correct curriculum will be one that is neutral in the sense that all possible views will be represented fairly. Students will decide for themselves what they believe, and they will become truly effective in the arts of self-determination by living through the experience of the "neutral dialogue." Ackerman's mythic "liberal educator" puts it this way:

> In exercising my power over the young, I have not used it to indoctrinate them into one or another of the competing ideals affirmed by members of our political community. In my capacity as liberal educator, I do not say that any of these ideals is worthy of greater respect than any other. Instead, my aim has been to provide each child with those cultural materials that—given his imperfect self-control and inexperience—he would find most useful in his efforts

at self-definition. After all, these children are citizens of our liberal state. Although they may be subjected to special limitations when necessary to assure their future standing as citizens, they may not otherwise be denied their right to pursue their good in the way they think best.[26]

Later in the book, Ackerman's deference to the child's own will becomes more attenuated. He acknowledges that "the task is not to undertake a vain search for the coercion-free educational system, but to consider ways in which the inevitably coercive aspects of socialization can be justified." He concedes that what liberals are searching for is "a theory that will enable decision makers to legitimize their uses of power without claiming the right to declare that one conception of the good is better than another."[27]

In these passages and elsewhere, Burt and Ackerman faithfully reproduce the ambivalence of the "neutral" educator who is so opposed to forcing students' minds that he compels them to hear what he thinks will free them. Too liberal to impose on anyone, he imposes on everyone. This paradoxical outlook allows its spokesmen to remain ambiguous as to who is really in charge. On the one hand, students "learn to think for themselves." On the other hand, there is some unidentified adult hanging around culling the necessarily finite number of ideas that will be thought about. Though his full commission is never made clear, this adult stranger at least is expected to exclude parents' moral and political views from school. We may not know who is running the place, but we know who is not.[28]

To put it delicately, these are questions here about the commitment to an ideal of liberty. Quite apart from the obvious paradox of compelling autonomy, there is an initial question of politics. A strategy of delivering even secondary education into the hands of a "liberal" elite strikes me as simply beyond the practical reach of democratic society— at least this one. It is worth remembering, as a starter, that no such educational regime currently operates in public education, nor has it ever. The notion that the public school is value-neutral is illusion, as has been observed by everyone from John Dewey to the Supreme Court. Nor do I take protagonists such as Burt and Ackerman to assert the contrary; what they are expressing is a longing for an ideal yet untried.[29]

By what stages could such an ideal become a general policy? It would first require frustration of the curriculum preferences of thousands of local majorities. A heroic legislature must begin by declaring the state's general commitment to a principle of value neutrality. This alone would require a political miracle. A second and greater one would be necessary to make this broad policy operational by enacting detailed legislation regulating instruction throughout the entire system. Even though there is no agreement among educators on proper content or method, very particular rules would have to be specified for both. Given the risk that some nonneutral teacher down the line would empathize with the poor or condemn the sins of George Washington, little could be left to chance. Such a reform seems unlikely in a majoritarian polity. Indeed, its nearest—if remote—approximation is a creature not of politics but of privatism. It is, curiously, the "independent" academy of the wealthy that is freest to aspire to a neutral curriculum. The last place that will ban Kurt Vonnegut or revive McGuffey is Phillips Andover Academy.

This is not a suggestion that private academies produce autonomous adults—or that they don't. Indeed, whether teaching of a "neutral" sort is effective to that end might be our next question. It may be that a fully Socratic secondary education is ideal, but there is little beyond intuition and reputation to suggest it. Plausibly the opposite could be the case. The most promising education for autonomy may be a "narrow" one driven by some distinctive ideology. The most liberated adult could turn out to be one who, throughout his or her school life, has experienced the steady and uncompromising faith of his or her parents—religious or secular. If, as many educators contend, the media impose upon children a shallow and marasmic ethic, a case is thereby suggested for a rather more pointed countereducation in school as a source of moral liberty. A strong value position defended by intelligent and committed adults could prove an exhilarating and toughening experience for a young person weaned on Fred Flintstone; it might do more for the possibility and practice of liberty than even a prolonged immersion in Socratic dialogue.

Neutral education is, therefore, both unlikely politically and problematic as an efficient instrument for producing autonomous adults. But we must add a third concern, one with which we might well have begun, namely, there is no consensus concerning even the model for autonomy.

Who is it that is supposed to represent this peculiar quality? If it is an adult with a penchant for seeing all sides of an issue, autonomy is essentially some attitude of mind—a virtuous intellectual habit. But autonomy may instead be seen as a matter of will and character—specifically, the ability to stand against a majority. If so, we may be describing rather different people. My experience tells me that law professors are a fair example of people who can perceive and enjoy diversity of thought and may even "think for themselves." If this be autonomy, they generally have it. But I know of nothing suggesting that law professors are especially good (or bad) at standing tall in a moral crisis. It could be one thing to think for yourself and another to act upon that knowledge with independence. Does the ivory tower intellectual qualify while Good Soldier Schweik fails the test?

No doubt this particular distinction oversimplifies, but it suggests how unhelpful it can be to see the "root values of the First Amendment" as consisting of something called tolerance and diversity of thought and then to imply their close association with a model of character called individual autonomy. In fact, the relation of autonomy to tolerance is murky partly because the meaning of tolerance is also opaque. Sometimes tolerance suggests a practical disengagement from moral issues in civic life. Once we decide with Dworkin or Ackerman that no one has "the right to declare that one conception of the good is better than another," it is a little hard to justify enthusiasm about reforming anything or even to imagine what reform might mean. Of course, in practice not all who espouse tolerance lack moral fervor; at least they are able to summon and express indignation against the intolerant, as by suggesting a lockout of parental ideas.

In the end, the ambiguity about who is intolerant—the parents or the professors—seems unfathomable. And this is but one example of the perplexity concerning tolerance and autonomy that is so richly displayed in the recent political debates over church and state, abortion, gay liberation, school integration, and so forth. But all this ambiguity leaves us wondering. In a state of ideological warfare, who is entitled to the prize for autonomy? If there is a scale for being liberated, how do we rate Phyllis Schlafly, Mario Cuomo, the Yoders, James Watt, and Linda Lovelace? Where on the scale should we put the eccentric who physically attacks abortion clinics? What about the Rajneesh, the Happy Hooker, or the Moral Majority? Who is liberated?

As I have offered no crisp definition, neither shall I throw the first stone. I am content that the examples of parental and child liberty used in this essay are relationships defined by law—rights, duties, and powers of children, parents, and the state. It is possible to speak clearly of liberty in juridical terms. Once we move beyond this to the protean moral models of autonomy, anything goes, and hence it goes badly. Liberty, self-determination, and autonomy continue to emote long after they have ceased to denote.

My sense is that the legend of the neutral school is really in the last analysis not about liberty at all. It borrows heavily from the idiom of liberty for the sound political reason that in this culture liberty is a rich source of value energy. But the legend is really an ark of the nineteenth-century covenant concerning schools. Earlier in this essay, and with some strain, I was able to give liberty a temporary and uneasy place within that covenant. But at heart this historic compact concerned the rather different enterprise of capturing from the family whatever was necessary to ensure that its barbarisms would become tempered by Yankee and professional virtues. The neutrality legend is best understood as a part of the nativist folklore that saw hope for the United States in the deliverance of immigrant children from certain ideological and religious baggage. This has never been said more plainly than by those who promoted the Oregon initiative that went down in *Pierce v. Society of Sisters*:

> We must now halt those coming to our country from forming groups, establishing schools, and thereby bringing up their children in an environment often antagonistic to the principles of our government.
>
> Mix the children of the foreign born with the native born, and the rich with the poor. Mix those with prejudices in the public school melting pot for a few years while their minds are plastic, and finally bring out the finished product—a true American.
>
> The permanency of this nation rests in the education of its youth in our public schools, where they will be correctly instructed in the history of our country and the aims of our government, and in those fundamental principles of freedom and democracy, upon one common level.[30]

The deliverance of the child from the family that was intended by Oregon would have spared us the discrimination between rich and poor by delivering all children without distinction to the state. This idea remains as plausible today as it was in 1920—or for that matter in fifth-century-BC Athens. But it is not an idea that should detain us here, for its connection to liberty is at best remote and problematic. Its real object is the building of culture and community by a particular coercive social instrument. I think its claim for that instrument is profoundly important and profoundly wrong, but, much more important, it is irrelevant.[31]

Enter the Justices

In modern times, the U.S. Supreme Court has had occasional encounters with the question of intellectual liberty in the schools. Since 1923 the justices have produced a sprinkling of endorsements for the limited autonomy of parents and their school children, some of which are relevant here. For all but the most recent of these decisions, it will serve to note the holding and pass on. These cases are familiar even to laymen, and my sole object is to suggest their limited scope:

1. *Meyer v. Nebraska* (1923): A private school teacher may not be forbidden to teach foreign language.
2. *Pierce v. Society of Sisters* (1925): The state may not forbid satisfaction of the duty of compulsory education in private schools; these schools may be regulated to a degree uncertain.
3. *West Virginia State Board of Education v. Barnette* (1943): Public school students with ideological objections cannot be forced to violate their consciences by reciting the Pledge of Allegiance.
4. *Wisconsin v. Yoder* (1972): Students with specific religious qualifications (namely, Amish) may be excused from a small part of the compulsory education laws where suitable alternatives are arranged.
5. *Tinker v. Des Moines Independent School District* (1969): Students in high school may not be disciplined for wearing controversial political symbols so long as they are not the occasion of serious disruption.[32]

There are other decisions that plausibly deal with intellectual liberty and might pretend to a place here. The issue of the rights of public school teachers to introduce or to exclude specific ideas provides an example. In *Epperson v. Arkansas* (1968), the Supreme Court was presented with a replay of the classic "Monkey Trial." Even in the 1960s, Arkansas still forbade teachers to present the theory of scientific evolution. The Court rescued the teacher. But teacher liberty is neither logically nor even practically connected with student liberty in any system in which the students are not free to seek another teacher. "Academic freedom" is irrelevant to the autonomy of those for whom the system presumably exists. It is at least as vexing to be tyrannized by an individual as by a school board. Racial segregation and discrimination cases are irrelevant for the same reason; the right vindicated has had nothing to do with student or parental choice. Indeed, the locus of liberty in the race cases is, if anywhere, in the federal courts.[33]

There is not a great deal that can be said about the contribution to liberty even of the few cases noted. Plausibly, *Meyer* and *Pierce* should not be considered with the rest. They are confined to private education. To the degree that they escape "reasonable regulation," private schools may be a source of liberty for those whose preferences they happen to represent and who can afford their tuition. But the *"Pierce* Compromise" does nothing at all for the bulk of families who perforce use public schools, and they are the concern and justification for this essay.

Barnette and *Tinker*, of course, are wholly relevant. Each represents a pure species of intellectual liberty—the former the right to forgo expression demanded by the school; the latter the right to engage in a certain kind of expression forbidden by the school. *Yoder* too represents a limited escape for particular nonconformists, and I should also concede that the exclusion of compulsory prayer from public schools is yet another example of liberty for at least some. Aside from the effect of *Pierce*, however, the strongest single impression from these cases is that of triviality. There is much less here than meets the eye, and the confirmation of this is the Court's 1981 decision in *Board of Education, Island Trees Union Free School District No. 26 v. Pico*. It is to date the most florid example of devotion to the symbols of intellectual liberty and, simultaneously, to the servile reality of school. The Court pledges its allegiance to student liberty while endorsing crude intellectual coercion. The decision deserves special attention.[34]

Pico involved a school board that had brusquely and awkwardly interfered with the administration of its high school library to remove a few volumes that (for reasons that were in dispute) fell out of favor with a board majority. Certain students sought an injunction. The Supreme Court produced seven opinions, the only result being that the case was sent back for trial (and ultimately settled). It may be inferred from all the opinions that a school board's power to remove books is not unbounded, but the substantive and procedural limits of its authority over the whole of the education process remain few and obscure. In the opinion announcing the Court's judgment, Justice Brennan, speaking for only three members of the Court, asserted a new student liberty right to receive information; this sounds important, but his opinion, to be fair, is not only cryptic but inconsequential. The case has been ably analyzed elsewhere, and my interest is limited to the curious light it shed on the liberty thesis.[35]

I said that *Pico* endorses crude intellectual coercion. By this I mean that, even the justices who voted to send the case back for trial went out of their way to emphasize that school boards have wide authority to impose their preferred forms of intellectual experience upon students. This is said of the library selection process, but more importantly it is said of the curriculum. Indeed, here the board is acknowledged to have a very broad discretion. Given this concession of essential school supremacy, there appears to be something paradoxical in the Brennan encomium to student liberty. In truth, however, this incongruity is required by the Court's simultaneous commitment to the existing structure and to the argot of liberty. It cannot bear to surrender its claims as the champion of speech, but it is unshakably loyal to the coercive system. The Court cannot afford to utter an intelligible rationale based in liberty, for it would be reduced to speaking in contradictions. Who cannot be sympathetic to its plight?

Facing this dilemma, the justices wisely chose to obfuscate the problem. Happily, the case came up focused upon the voluntary use of the library collection; this made the Court's escape from the basic issue relatively easy. The justices could distinguish and isolate the embarrassing implications of a compulsory curriculum. That they did so is understandable. Unlike the library, the curriculum is in every dimension a form of intellectual constraint; it is the full measure of the "inculcative" system operating in its most typical mode. It is what children actually experience on a daily basis.[36]

This is not a suggestion that compulsory education or minimum standards violate liberty. These devices need be no more authoritarian in effect than rules against child abuse; they can protect the child by assuring an intellectual safety net. They could be viewed as a part of the very structure of liberty. What could not be justified as liberty is the conscription of a child to attend a particular public school, when the child and/or parents would prefer another school—public or private— that would satisfy the state-determined minimum standard.

Suppose the next plaintiffs object straightforwardly to ideas odious to them, which they are forced to study in class, or complain about the exclusion from their classes of ideas they wish to study. Justice Brennan has assured them that, in the library they have a "right to receive information." Regarding curriculum, however, he is prepared to frustrate this same right in order to protect professional control. Obviously, there is a liberty interest in the child's having access in class to the ideas she and/or her parents want learned. How can Brennan's distinction be defended on liberty grounds?

The reality is that once the existing framework of coercion is accepted as legitimate, no judicial remedy can satisfy the liberty interest. This would remain so even if (or especially if) the judges themselves decided what should be studied. No judicial order could promote liberty of the child, unless it secured to the representative of that liberty the capacity to secure the education of his or her choice. The autonomy principle cannot by its nature be honored under the present regime of compulsory attendance at a school chosen and run by strangers.[37]

Even in the limited library setting of *Pico*, the inevitability of intellectual conscription forced the justices into grotesque positions. Brennan, for example, would authorize judicial intervention only within the zone of "voluntary" student inquiry, which he asserted is typical of a library and untypical of the classroom. There is, to be sure, a distinction here, but the pervasive fact of compulsory attendance saps much of its force. But, even accepting Brennan's point, the overall effect is peculiar, and the protective force of the new right is inconspicuous. For the constitutional guarantee then becomes effective only when it is least needed; indeed, the particular library books could have been procured elsewhere, but liberty in the classroom—for most families—could not. Brennan declines to rescue student choice exactly where it is most beset. When a curriculum case eventually arises, will the Court relent, go further, and recognize a student right to receive (or avoid) particular communications in class? I think certainly not, for such a protection would cripple the very system of intellectual constraint the Court accepts as a given.

There are other peculiarities about the Brennan opinion that betray an acceptance of systematic coercion. It specifically recognizes that, in spite of the liberty interest, government may require student attention to very particular ideas (presumably excluding others) because of the school board's "duty to inculcate community values." Now, that duty in most states is only statutory. How it could outweigh the student's First Amendment liberty right is puzzling. Is the statute conceived to justify itself? In other First Amendment settings, the government has been required to demonstrate both a compelling interest of its own and the absence of any alternative solution less onerous to the enjoyment of the protected interest. Why not here? It could scarcely be a compelling interest of the state that families not exercise their First Amendment rights.[38]

The Brennan opinion would test a school board's power to remove books by examining its motivation. The rights of the students turn on whether the board had its hearts in the right places. How is this to be determined? On the one hand, say the justices, a board can properly wish to inculcate fundamental values and community aspirations, and it may promote "respect for authority and traditional values be they social moral or political." On the other hand it cannot aim to suppress ideas or to prescribe the "orthodox in politics, nationalism . . . or other matters of opinion." Much has been said about what this collection of phrases might mean. I will say nothing, for I do not understand it. It seems a wholly elastic notion by which any result will be possible in almost any case. Nor do I grasp still another distinction proposed between censorship in ordering books and censorship in their removal, except perhaps as a pragmatic perception that motivation may be easier to prove in the latter case, thereby easing the Court's task. What can be said with conviction is that all such niggling and marginal distinctions are precisely what could be expected in an arena where candor would be a hero's (or a fool's) calling and in which the Court cannot afford to get serious about the very liberty interest it proclaims. The plurality opinion in *Pico* is a distracting liberal gesture, nothing more.[39]

I should not leave the impression that the Brennan opinion is the only puzzle in the case. The concurring opinions and dissents seem equally bewildered by the effort to square the First Amendment with the structure of the school system. Justice Rehnquist, in dissent, for example, thinks it useful to distinguish government acting as sovereign from government acting as educator. The implication may be (it is impossible to tell) that government's role as educator is less a threat to First Amendment values. School is a consistently benign institution; it is not the military draft or a code of television censorship. Rehnquist would have it that government acting as schoolmaster is much like government acting as a private property owner; it is free on its own property to do what it could not do elsewhere. He views the system as if the pupils come by choice as willing customers. There is here no perception that the process requires the incarceration of persons without consent in order to carry out the "inculcation" that is given judicial blessing. To Justice Rehnquist, public school is a tame and virtually private concern of the owner of some buildings that he happens to use as schools.[40]

What is it to act as "sovereign?" Public school is the primary social instrument for the most comprehensive nonpenal system of compulsion known to our society, not excluding the military. School is the lever of intellectual control, the tool of a conscious collective effort to induce citizens to think correct thoughts. This may be good, bad, or indifferent, but this is sovereign, or nothing is sovereign. If the school board, nevertheless, enjoys a special exemption from the First Amendment, this can be only because the interests of such a system precede in constitutional dignity the liberty right of parent and child.

The school system and the declared student right cannot peacefully coexist; the government's "special role as educator" in its present structure requires that it act as selector, inculcator, and indoctrinator, in short, as a restrainer of intellectual liberty. Nor can euphemisms about neutrality alter the reality that teaching involves the transmission of specific values. The only question is who shall get to choose and impose them. Still, I concede that all this may be virtually invisible to persons of the age and peculiar experience of the justices. Perhaps their own families have for the most part been able to choose where to live and where to send their children. They could be forgiven for imagining that the public schools are part of a system of liberty enjoyed even by the nonrich, because they have never been challenged to consider any other possibility. And they have missed the reality.

But in any case, little can be expected of the Court. The justices cannot protect the liberty interest of child and parent unless they have the temerity to condemn the system itself. Short of that they are reduced to the role of occasional sniper. The Court can gesture at the margin, rescuing a few books for the library; it can provide some procedural harassment on behalf of students in trouble; it can approve their nondisruptive badges and pins. Meanwhile, however, it will reassure the system by authorizing batteries by teachers upon their pupils — batteries that might violate the rights of prisoners. (Are even prisons more libertarian?) Indeed, under the Constitution, according to the Court, the school may and does beat children even in the face of parental objection to corporal punishment. And what it may visit upon the body as an exceptional matter, it visits upon the mind in the regular course of school business.[41]

Even if the Court were inclined to heroics, there is little it could do to insinuate fundamental First Amendment values into public education. So long as the system retains the capacity to force the average family into state institutions, the Court is basically helpless. Theory may suggest that, in some activist season, the justices could embark upon a course of institutional restructuring. Arguments are sometimes made that the First Amendment excuses all dissenters from the public school regime. Fair enough. Perhaps there are adumbrations of such a liberty in *Barnette*. But how then is the child educated if the family cannot afford tuition? Is the Court prepared to find a complementary Fourteenth Amendment right to a subsidy the parents can spend in a school of their choice? It may move that way. But not much and not soon.[42]

CONCLUSION

Will the education of children remain inevitably an exception to a general commitment to individual autonomy? Perhaps not. The present reality may be politically contingent. Arguably, for only a few generations has the system served the set of interlocking political and economic interests that so conflict with the liberty of parents and children. If these interests are beyond the Supreme Court's reach, they are not necessarily beyond that of politics. It now is plausible that half the population would desert public schools (as currently operated) were it not for economic compulsion. And it is by no means certain that public school teachers are satisfied with their own or the public's perception of their place in our culture. The role of monopolist is a source of regret to many in the profession and not merely for the limits it places on economic reward. If the mythology of intellectual liberty begins to erode, reconciliation of schooling with a constitutional ideal of autonomy could be politically imaginable.

CHAPTER TWO

Making Schools Public

I would like to share a recent discovery of mine. Why I did not perceive it sooner astounds me. It couldn't be plainer, if it were my own ear, except that, like my ear, I was not able to observe it directly. My head kept getting in the way. That same dense object has blocked my perception of a basic truth about the schools called "public."

An old story may illuminate my point. Patrick and Mary O'Toole had been long and happily married. They had four strapping sons who all went to Notre Dame and became all-Americans, living out Patrick's dream. Regrettably, a fifth son turned out badly. He was weak of sight and of limb and inordinately fond of books. He went to Harvard and took honors in poetry. Patrick was long suspicious about the boy, and when at last poor Mary was on her death bed he urged a confession. "Mary," he said, "you're going to meet your Maker. Now is that boy an O'Toole or is he not?" He got his response: "Faith, Patrick, that boy is an O'Toole; the other four are Finnegans."

This chestnut illustrates the eternal verity that labels do count (with apologies to Juliet), and that an onion called a rose can be admired for its aroma. So has it been with me and "public" schools.

When the tax-supported schools were born more than a century ago, they were, of course, christened. I am now convinced that they were wrongly christened. I don't argue that they should have been called "Finnegan," nor should we indulge the temptation to call them

Originally published in *Private Schools and the Public Good: Policy Alternatives for the Eighties*, ed. Edward M. Gaffney (University of Notre Dame Press, 1981)

illegitimate. But this much seems sufficiently clear: whatever we call our tax-supported schools, we cannot fairly call them "public."

What is it to be "public" except to be accessible to all regardless of wealth or place of residence? Access, that at least for me is an essential test for a public institution. Who is eligible? May any child hope to enter the school or only a privileged few? Perhaps I am quaint in my sense of what it means to be "public," but I take some consolation in Webster, to whom I invite your attention.

Now, if access be a necessary criterion, how public are tax-supported schools? We in California have arranged ourselves in 1,041 school districts with maybe ten times the number of attendance areas. Some of the districts are famous: Beverly Hills, Palo Alto, Huntington Beach, San Clemente, Sausalito. How does one get to choose the school in such a place? By purchasing a home there. Perhaps one in ten California families can afford to live in the area where they please. They have the power to cluster their children in isolated tax-supported schools called "public." And when they have paid their school property taxes, they can deduct them on their federal tax return.

Some well-to-do families don't worry about what school district to live in because their children's schools are called "private" and they pay the tuition. What they share with the burghers of Beverly Hills is the ability to choose. They cherish it and they exercise it, and who can blame them?

I do not wish to suggest that all the well-to-do families of California arrange to share one another's company to the exclusion of others. Many exercise that option so as to give their children contact with children of all kinds. Thus, some choose to live in residential areas that include various income classes and races, and they use the local tax-supported school. Others use Catholic schools that enroll a higher percentage of minority children statewide (44 percent) than do the tax-supported schools (41 percent). But whatever these families do, they do by choice. And they alone do so by choice.

Those who lack the means (or a church subsidy) must go to the government schools in the neighborhoods where they can afford to live. For their children, connection with the school and teachers is not made by adults who know them, or, for that matter, by any human at all. It is determined by the place of their residence. The decision is unsullied by human intervention and is best handled by a computer.

What California has managed to create is a system designed to serve private preference of a relatively few people. They have choice; the rest have their marching orders. This system of tax-supported schools is "public" only in the vapid sense that is a creature of the law. Viewed in terms of its structure and functions, it is simply a monopoly reigning over the education of the nonrich, and it is a monopoly making an offer the ordinary family can't refuse.

Monopoly over the common family was once justified by nineteenth-century designers working on two premises. One was that education would become a science, like physics; many thought they were on the threshold of decisive interventions that would end illiteracy and ignorance. The other premise was that Americans agreed on the good life; there was a value consensus that would hold and increase. Thus there was little embarrassment that the system was grossly illiberal and undemocratic; they were merely imposing scientific efficiency on what everyone wanted done anyway. It was, as David Tyack has described it, "The One Best System."

Neither promise remains today, and instead of one best system, dozens compete for teaching reading, writing, and arithmetic. In place of one work ethic, we have a dozen ethics, only some of which value work for its own sake. Of course, we agree that we should pursue the best interest of the child and foster learning, tolerance, consensus, and racial integration, but there is little agreement as to what these ideals mean or how to achieve them. Education is indeterminate in its means and pluralistic in its ends. Nevertheless, we plunge on. Those who can afford to do so choose the means to the ends for themselves; the rest choose neither, and in all things await the pleasure of the educartel. More and more clearly we see that the system is animated by a third premise: only those who can afford choice can be trusted with it. It is that creeping recognition of this systemic bias against the common man that is the bitterest pill for the managers of the system. After the rivers of democratic mythology have baptized "public" schools, it is asking a great deal of the schoolmaster to accept with good humor being perceived as despot.

What emerges from this analysis is not a simple answer to the educational problem but a clearer question. Insofar as the purposes and means of education remain conflicting and obscure, the policy question is not, "What is best?" Rather, it is, "How do we allocate authority to decide for the individual child?" Beyond that vague minimum about which society does agree, who should decide what and where the child shall learn? There are two candidates for this authority: the educational managers and the family. Are there reasons to prefer one to the other, or some combination of the two?

The answer could be sought on the high plane of political theory. Here everything depends on the assumptions with which one begins. From an aristocratic preference, one favors decisions by the few for the many. Of course, to the extent that the educational aristocracy is itself in deep conflict, such a paternalistic decision model would seem a bit arbitrary; it means handing children over to schools almost because their managers have acquired certain credentials and not because they are the guardians of any particular ideals or because they claim any particular skill.

Every teacher in every school today *does*, of course, hold some specific ideals of his own and *does* claim some specific skills, but the child does not come to that teacher's classroom for either of those reasons. The child comes simply because he lives on Thirty-Fourth Street and is told to come. And whether he gets a touchy-feely or a back-to-basics school is just luck of the draw. Our present system thus fails the historic definition of aristocracy, for it lacks a common commitment among those in authority. I have on occasion called the educational order "elitist." I apologize. It is, instead, Hobbes's jungle of petty tyrannies imposing private judgments. It is for the ordinary family an experience of chaos and coercion.

The alternative to Thomas Hobbes is basically Jeffersonian and democratic. Thomas Jefferson thought in terms of sturdy individual farmers. We must translate this eighteenth-century image into individual families, few of whom are close to the soil and not all of them sturdy. But like it or not, family choice is the only democratic model available to an educational world so divided. If there were consensus on specific learning goals and the tools to reach them, we could imagine an educational system that could be called democratic in the sense of majority rule. For better or worse—and I think better—the United States in 1981 cannot assemble a consensus for any but the very broadest set of educational objectives and no consensus whatsoever regarding means. The only sense, then, in which democracy is possible is that of the individual choice of free and equal citizens.

If we descend from political theory, it may be possible to say something more practical about the proper allocation of power over children for the pursuit of such broad majoritarian aims as can be identified. I will try. What I say will not rise to the level of theory; nonetheless, I say it because it has helped me to think about the issue, and it might help others who are similarly puzzled.

Here are my candidates for these dimly perceived social objectives. Education should promote the following: the best interest of the child, high-quality learning, parental liberty paired with parental responsibility, social consensus, racial integration, and the good of the teaching profession. I commence with by far the most important—the child's own interest. It is the necessary (and perhaps sufficient) justification of any educational system. But, except for mastery of basic academic skills and some sense of our political institutions, what can the "child's interest" mean? In the absence of any social definition of a good education, it means whatever the adult with power to choose for the child would have it mean. We've made the circle again.

But not quite. I think it is possible in a rough way to evaluate decision-making about the child's interest simply by observing and comparing the way decisions are reached by professional systems, on the one hand, and parents, on the other. At least one primitive principle for the allocation of power emerges from that experience. By and large, individual assignments made by an adult familiar with the child are superior to assignments determined by the impersonal fact of residence. Human judgment may be fallible, but it improves upon random selection. I suppose it is too clear for argument that it is the parent who is in the better position to make a personal judgment about *this* child. Bureaucratic systems can provide individualization for only a very small portion of cases—and then only at great cost. If personalistic judgment is important, the parent has a great advantage.

Further, human judgment about children tends to be improved by three rather specific qualities that occur in different degrees among adult deciders. The first is the decider's capacity to hear the child's own opinion; Steve Sugarman and I call this "voice." The second is the degree to which such a decider is likely to act with altruism; we call this "caring." The third is the degree to which the outcome of the decision is mutually baneful or beneficial for child and adult; we call this "responsibility." I won't restate all the arguments one can make for the family in terms of voice, caring, and responsibility. They are mostly obvious. It is the parent who in most cases hears the child's own opinion, it is the parent who cares the most, and it is the parent who suffers with the child when the decision is bad. It is also the parent who is most likely to take the initiative to get the child out of a bad situation; it is seldom in the interest of the managers of the school system to see students disappear from the average daily attendance count.

These arguments are not antiprofessional. They merely recognize that professionalism only becomes possible when the client is free to sever the relation. Family choice, indeed, is the only way to introduce professionalism into government schools. Nor would I argue that parents do not need professional counseling in making decisions. That is precisely what they do need; what they don't need is subordination and domination by bureaucrats who have them as a captive audience. Under such conditions, the interest of the child tends to become secondary to the interest of the system.

My conclusion so far is that the empowering of parents would not only make it possible at last to create a public system of education but would also seem quite consistent with the best interest of the individual child. Before going on to ask whether family choice is consistent with consensus, integration, and other broad social values, let us pause to ask what a system based upon family choice might look like. There is no need to describe every possible model (but I do exclude some, such as individual tax credits, which are useful principally to wealthier families). What I will describe is the plan for my own state, which many think technically feasible and politically attractive. This plan, which I will call it the "California Plan," is reproduced below.

The structure of this plan is, first of all, conservative in this sense of that word. Unlike other reform plans, it destroys no institutions and it favors the existing government schools. These would justly be labeled "public," for no child would now be subject to an assignment forced upon him by his family's circumstance. Those who wished not to attend public schools could attend any of three other types of schools. They could, as today, opt for the traditional private school financed by tuition. In addition, however, they could choose either the private or public form of what we call the "New Schools," both of which would be financed by state scholarships provided to families.

The important institutional innovation here is the New *Public* School, which is a novel legal creature; each such school would take the form of a separate public corporation organized and designed by a local school board (or public university) and financed by the scholarships of its patrons. Its counterpart in the private sector would be the New *Private* School operating according to the same rules, except for its entitlement to teach religion.

The traditional public school—that is, the present model of state-owned—would be relatively favored over the New Schools, first, with more money. Scholarships for the New Schools would be worth 90 percent of what would be spent statewide in the traditional public schools for children of similar age, grade, and circumstance. Traditional public schools could also, as today, prefer children who live in an attendance area chosen by the school board. Likewise, severely disabled children could be redirected to schools convenient to the system. New Schools, by contrast, would be open to all children, regardless of residence and disability.

Unlike the public schools, the New Schools would also be required to set aside at least 25 percent of their spaces, in which spaces priority would be given to the applications of children from low-income families defined as the bottom 25 percent on the income scale. (These children would also be entitled to reasonable cost of transportation.) The rest of the spaces in a New School would be filled by application of criteria valid for public schools under the U.S. Constitution other than residence and disability.

The California Plan is, then, a way for families to choose freely among existing and new institutions. If change occurs in enrollment patterns, it will be because consumers did not like the services offered in a particular school. At last, there would be a way for public institutions that have suffered brain death to expire peacefully, as do private schools, instead of having life sustained by artificial means, including a captive clientele. Conversely, there would be all the rewards of popularity for the schools that people like. This phenomenon is called "competition," and I believe that in our society it is regarded as normal and healthy.

Another special and important feature of the New Public School, in contrast to traditional public schools, is that it is permitted to operate as much like a private school as its founding school district desires. Its articles of incorporation can bind it to the parent district very closely or very remotely; thus its management could be lodged in the parents and children or, conversely, left in the hands of district administrators. Many models of governance could flourish, including management by the teaching staff. If permitted by its charter, each school could hire whom it chooses and deal with employees solely by contract instead of by statute and regulation. It could set its curriculum to different specialties, and it could set a code of discipline and enforce it.

California law has burdened its private schools very lightly. A fear of some opponents of educational subsidies to families has been that private schools would run too great a risk of heavy state regulation. With this fear in mind, Sugarman and I have inserted the following language into the initiative:

> New schools shall be eligible to redeem state scholarships upon filing a statement indicating satisfaction of those requirements for hiring and employment, for curriculum and for facilities that applied to private schools on July 1, 1979; the Legislature may not augment such requirements.

This language, which would become part of the California Constitution, not only would prevent such an outcome, but for the first time offer private schools complete protection against legislative control of hiring, curriculum, and facilities. The more important effect of this provision, however, is to open the possibility of deregulating some portion of the *public* sector; just how large a portion would depend upon the preferences of consumers. Some families will want public schools that continue to be heavily regulated; they believe such regulation contributes to child protection. Some, by contrast, will want New Public Schools that are deregulated to permit variety and flexibility. Consumers could have their individual way without leaving the public sector.

Other than the admission rules, the only significant regulation of the New Schools—public and private—would come in the form of information requirements and limits upon the ways in which tuition can be added on top of the scholarship. The information demands are of course crucial if the market is to be self-regulating. Consumers must have adequate knowledge to make choices, and they must be able to punish the school that deliberately misinforms them. The California Plan would permit parents to levy that punishment by transferring the prorated portion of their scholarship at any time to another school; it would permit the state, upon proof of deliberate fraud, to punish by terminating the school's eligibility to redeem scholarships.

The California Plan also requires an agency independent of any particular school to distribute information about all the options available to parents, and it guarantees an additional subsidy to families with "special information needs"—an information voucher—to purchase counseling services in the market. The initiative is based upon respect for the judgment of all parents, but it recognizes that some families will need to overcome barriers to full participation. Some will not speak or read English well. Some will be quite unsophisticated about education, since strangers have always decided for them. Personal counseling will be the most effective means for such families to raise their level of knowledge about schools, and the counselor should be of the parent's own choosing. It is expected that a new profession of educational advisers would arise; unlike the old counseling system, it would answer to the family instead of to the school. It is also predictable that volunteer organizations ranging from the YMCA to the League of Women Voters would find counseling of disadvantaged parents a rewarding activity. And private accreditation groups would make it their business to rate schools based on criteria to which different parents will give varying weight.

The New Schools would be limited in another way. They could not charge extra tuition to low-income families, and the other families could be charged only according to their ability to pay. Unlimited freedom to charge add-on tuition would frustrate access by the ordinary and low-income family; it would re-create the present system in new form.

The scholarship would, today (1985), average about $2,300 (but the amount would vary among children according to legislative judgment of need and other considerations). It is likely that some schools will be able to find families content to pay an extra thousand dollars or two. And although their payment would in part be a subsidy for others in the school, they would be paying far less than what it costs them today for private schools that spend at an equivalent level. The sole disincentive, if any, for such families would be the presence in the New Schools of children from all classes and races; we hope that for most families this social mix will be viewed as an opportunity for their child. For the unready, there would still be the option to stay in the old private school and pay for it (or, of course, their present public school).

The New Schools would be subject to one more limitation. They could not dismiss a child for academic reasons unless he or she were acquiring no substantial benefit; the school, however, could itself regulate the process of dismissal so long as its procedures were fair. Most schools would very likely establish an arbitration system for serious disputes. The school could also—with notice and fair procedure—set a code of conduct and enforce it.

For the child dismissed for academic or behavioral reasons, the California Plan represents new hope. Hitherto, he or she has been relegated to "opportunity" schools or "continuation centers," some good, some not so good, but in any case with few options. There would now be a strong incentive for public and private providers to organize to serve such children in new and creative ways. We should remember the historic parallel of children with learning disabilities; until the recent intervention by the federal courts and Congress, the hope, if any, for such children lay largely in the private sector. For any child who is "special" in the many senses of that euphemism, the best system is the one that can adapt and reorganize flexibility, whether the providers be public, private, or both.

Let me sum up what I have said about the California Plan. It delivers as much power to the consumer as our ingenuity could devise. And for the producer it guarantees as much liberty as is consistent with the primary right of the family. Such a system should truly put the family in the saddle. It will at last be "public" in the fullest sense and will serve the best interest of the child.

But will it serve the other broad goals of the social order? Let me add a word as to each, beginning with the need for consensus and tolerance. Some claim that giving ordinary families the choice that the wealthy now employ would divide us as a people. Two flawed assumptions underlie this assertion. The first is that, thanks to the public schools, we are currently unified and tolerant; the second is that ordinary people tend to be bigots. There is no evidence supporting either assumption, nor is there any reason to believe that government schools are fostering consensus.

My own belief is that a government that despises the values of ordinary people and wishes to erase them by compulsion is likely to generate more conflict than it cures. Conversely, a government that plainly respects the cherished differences among people is not necessarily divisive. Indeed, the manifestation of trust by the government will beget trust in return from families. To know that the society supports the transmission of one's special values is to have a reason to support the transmission of one's special values, which is to have a reason to support the social order, not to upset it. E pluribus unum is not a statement of satisfaction that we have abolished all differences; it is a recognition that in human society—as in the biological order—variety is not weakness but strength.

As for racial integration, the question can be plainly put. When we are through doing whatever it is we will do through the courts, should we deny opportunities for integration for those who will seek them beyond the judicial reach? Consider the District of Columbia. Would we have more or less integration if the children of the District were entitled to scholarships and a bus ride to the private school or public school of their choice, either in or out of the District? In many parts of California and elsewhere, there are spaces in private or public schools within reasonable distance of children whose presence would be an integrating presence. I should add that the most stable integration our society has experienced is voluntary integration, and there is more of it today than is acknowledged by those committed to busing orders as the principal, or worse yet, the only tool in our legal quiver.

What would family choice do for teachers? I have already said it could make public school teaching a true profession. Let me add that it could make it a prosperous profession. At least it would do so in California, where the cost per classroom is now approximately $85,000 and the teacher is paid less than $25,000. In a world of free consumer choice, state systems characterized by an enormous commitment to administrative and paraprofessional personnel who operate very large schools would begin to get competition. Many families prefer smaller schools, and given free choice, they could get them. Such schools would be characterized by a heavier proportional investment in teachers as is characteristic of private schools today. Imagine a school of ten teachers serving two hundred children who bring, on the average, a $2,300 scholarship;

it doesn't take a computer to perceive that teacher salaries could rise. To the objection that somebody else would then lose, I respond that the consumer is the best one to decide which laborer is worthier of his hire.

Teachers, by the way, could be expected to form many New Schools, acting either on their own or through their unions. In the present order, teachers are not often entrepreneurs; some observers think they lack the temperament. I think they lack the capital. Who is in his right mind would offer risk capital to finance a school today? But given a system of scholarships, there would be every reason for private (and public) sources of capital to invest in good teaching. This would be assisted by a special provision in the California Plan making unused space in public schools available for rent at cost to the New Schools. In an era of surplus capacity, this is another important incentive. Finally, it is inevitable that the formation of New Schools will be advanced by the expertise of unions and of management consultants who will offer entrepreneurial services to teachers and to the families who wish to obtain their services in various kinds of schools.

It is crucial that this society do something for the teaching profession, which is seriously struggling. Since we lost the indentured service of many of our brightest women through the women's movement, and since the baby bust wrecked the teacher market, too few of the most talented young peoples are pursuing the path to the teaching degree and certification. Unless we change the system, within ten years it will be entirely in the hands of well-meaning mediocrities. The frightening details of this problem may be read in the recent work of Timothy Weaver of Boston University. The remedy may be read in our California Plan, which abolishes credentialing and tenure as requirements of law and which gives to teachers both the dignity of a free relation to a parent client and the opportunity for economic gain.[1]

I will shortly describe how the plan is a blessing to taxpayers; let me now point out that the present scheme of things unnaturally depresses the level of national commitment to education. So long as the public and private sectors are arrayed in mutual economic hostility, education will be shortchanged. It has become dangerously fashionable to view education essentially as a zero-sum game. According to this view, every dollar now spent for private schools diminishes the political and economic support for spending in the public sector, and vice versa. I would like to suggest, however, that a system in which the choices of families in both sectors are funded by the legislature would assemble the largest possible constituency for education. Even those who operate traditional public schools ought to grasp this fundamental lesson in economics, un-less, of course, they perceive change itself—any change—as threatening. For the California Plan is in the best interests not only of the students, but also of teachers and administrators in the public and nonpublic schools alike.

As for the effect on the institution of the family, consider first the effect of the present system on the parent of ordinary means. Until age five, the child experiences that parent as authoritative and protective. At that vulnerable age in the child's life, the parent is suddenly stripped of all power, and the child is directed by strangers to report to strangers who will teach him what the strangers think best for him or her. Should we be surprised if the child loses her healthy faith in the only people who have been her primary advocates? Can we blame children for view-ing their parents as impotent, when parents can do nothing to affect the basic character of the institution that claims the prime hours of their day? There could be no more efficient device for discrediting the family in the eyes of its own members than the present regime in education.

By contrast, the family that maintains control of education has a better chance of remaining effective in all of its functions. In such a family, the opinions of both child and parent can count for something; they thus become worth discussing. The family can function as the political incubator in which important questions are aired and shared. This society could do nothing better for the battered and beleaguered American family than to give it the capacity to decide for its own chil-dren. Give it counseling, give it information, give it limits, but give it power and responsibility.

Therein lies sanity and a stabler social order. Don't tell us that many poor families are apathetic, stupid, and delinquent. Of course they are, as are many wealthy ones. Don't warn that they will make mistakes. Of course they will; the rest of us do, with embarrassing regularity. Per-haps the difference between us and the poor is that we are permitted to make our own mistakes—and learn from them. The poor are permitted no mistakes and thus have nothing to learn; their apathy and hostility is a perfectly rational response, just as the failure, violence, truancy, and apathy of their children in school are responses to the indignity and foolishness of compulsory and often arbitrary assignments. If you want parents who try, and if you want children who try to learn, the surest medicine is to link them to their teachers by family choice.

I would be remiss if I said nothing about the economic cost of a system of family choice—the California Plan in particular. Let me first say that I am more interested in efficiency than cost. Let me also restate my belief that society ultimately will support education more generously if the private and public sectors can be brought more into economic harmony. But then let me stress that any plan can be designed to limit cost through a variety of devices. One is a simple clearing of public expenditure; the California Plan, for example, would impose a six-year freeze on additional spending, except for inflationary adjustments. Eligibility for scholarships would be phased in over that period, and the introduction of an additional percent or two of children drawn from the private sector each of those years would have a minimal effect on average spending per pupil. Information and transportation would cost something, but these costs would be minor and would be well worth the price given their importance to making choice effective for poor families. Even the enemies of choice have estimated the maximum added cost at less than 4 percent of the total public cost of education, and these critics have never begun to consider the savings.

These savings are potentially massive. There would be two important sources of efficiency: the size of the scholarship and the effects of deregulation. Since the scholarship is set at 90 percent of the cost in the traditional public school, student transfers from public schools to a New Public or New Private School would offset some or all costs of private school entrants. More important, the elimination of heavy statutory controls over curriculum, credentialing, tenure, and facilities would permit New Schools to operate with the efficiency characteristic of private schools. Today, spending per pupil in private schools is less than half that of their public counterparts, yet these low-budget schools achieve what James Coleman and Andrew Greeley tell us are consistently superior results in learning. The costs of such schools will (and should) rise as they enter the system, but competition will assure that their efficiency will be maintained with consequent benefits to their pupils and the society. Thus, a legislature that wished to maintain educational output could expect to do so without changing the present public investment. In spite of deregulation, there will be interesting and important decisions left for lawmakers.

Even if public education has had a checkered past in this country, it certainly has a future. The United States desperately needs true public education, and I am convinced that it is politically possible to achieve it. The principal barrier is the "public" halo with which the monopoly has crowned itself. The lawmaker and the executive are in an effective position to expose this mislabeling, but they obviously run political risk in doing so. It will be interesting to observe their contributions to the formation of public awareness and public opinion in the decades before us.

APPENDIX

An Initiative for Education by Choice

The following section shall be added to Article IX of the California Constitution:

Section 17. The people of California have adopted this section to improve the quality and efficiency of schools, to maximize the education opportunities of all children, and to increase the authority of parents and teachers.

(1) New Schools

    (a) In addition to the public schools and private schools currently recognized by law, there shall be two classes of schools, together known as New Schools.

    (b) New Private Schools are private schools eligible to redeem state scholarships.

    (c) New Public Schools are schools organized as public corporations eligible to redeem state scholarships.

    School districts, community colleges, and public universities may establish New Public Schools. Each shall be a public nonprofit corporation governed by rules fixed by the organizing authority at the time of incorporation. Such schools are free common schools under section 5 of this article; section 6 of this article shall not limit their formation. Except as stated in this section, New Public Schools shall operate according to the law affecting New Private Schools.

    (d) New Schools shall be eligible to redeem state scholarships upon filing a statement indicating satisfaction of those requirements for hiring and employment, for curriculum and for facilities that applied to private schools on July 1, 1979; the Legislature may not augment such requirements. No school shall lose eligibility to redeem state scholarships except upon proof of substantial violation of this section after notice and opportunity to defend.

No New School may advocate unlawful behavior or expound the inferiority of either sex or of any race nor deliberately provide false or misleading information respecting the school. Each shall be subject to reasonable requirements of disclosure. The Legislature may set reasonable standards of competence for diplomas.

No school shall be ineligible to redeem state scholarships because it teaches moral or social values, philosophy, or religion, but religion may not be taught in public schools or New Public Schools; a curriculum may be required, but no pupil shall be compelled to profess ideological belief or actively to participate in ceremony symbolic or belief.

(2) Admission to New Schools

(a) A New School may set enrollment and select students by criteria valid for public schools under the U.S. Constitution other than disability and place of residence within the state.

(b) Each New School shall reserve a least 25 percent of each year's new admission for timely applications from families with income lower than 75 percent of California families. If such applications are fewer than the places reserved, all shall be admitted and the balance of reserved places selected as in paragraph (a) of this subsection; if such applications exceed the reserved places, the school may select therefrom the reserved number.

(3) Finance

(a) Every child of school age is entitled without charge to a state scholarship redeemable by New Schools and adequate for a thorough education as defined by law. Scholarships shall be equal for every child of similar circumstance differing only by factors deemed appropriate by the Legislature; they shall reflect the educational cost attributable to disability, and, for children of low-income families, the cost of reasonable transportation. Except for children enrolled in schools in which parents or other relatives have primary responsibility for instruction of their own children, no scholarship shall be less than 80 percent of the average scholarship for children of similar grade level. A New Private School shall use scholarship income solely for the education of its students. The Legislature shall provide for an appropriate division of the scholarship in the case of transfers. Nothing required or permitted by this section shall be deemed to repeal or conflict with section 8 of this article of section 5 of Article XVI.

(b) New Schools shall accept scholarships form low-income families as full payment for educational or related services. Charges to others shall be consistent with the family's ability to pay.

(c) The average public cost per pupil enrolled in New Schools shall approximate 90 percent of that cost in traditional public schools. "Public cost" here and in subsection (3)(d) shall mean every cost to state and local government of maintaining elementary and secondary education in the relevant year as determined by the Department of Finance according to law; it shall not include the cost of funding employee retirement benefits that are unfunded on June 3, 1982.

(d) For school years 1982–83 through 1987–88, the total public cost of elementary and secondary education shall not exceed that of 1981–82 adjusted for changes in average personal income and total school-age population. The Controller shall authorize no payment in violation of this subsection.

(e) Excess space in public schools shall be available to New Schools for rental at actual cost.

(4) Rights

(a) A pupil subject to compulsory education who attends a New School may continue therein unless she or he is deriving no substantial academic benefit or is responsible for serious or habitual misconduct related to school. With fair notice and procedures, each school may set and enforce a code of conduct and discipline and regulate its academic dismissals. No pupil enrolled in any such school shall suffer discrimination on the basis of race, religion, gender, or national origin.

(b) The Legislature shall assure provision of adequate information about New Schools through sources independent of any school or school authority. Parents with special information needs shall receive a grant redeemable for the services of independent education counselors.

(5) Transitional Provision

The Legislature shall promptly implement this section, ensuring full eligibility for scholarships of at least one-fourth of all pupils in school year 1984–85 and a similar additional number yearly thereafter.

CHAPTER THREE

School Choice as Simple Justice

SCHOOL CHOICE AS SIMPLE JUSTICE

The media have at last grasped the fact that test scores and graduation rates improve where schools are freely chosen by families. But what many people still fail to appreciate is that the case for choice in education goes much deeper than market efficiency and the hope to overtake Japan. Shifting educational authority from government to parents is a policy that rests upon basic beliefs about the dignity of the person, the rights of children, and the sanctity of the family; it is a shift that also promises a harvest of social trust as the experience of responsibility is extended to all income classes. So far, that part of the message is not making it into the current great debate about schooling.

Even the work of John Chubb and Terry Moe, authors of the celebrated *Politics, Markets, and America's Schools*, has contributed to the lopsided picture of educational choice as an efficiency device aimed primarily at economic growth. Their book treats consumers of education as potential instruments of producer autonomy; the declared objective is liberation not of the family but of the school. In their telling, choice becomes, almost by inadvertence, a tool of supply-side economics: we could almost suppose that the only serious aim of school reform is to maximize those outcomes that we now measure in our econometric models. Test scores, courses taken, attendance, and graduation rates are allowed to exhaust the definition of the objective.

Originally published in *First Things*, April 1992, 193–200

This is troubling on several specific grounds. First, putting the focus on the school instead of the autonomy of its clientele suggests that we can achieve the same objective by giving each existing government school the powers of an independent feudal baron. Choice would be superfluous. The reasons given by Chubb and Moe for believing that such local dynasties could not survive might be right, but nobody knows for sure. Second, their arguments are largely indifferent to the participation of private schools. For reasons that I will elaborate, the possibility of parents' choosing in the private sector is crucial both as justice and as policy. Third, and most important, in the end choice comes off merely as an interesting policy gadget, further obscuring what its earlier supporters had supposed to be its central humanistic justifications.

School choice, in short, has been treated like the teenager with the keys to the convertible. His friends see that he is useful, and for the moment he is popular. One day, however, he may need to be admired for less ephemeral reasons. Choice, too, needs to be loved for its own sake, or at least for a reason more noble than its capacity to make life better for the producers. In fact, there are larger reasons for believing in choice—reasons equal in dignity to those that underlie our great constitutional freedoms. A humane democracy, however, should not leave its realization to the vagaries of constitutional litigation. What follows is a brief sketch of some of the more obvious social and political arguments in support of parental choice.

Our system of tax-supported education has for 150 years provided many of the primary embarrassments to the image of the United States as a just society. The United States, for example, is still resolutely unfair to the children attending government schools in those districts that are disfavored by the poverty of their tax bases. This form of fiscal discrimination is unique among Western nations; foreign visitors find it incomprehensible, and, of course, it is. It also happens to be constitutional.

So also was the official racial segregation that lasted in the schools from their beginning until the courts removed the option in our own time. Not that the reality of segregation is behind us. Those who know Detroit, Kansas City, or the District of Columbia will affirm that the same exclusive effect can issue lawfully from the impermeability of district boundaries.

Until yesterday it was also the practice of our schools to force dissenting and nonbelieving children of the poor to behave like Protestants.

Eventually the courts said no. That particular tyranny is behind us, only to be replaced by another: children of whatever belief now must study the gospel of secular neutrality.

Finally, we still arrange education so that children of the wealthy can cluster in chosen government enclaves or in private schools; the rest get whatever school goes with the residence the family can afford. This socialism for the rich we blithely call "public," even though no other public service entails such financial exclusivity. Whether the library, the swimming pool, the highway, or the hospital—if it is "public," it is accessible. But admission to the government school comes only with the price of the house. If the school is in Beverly Hills or Scarsdale, the poor need not apply.

Choice is the obvious remedy for such maldistribution and discrimination. A system of universal state scholarships, properly designed, would remove the anomaly of the impoverished district and the imposition of state ideology upon dissenters. This is the primary hope for ending the balkanization of children by race and family wealth. Choice, indeed, is the specific therapy for every historic pathology of the schools.

It is also the key to redirecting the schools toward positive but neglected social missions. The real case for choice begins with the significance it places upon free expression and the effects of that emphasis. Raising our children to represent our own values is the most important form of speech most of us will ever experience. That this point is almost wholly neglected by civil libertarians and by most literate people is a puzzle. One wonders if they are blinded by the hermetic separation of their professional work from their family life. The adult members of our elites tend to experience significant parts of their daily economic roles as forms of cherished and protected speech; in a market economy, their work often has a public dimension, or in any case tends to provide opportunity for discourse on public affairs. By contrast, communication within the family to their own children can easily seem remote from First Amendment values. Given its natural privacy, such speech is seldom constrained by external influences; hence it is seldom evaluated in political terms. Communication within the educated family is essentially cloistered, and its organic role within the system of speech is not easily appreciated.

It is ordinary parents who grasp this point most easily. They wear no cultural blinkers in their daily work. They have little reason to fantasize that the ideas they profess will reach influential ears or be disseminated by the market or the media. For most parents it is obvious that their chance to influence the world abides largely in the message they are able to embody in their descendants. Children are the books written by the poor. One day, perhaps, civil libertarians will discover this; the ACLU might even convene a great conference on family speech and the First Amendment—but certainly not tomorrow.

Note that there are two distinct aspects to parental speech. There is, first, the communication to the child—the ordinary private act of personal speech. Second, there is the message the parent hopes to embody in and disseminate to others *through* the child. Later in this essay it will be argued that this latter conception of the child, not as audience but as medium, constitutes an independent justification for educational choice, and that, when schools are freely chosen, they constitute a marketplace of potential ideas.

For the moment, however, let us concentrate on the purely personal and private dimension of parental speech. Here it is sufficient to observe that a society that truly cherished freedom of expression would ensure that options were provided to the family within the educational economy. For the school itself *could* represent an important personal message from parents to children; that is, it could serve this function to the extent that parents are economically able to express themselves in the act of selection. Today those families with the means to do so use schools in exactly that manner, and our law supports this precious liberty while carefully arranging to deny its practical enjoyment by the poor. This aristocratic policy is especially problematic given the reigning system of tax-supported compulsory education in which government providers dispense a set of ideas that is politically filtered. Choice is the obvious therapy. Indeed, viewed as free communication from parent to child, the choice of the school is not merely a means but a significant constitutional end.

Simultaneously, choice is therapy for the family's sense of its own dignity. It seems safe to assume that we have no present plan to replace the family as the social unit that bears primary responsibility for the child. Even the widely defamed "welfare mother" continues to bear both the right and the duty to decide everything about her child's life. She decides everything, that is, except the institution, the teacher, and the curriculum to which the child will be bound for the prime hours of the day.

This disenfranchisement of the poor (and not only the poor) comes at a cost to both parent and child. The parents learn that they are not trusted; they are not taken seriously. Society tells them instead that even utter strangers are better judges of the school that is most suitable for their child. A more disheartening message is hard to imagine.

From the child's point of view, the picture is equally dispiriting. For five years he or she has experienced the parent as friend and advocate. This dependence is complete, and normally it is wholly positive. In the case of the child whose family can afford to choose, that relationship extends beyond infancy when the parent selects the institutional agent— public or private—that will provide him or her with formal education. For the ordinary family, the opposite obtains. The relationship of trust and confidence terminates when the child sees the parent subordinated to strangers who command his or her presence for purposes of their own.

This is horrendous social policy, and it could be reversed without great technical difficulty. Over time, much of the damage to the family could be undone simply by a social commitment that human dignity be respected through an intelligently designed system of choice. No doubt the new experience of responsibility may prove painful for some parents; it generally has for the rest of us. But that way lies the possibility of maturity and autonomy. Not all of us make it, but no great purpose is served in denying the poor their chance to fail. The present policy succeeds only in maintaining that passive dependence of which we all complain. Some say the poor prefer and deserve it, but how would we know, so long as we withhold their opportunity to do otherwise?

For my part, I have yet to meet a poor parent who prefers such impotence. Anyone who claims to speak for the poor should think twice about supporting a system that assumes them to be invincibly incompetent in their evaluation of educators. Obviously, people who have never been allowed to choose may need access to good advice, and ensuring good information and advice may usefully enlist the agency of the state. In designing information systems, we need only remember that choice is the goal and the state is only its occasional instrument.

Now, change the focus slightly and consider parental speech specifically as a collective good. Protecting the speech of all parents as we protect that of the rich is a social end that can be realized only through choice. Schools that are freely chosen are the proxies for parental ideas that seek entry to the public dialogue. Today those who can afford to do so often choose a school precisely because it preserves and projects a certain deposit of belief. The parent has two distinctive interests in that belief. *Qua* parent, one seeks transmission of one's beliefs to the child. *Qua* citizen, one chooses a school that puts one's particular beliefs into the ideological market. The school is a loudspeaker for those who freely support it with their presence and wish to cooperate in its message.

The nonrich are currently denied this medium of expression. They are conscripted for schools that impose upon them a narrow curriculum produced by a political process. By political necessity the content of that curriculum is a matter for lobbying by, and must emerge inoffensive to, feminists, business interests, gays, lesbians, unions, racial minorities, seniors, Jews, Christians, scientists, and Christian Scientists. In short, it must be censored. The curriculum of the public schools is whatever survives this comprehensive system of prior restraint. It is an abuse of language to describe such denatured communication as a marketplace of ideas.

If we seek the specific therapy for this monopoly of expression, it lies, again, in the extension of choice to all income classes. Such a policy would serve the common interest in a dynamic system of free speech. Society at a stroke could eliminate the censorship of family expression and establish a robust marketplace of ideas embodied in institutions that are freely chosen by parents from every corner of society.

A counterargument is sometimes made that, although school choice would produce a marketplace of competing ideas, the individual child would experience its benign effect only if the parent chose a school that strove to embody the spectrum of ideas in its own curriculum. Most, they fear, would choose a school with a particularized method and ideology. Therefore, we should conscript the poor for whatever it is that is represented in the public school.

Unfortunately, a curriculum that is politically determined—that is, any public school curriculum—cannot aspire even to be neutral much less to be a marketplace. Its highest ambition is to avoid offense. An open market of ideas inside PS 102 is unthinkable quite apart from the insufficiency of classroom hours. If the state were to double the school day, there would be crucial ideas that for constitutional and/or political reasons could never enter the public classroom. Nor would all these censored ideas be about controversial topics like race, religion, homosexuality, immortality, abortion, and gender roles. There are subtler heresies abroad that suggest limits to the ambitions of science and even presuppose the objectivity of morality. On such matters the public curriculum is not merely neutral; it is silent and will remain so. If there is to be a marketplace, it will be provided by schools that teach sharp-edged ideas of the sort that are offensive to the public censors and the lobbyists; these schools will be freely chosen by parents from among the alternatives allowable only in the free curricula of a private sector.

Another response to the speech-based claims for choice might be put this way. Censorship is, to be sure, a structural feature of the government school, but, if this is an objection, it is one fairly to be levied also at a system of choice that merely enthrones the parent as censor.

Left in this naked form, the objection is obviously true. Today when a rich family chooses a school—whether public or private—this is an act of censorship. But to see this clearly is an awakening. We grasp the reality that some adult is going to be determining the content and form of the curriculum for every child; in the designing of schools, young people will necessarily be dominated by older people. Insofar as it is inevitable, this is no objection, but it does allow us to see that the correct formulation of the question must be this: Who should dominate the children of the ordinary family? Ought we to strip the working parent and the poor of the censoring authority that we blithely confirm for the rich?

In saying all this, we are still discussing choice in the context of liberty—and specifically of free expression—as a central social value. In relation to children, however, liberty is a tricky idea. I have just said that children will inevitably be subject to adults, but what would be more precise is to say that adults will determine the formal characteristics of the institutions of society. It may nevertheless be possible and desirable to have a care for the child's own autonomy. Paradoxically, if we do have such a care, we must (at least in some cases) proceed by preferring the distinctive interest of the child in remaining relatively dependent and protected even against his own will. That is, even to maximize the over-all autonomy of a child, we may in the short run be required to limit his opportunity to risk injury—whether physical, intellectual, or moral. What society must seek from the institutions of childhood is the preparation of an independent adult. In pursuit of that end the question becomes when to restrain and when to enfranchise the child along the way. Note, again, that in the case of wealthy parents we pursue the child's own autonomy precisely by giving the parents complete sovereignty. At least for those families, we have concluded that patriarchy is liberating.

Where education is concerned, any general argument for parental sovereignty as handmaiden to autonomy must be sensitive to the liberty interest of both parent and child and must extend to families of all classes. This argument would have various parts—one negative, several positive. The negative step is simple enough. Any claim for systematic state hegemony assumes a preexisting social agreement about the proper content and method of education; subordination of the family rests at a minimum upon a consensus about what the state should command. Of course, no such consensus exists. This society is deeply pluralistic, not merely concerning the aims of education but even regarding the proper means to convey effectively that content on which we do agree. On this ground alone our constitutional traditions should support parental sovereignty. What excuse have we for frustrating the interest of the low-income parent to select any of the experiences that we concede to be appropriate for the fortunate? Surely the public educator claims no offsetting liberty right of his own to conscript somebody else's child for the bureaucrat's private vision of the good life.

However, the argument for broad parental authority is much more compelling than the selfish individual liberty interest of mothers and fathers. The central—and wholly positive—proposition is that in most instances the liberty interest of the child is advanced more by decisions of the sovereign parent than those of the sovereign bureaucrat.

The reasons for the parental superiority are not difficult to specify. First, growth in the child's own autonomy is generally in the direct self-interest of the parent; it is not so often in the self-interest of the professional. Normal parents seek to bring the child's subordination to an end by extending each petty liberty—the bicycle, the car, the hours—

at the point where the child shows readiness for autonomous choice. Regarding selection of the school, for example, it is common at some point in the high school years for those who can afford it to let slip the reins and to honor the child's own preference. There is no reason to predict that less affluent families would vary from that pattern. Subsidized choice thus would mean that many more adolescents would achieve influence over their own education. They would by stages enter into an adult relation of cooperation with their own parents.

Prescinding from the liberty issue for the moment, it is also clear as a general proposition that—in terms of child welfare—better decisions tend to be made by decision-makers who themselves stand to benefit by decisions that are good for the child and who conversely stand to suffer when a mistake is made. On the whole, such accountability is characteristic of parents. They must live over the long haul with the success or failure of the child's formal education. Their advantage as decision-makers is, of course, augmented by their unique personal knowledge of the child and by their natural affection.

None of these relationships characterizes the professional educator. In general, he is not accountable for his mistakes and may even prosper from the child's continued floundering dependence. He may have personal affection for individual children, but this is unpredictable and, for various good reasons, ought to be restrained. (For one thing, given budget realities, the professional often and quite properly must sacrifice one child's interest for that of another; sometimes we can't have both volleyball and violin.) Finally, his knowledge of the child's needs is relatively abstract. I do not mean that the professional's knowledge is unimportant. What I do mean is that his proper contribution is like that of the architect: so long as the client is free to follow or disregard it, it is useful. That is what professional advice is for; the professional is our agent, not our boss.

Now these claims about the best interest of the child may seem like a reversion to the "efficiency" arguments for choice that I originally criticized. In part, this is correct. To assert that parents make the best choices of schools for their own children is to echo the findings of Coleman, Chubb and Moe, RAND, myself, and everyone else who has asked the question—including even the enemies of choice. The point has special application here, however, because the liberty interest is intimately linked to the overall welfare of the child. Both interests must be simultaneously served through an adult authority, and parental choice most nearly achieves their harmony. Please note: I have not argued that parents are necessarily good deciders. They are merely the best.

Critics of choice often invoke another set of American metaphors to justify the exclusion of nonrich families from the marketplace of ideas. They assert that, by expressing their preferences in education, the poor will foment ideas that are dangerous to society. Some of them, indeed, will prove intolerant of others. Before I address that claim, I would like to comment on the particular contribution of public schools to intergroup tolerance.

The machinery of public monopoly was chosen specifically by Brahmins such as Horace Mann and James Blaine to coax the children of immigrants from the religious superstitions of their barbarian parents. Today that antique machinery continues its designated role, and if this function was ever benign, it has long since ceased to be so. What has endured is the public school system's peculiar legacy of intolerance, racial segregation, religious bigotry, discrimination against the poor, irrational fiscal distinctions among school districts, and—over and against all this—the careful buffering of the freedom of the rich to decide for themselves.

This masterpiece of social hierarchy is a source of intense mutual antagonism among those whom it throws together by their common poverty. Seeing that their own opinions count for nothing, its victims are easily moved to a similar contempt for the ways of others different from themselves. Those others they encounter at close range, conscripted like themselves for compulsory institutions. The hostilities generated among students and among parents are replicated at the macro level by conflict among organized minority groups struggling to control pieces of the educational juggernaut for their own parochial purposes. Who can blame them? By mistrusting them, society has encouraged them to mistrust one another.

Subsidized choice, again, is the specific therapy for such discord. In part this is simply because schools perform their pedagogical tasks better when families are there by choice. It is only by contract and mutual accord that families are able to form and maintain those fragile communities of learning that James Coleman has found to be the single most important stimulus to the disadvantaged child. Nor is it even relevant to object that the families in private schools are self-selected. This is true by definition, but so what? Indeed, self-selection is the very point; choice does work for those who use it.

And many more do want to use it. What we know from the polls is that most families would covet the opportunity to join or form such learning communities. Except for the wealthy few, this yen for family autonomy has until now been incapable of satisfaction. We can only guess how many families—given the chance—would emulate the pioneers.

The literature confirms that these private communities of learning are efficient, but I wish to emphasize that they are socially healing. Corrosive intergroup enmities are seldom replicated in private schools. Whatever the mix of race and social class represented by their families, hatred is not their most important product. So far as anyone can tell, their graduates are at least as tolerant of racial, religious, and ethnic differences as are their public school counterparts.

For my part, this civic virtue seems the natural outcome of an education that is allowed to focus upon a coherent set of human and/or religious values, even where those values are strongly sectarian. The child who studies justice in a simple focused model filled with live adult exemplars may be the readiest in later life to recognize that justice is a problem involving all of us. Karl Barth put it that "a will to unite cannot be developed by people who have not yet taken themselves, to say nothing of the others, seriously."[1] To begin to treat ordinary citizens as responsible—to take them seriously—is an investment in social unity.

All this is not being asserted as a universal psychological law; possibly for the moral development of certain children, the blandest and most irenic of curriculums is the ideal. In any case, it is an admirable thing for a school to teach that those who disagree with its message have dignity and are worthy of respect, and not every private school does or would do so. Private school offenders, however, are not noticeably different from the public systems that systematically separate off the poor and that, by political necessity, relegate a range of religious and other values to a kind of limbo. Those who claim that compulsory state schools in general work to increase the civic virtues will find me a tolerant but skeptical listener. Meanwhile, we pass on to the particular question of tolerance among the races.

For this purpose, it will be useful to retell the brief sad tale of Kansas City. In 1986, the public school district of that city and the state of Missouri were both found guilty of deliberate racial segregation. The nearby white suburbs were found innocent. The federal judge distributed the white children in the district to achieve what desegregation he could, but they represented only 25 percent of the children. He offered the Black students a free ride to the suburbs with fat tuitions for the suburban public schools, but those schools would not have them. In 1989, fifty private schools offered these same children 4,100 racially integrated places at an average cost one-third that of KC public schools. Black plaintiffs thereupon sued both city and state, asking for scholarships that would allow them to vindicate their Fourteenth Amendment rights in private institutions while saving the taxpayers money. Each defendant promptly engaged two major law firms in addition to its own legal staff to oppose the suit. The teachers' union hired a fifth firm for the same purpose—to frustrate the choice of an integrated education for these children. So far the defendants have managed at enormous cost to avoid a decision on the merits.

The lesson is plain enough. Choice can be—and generally is—an instrument of social peace. In the case of Kansas City, it is the *only* instrument. One can imagine its adaptation to the predicament of disadvantaged minority children in Detroit, the District of Columbia, Los Angeles, Seattle, and many other urban areas in which minority children are immured by the monopoly. Here is tolerance for the asking, if only the civil rights establishment will ask for it. So far the establishment has lined up in opposition. Civil rights lawyers in Kansas City admit that the plaintiff children would be better off if given a choice. However, they cannot in conscience support anything that might facilitate the flight of the poor from the public sector. And they augment this noble objection with the observation that most of the schools available to help the poor are religious. Q.E.D.

All these kind words for choice rest on the assumption that the particular system of subsidies to be legislated will follow certain simple operational criteria. First, the subsidy must go to families and not to schools or other institutions. In the case of religious schools, this will be sufficient to insulate the subsidy from constitutional attack under the First Amendment's establishment clause and, possibly, some of its state counterparts.

Second, private schools must be included as legitimate choices. This was implicit in my observations on the limited free market now constituted by private schools. Only private schools can satisfy the legitimate interests of many families in exposing their children to ideas that would be politically or constitutionally censored in the government schools. However, the presence of private schools is also necessary as a matter of elementary economics. Without them, it is unrealistic to expect the custodians of the public monopoly to purge the system. Among the recent legislative proposals for "public school choice" there is not one that would threaten anyone's job. The "educartel" has no intention to disengage public systems from the respirator. It will harbor and promote those whom competition would instead encourage to find more suitable professions. Eliminating incompetence and redundancy is not the whole of the matter, but it is a necessary element of any serious reform.

Third, private schools ought to be protected from regulation of curriculum, hiring, and choice of facilities. The point of reform is not to reduce them to the role of Leviathan's apprentice, but to encourage their self-definition and thus their special contribution to our intellectual and social life.

Fourth, public educational authorities must be liberated to organize schools and to instruct children with the freedom characteristic of the private sector (the exception here is religious instruction). Most parents will probably wish to choose government schools, and these schools must, therefore, be given the necessary opportunity to perfect their product. To that end, the various initiatives that Stephen Sugarman and I have designed over the last generation would give school district boards an option. The district could—if it chose—stand pat with its present arrangements, including student assignments based upon geography or other criteria. On the other hand, the district would now be empowered to create deregulated, subsidiary, not-for-profit schools in whatever numbers the board saw fit. Each of these new schools would be a separate public corporation with articles of incorporation and by-laws that tailor the school to whatever management style and educational mission the district board wishes to try in the market.

These new public schools would survive on their capacity to attract customers, each of whom would be eligible for a state scholarship worth 90 percent of the average statewide expenditure for a child of similar grade level and circumstance. In such schools, residence could no longer be a criterion for admission. The playing field for public and private providers would be effectively leveled.

Fifth, the system must, nevertheless, tilt toward the poor. Sugarman and I reject the sunny prediction that a wholly unregulated system of scholarships would serve all classes equally well. The primary object of reform is the provision of good education to those who are currently most disadvantaged; these are the children who will be least attractive to the most popular providers in an educational market. Others may well believe that the benign intention of providers is enough to assure sufficient places for the poor in the best schools. I concede these good intentions, and I intend no offense by my skepticism about the outcome. I would insist, however, on a provision setting aside in each participating school (public and private) a substantial proportion of new admissions (say 25 percent) for low-income families. In addition, it would be crucial to ensure the affordability of enrollment either by forbidding charges beyond the amount of the scholarship or by requiring that such charges be scaled according to the family's capacity to pay. These are the only restrictions that I would insist upon for those schools—public or private—that are organized to accept state scholarships in exchange for education.

Finally, the subsidy to the family must be sufficiently large to stimulate the establishment of new schools in order to provide alternatives and competition. The national average per-pupil expenditure in public schools in 1991–92 is roughly $5,800, of which $400 is federal money. An average state scholarship of $4,800 would ensure formation of new producers in both sectors in most areas and could be phased in with little or no additional tax burden. Conservatives and libertarians often propose subsidies in the range of $1,250. These may be useful to let a modest number of low-income urban children fill up spaces in existing parochial schools, and it will be lovely for middle-class families who already use such schools in the suburbs. It will do little to expand the alternatives necessary to make choice meaningful for the mass of working-class and low-income families.

If our recent political experience means anything, several of the previous points will be misunderstood by certain professed friends of choice. For example, an admission preference for the poor will draw someone to his feet shouting, "Quota!" This is natural, but it is wrong, and here are some reasons why it is wrong. First, a set-aside for low-income children is utterly unlike a racial quota. Race and gender are immutable natural characteristics; hence, for various reasons—rational and historical—legal classification by race or sex is always suspect and needs strong justification (e.g., prior deliberate discrimination). By contrast, poverty is a circumstance that may occur to any of us and, by the way, occurs among more whites than among minorities.

Second, poverty is *by definition a disabling circumstance.* It is a condition that puts undesirable limits upon the individual's capacity to fulfill either his responsibilities or his legitimate aspirations. Race, by contrast, is not disempowering by its nature and can become so only in specific cultural settings; being minority or female can even be an advantage in some circumstances. When we favor or burden persons by skin color, therefore, we run a serious risk of injustice precisely because race by itself is not a reliable indicator of anything important. Involuntary poverty is such an indicator. It specifies a significant human disability.

It is for this reason that poverty historically has been used by governments of every stripe as a legal classification. In aid of their personal autonomy, the state has made the poor eligible in countless ways (mostly ineffectual) for special public benefits. Whatever one thinks of Milton Friedman's own proposal for a guaranteed income, it was advanced within this historical tradition. Being for human liberty does not always exclude giving the poor a helping hand on the way to independence.

Conversely, there are pragmatic considerations affecting the operation of private schools for the poor that make the resulting burden of a limited preference easily manageable. First, this is a preference respecting admissions only; it gives the child the *opportunity.* If either the academic work or the discipline eventually proves too much for the occasional misfit, the school can discontinue the relation. Second, many or most of the private schools already have substantial and successful experience with children of the poor. Third, by recruiting a larger pool of low-income applicants, the school can have an unencumbered choice among them. The energetic school thus could pick and choose all of its students, so long as its new enrollments each year included one poor child out of four. Fourth, since the school could advertise its specific practices and curriculum, any fear that it would attract misfits is far-fetched. In an open market with a variety of schools available, why would families hostile to its message want to enroll in the first place? Fifth, the poor desperately need precisely the kinds of learning communities that are now represented in the private sector.

Would the private schools lose some autonomy? Obviously—to some extent and in certain particulars—they would. The question is whether both they and the families of the children in them would experience an overall increase of freedom. In addition, it is unsettling to suppose that private schools would seek access to state scholarships but remain unwilling to share the common burden of educating disadvantaged children.

Having said all this in support of favoring the poor, I want to add the political observation that this issue may be the rock on which reform will founder. On the one hand, if the poor are not specifically favored, the usual suspects—the unions and the professoriat—will declare choice to be an instrument of class dominance, and the media will naively affirm this canard; the monopoly will have been handed a political stick it does not deserve. On the other hand, if the poor are in fact favored in the proposal, those now holding the political throttle will be tempted to cry, "Quota!" I hope both sides will be restrained in their tribal responses.

There is at present little evidence that they will. In 1991, after eight months of apparent consensus among all interested factions, a balanced ballot initiative for California was quietly dumped at the final moment in favor of a $2,500 scholarship with no protections for the poor. It will be supported by libertarians, Chubb and Moe, the Heritage Foundation, Milton Friedman, and most religious, but non-Catholic, schools. At this writing, the Catholic bishops are deciding their own position. For their suburban schools, the initiative would add the scholarship amount to tuition, at last making Catholic schools financially competitive and more attractive to the middle class; in the inner city, it would allow the struggling low-tuition Catholic schools to fill thousands of unused spaces with low-income children, improving their lot considerably. The overall effect on the poor will be modest but benign.

The difficulty with the proposal is that the poor will be largely segregated in schools that spend $2,500 while the middle class will be largely segregated in schools that spend $5,000. At $2,500, few new schools will be started in the inner city. The continuing social division may be as thoroughgoing as that sponsored today by the public system. This is unsettling to some of the bishops, and the ultimate interest of the Church is unclear. The most vocal and affluent Catholics will probably approve, but the media are likely to take a dim view, with at least some justification. It is all a great pity, as the proposal could have been—and nearly was—designed to better express the interest of both the schools and the poor. It will be fascinating to monitor the arguments that get pressed in the campaigns for and against this initiative if it makes it to the November 1992 ballot.

Whatever happens to this well-intended conservative venture, there will in the future be political hope for better-designed systems of choice. That hope lies in a full-scale scholarship, phased deregulation of the public schools, and a modest tilt toward the poor in matters of admissions and add-ons. These policy impurities favoring the disadvantaged could be absorbed without damage to the identity of private schools so long as employment, curriculum, and every other educational aspect of the school's life are left untouched. Perhaps those who worship pure competition will come to appreciate this; perhaps those who have claimed to speak for the poor will come to recognize opportunity when it stares them in the face.

CHAPTER FOUR

Education

Intimations of a Populist Rescue

Civility is breaking out in a hotly contested sector of the culture war. For thirty years, armies of authors have savaged one another over the incendiary notion that society should assure have-not families free access to all schools. The extravagance of the claims made for and against subsidized choice is all too familiar. Now, belated but welcome, comes a balancing covey of altogether serious works from mainstream intellectuals. These voices, though tentative and discordant, all respond to the insight emergent among the urban poor and working class: parental choice is an issue of civil rights and basic justice. The populist impulse may yet receive its fair hearing.

My assignment is to review four of these recent works (there are others deserving attention) and comment on their significance for the future of school choice. I sandwich my assessment of the books between two thin crusts—the top an orienting bit of ideological history, the bottom my conclusion that this debate, though promising, remains hobbled by the false assumption of a coherent moral curriculum in our state schools.

Originally published in *First Things*, November 2000

THE LITERARY HISTORY OF SCHOOL CHOICE

For practical purposes, the debate on parental choice began in 1962 with Milton Friedman's *Capitalism and Freedom*. The book was a libertarian creed, an apotheosis of the market; in education as elsewhere, consumer freedom was portrayed as virtually a good in itself. Almost immediately, however, welfare politics was to reduce the idol to instrumental status. Lyndon Johnson Democrats seized vouchers as a weapon to be wielded in the War on Poverty. As a result, the literature on school choice for a decade remained suffused with a practical and Fabian tone. The primary issue for Stephen Sugarman, Christopher Jencks, and Stephen Arons was to specify institutional designs whereby choice in both private and public sectors could aid nonrich families to rescue their children from the failed system of conscription. At one memorable moment, Daniel P. Moynihan suggested that Congress convert federal educational subventions into vouchers for the poor.

The Democrat Party flirtation with the idea fizzled, and Friedman was to enjoy his libertarian revenge with a paradoxical assist from the teachers union—an affiliation unintended by Friedman and deadly to the hope for choice. It happened this way. In the political ascendance of economic theory in the 1970s, the limited understanding of the market as one practical tool among others lost center stage. Choice was elevated from means to end. Arguments specific to school choice were subsumed into the mechanistic justifications offered for the deregulation of banks and airlines. Along with travel and finance, schools were another consumer service in which to reduce friction.

Government educators and their unions shrewdly perceived their political opportunity; they simply confirmed and then exaggerated this truncated image of a school market. On occasion, the National Education Association and the American Federation of Teachers conceded that the invisible hand, in its Darwinian fashion, might achieve more efficient delivery. What it could not do, they said, is tell society what it would be good to deliver. Among the school folk and their collaborators in the media, the favored comparison was that between franchised schools and franchised hamburgers. Education is not like fast food or airlines; it has values apart from personal preference, and the entrenched unchosen professionals know what these are.

The debate between the marketeers and the school monopoly sputtered on in this polarized and vacuous form through the late 1980s. The economists wrote books about efficiency, and the schoolmasters responded with books about democracy, as if the two were oil and water. (Even as I write, another such puff arrives on my desk subtitled *Market Ideology versus Democratic Value*. Don't bother.) The marketeers compounded their own isolation by repeatedly rejecting coalition with liberal Democrats who argued that the politics of choice could only benefit from presentation as a hope for the underclass. In four states and the District of Columbia, libertarians sent initiatives to the ballot after stripping them of all regulation that would protect low-income families. These provisions had been a condition of support by the moderates, who now stood aside. Albert Shanker expressed to me his delight at this self-marginalization of choice; he accurately forecast the 30 percent of voters who would support the libertarian petards.

The phony polarity of this debate has now evaporated in the heat and light of the Milwaukee voucher program and its sequels outside Wisconsin. Once again the question may be asked whether school choice, properly designed, can serve a range of democratic and human values—including efficiency—in a manner superior to the traditional school monopoly. Our four authors approach the question directly and indirectly in ways that conflict but illuminate. The first two come upon the stage expressly as "liberal" philosophers; for them this word has ultimate moral significance. Once you understand what is truly liberal, you know what to do with the schools.

Four Books on Choice: From "Well, barely. . ." to "Yes, but . . ."

Indeed, Meira Levinson aggressively entitles her book *The Demands of Liberal Education*. To understand how liberalism gets so demanding, the reader must join the author inside the unisphere that is liberal thought: "I have not tried to convince individuals of the desirability of liberalism itself. . . . I took liberalism as a given." Nevertheless, she is keen to distinguish herself from shipmates less correct, especially "political liberals" who tend to be soft on the sorts of ideological crime that swarm out there in a pluralist society. She seems more comfortable around "comprehensive liberals," who might hope to extend their influence beyond the public square. It would take a more perceptive reviewer to toll the differences among the sects. Here, I focus only upon her institutional ideal for delivering education in the liberal mode. Its real-life chances are zero, but the view is instructive.

Levinson tells the reader that the core purpose of liberal education is the flourishing of personal autonomy; all else is subordinate. Happily, other benign civic ideals, such as tolerance, are also best served by the liberal program of schooling as it goes about the nourishing of autonomy. The embodiment of that program in a working system becomes quite complex in a pluralist social order. There are versions of the good life and the civic ideal that compete with the liberal vision. That is, they rest upon philosophical or religious premises that reject the right of the individual to choose his or her own concept of the good. Much of the book is given over to lamenting irreconcilable conflicts between certain Christians (especially fundamentalists) and the author's own liberal "demands." These practical threats from the Christians are largely unspecified but, for her purpose, may remain so. It is enough that these religious folks would hold the free individual child responsible to an external moral authority; parental hopes of this sort could never satisfy the ideal of autonomy, hence are properly (could one say "morally"?) excluded from the liberal curriculum. But she sees that childhood complicates the liberal solution. Children stand in special need of liberal deliverance; yet their very autonomy requires resources that are hard to duplicate outside the family. These include not only the means of survival and safety but also the "cultural coherence" and "identity" that make us real selves. This seems a dilemma, for, when parents are allowed to create the coherence that comes simply from being themselves, they notoriously thwart autonomy and frustrate little liberal identities.

The best a liberal can do is to cabin these opportunities of parents to act as bearers of specifically illiberal ideas, while educating the society toward the emergence of a new social consciousness (even among parents) that will support the assignment of every child to a "common school," meaning one that presents every reasonable idea, but no other. These schools, when they arrive, will interdict all "fundamental conceptions of the good," for autonomy requires the "sense of detachment," even— or especially—from one's own beliefs; the autonomous child is one who holds his own convictions in constant and liberating suspension, "detached from local and parental control." *Liberalismus macht frei.*

This regime need not entail complete neglect of the child's need for "cultural coherence"; again, the family must be respected in some dimension, if his or her identity is to be confirmed. This is not impossible even in a pluralist society, so long as the liberal school confirms only that part of the family repertoire that is neither philosophically nor religiously fundamental. This means that some families will have few or none of their values confirmed inside the school, but many children from these morally oppressive home environments may discover a coherence and identity—a substitute family—right there in the school.

The liberal educator anticipates that families who are diverse in belief will value choice in education. To a degree, this impulse can be harmlessly indulged. Individual children respond to different teaching methods in the pursuit of autonomy. There is reason, then, to allow pedagogical options—even through vouchers—so long as all schools embrace the liberal curriculum of sound ideas. Of course, as Levinson laconically observes, there would be "little if anything to distinguish private" from state schools. And, by the way, with or without vouchers, she would impose regulation upon all private schools so as to secure the liberal objective. Furthermore, the United States needs "to embed children's rights to an autonomy-promoting education in the constitution." Meanwhile, primary judicial declarations of parental rights, such as *Pierce v. Society of Sisters* (1925) must be "interpreted." In the end, she is happy to impose the liberal ideal by force, but for this we first "must change . . . beliefs and values." Levinson is certainly correct about the chasm between this vision and the hopes of those outside her liberal cloister. The book is heuristic and provocative. One wishes only that Orwell could read it.

Stephen Macedo holds the chair of Politics and Values at Princeton and returns to a favorite theme in his *Diversity and Dissent: Civic Education in a Multicultural Society*. Like Ms. Levinson, he lodges under the dome of liberal thought and fears the influence of kerygmatic religion out there in the public square. Inside the fraternity, he is distinguishable as a "civic liberal" whose stewardship of schools would be a hair more trusting of the poor and dissident. He hopes he is consistent with John Rawls's "political liberalism" but "goes beyond" in his own work by specifying "an account of the political and social structures that help promote a publicly reasonable liberal community." Macedo's ambitions are cosmic: "We work to transform the whole of the moral world in the image of our most basic political values." One braces for a big bang, but the pace is measured.

The book commences with specifics about the threat from religion, at least in its historical forms; Macedo recounts the educational sins of Catholic bishops of the nineteenth century. His flagship example from the 1840s is the rejection by New York's Archbishop Hughes of a proposal for religious neutrality within the state schools. Hughes deemed neutrality unfair to believers and—in any case—impossible to achieve; the just and equitable solution, he said, would be the support of all ideas without discrimination. This was not to be, and, given mid-century fears of an impending American Catholic majority, the decision of the states to monopolize tax-supported education can be glossed as a hedge for freedom. Macedo, however, does not bless the ensuing century of Protestant state curriculum and carefully applauds the Catholic social outlook of our own time as it recrystallized in Vatican II. For this transformation of the Church he credits the United States itself, but just how a state-school monopoly segregated by race and class helped Rome to see the light is unexplained.

For Macedo, this nineteenth-century history stands principally as a cautionary tale for moderns, one in which Jerry Falwell is made to play Pio Nono. Whatever the reality of the old Roman menace, this demonization of contemporary Christian enthusiasts seems far-fetched, and the scarcity of citations to specific offenses confirms that impression. Both Levinson and Macedo make too much of a few publicized courtroom skirmishes, notably the federal litigation entitled *Mozert v. Hawkins County Board of Education* (1987). In that case, fundamentalist parents in Tennessee discovered what they considered antireligious themes in the local public school curriculum. Like the Amish, Jehovah's Witnesses, and others before them, these plaintiffs were content to have the rest of the students learn the material, merely seeking an exemption for themselves (they lost). To conjure a threat to liberal values from a few requests to be excused seems out of proportion.

In any case, religious dissenters make an odd primary target. How much, if any, do these outliers and their beliefs contribute to our present culture of incivility? Most of America's very real anxieties concern not bad beliefs but bad *conduct*, posing three very earthly—and earthy— questions for the educational mission: (1) What *behavior* is correct? (2) What *source*, if any, obliges humans to pursue it? (3) In cases of doubt, how does one reason toward it?

Unfortunately, these questions are alien to the liberal, at least in public space; these good deeds are not something to be identified in some preinstitutional order of real moral relations. Indeed, for many liberals, the good is not a discovery at all but, rather, the imaginative conception of some possible state that the individual may or may not choose to seek. The creative process begins "by defining an objective human good." In this view, "the law is the only public morality we have."

This effort to detach the good from natural (much less religious) sources and from specific moral content is, of course, familiar. Liberals would have us invent the terms of public life without regard to conceptions of the good that are inaccessible to unaided reason. This does not mean that they are personally allergic to real morality. Indeed, in their families and private lives, many treat proper conduct as if it were something nonnegotiable; it may be this experience of the authentic good that often makes the institutions that liberals propose more sensible than the arguments they offer for them. In any case, they need broad consent for their inventions; hence often they respect in practice the plebeian premise they reject in theory—that human freedom is a thing given and bounded.

Our authors nonetheless see parents in general as a threat to the primary liberal objective of autonomy. (We gather that neither author has children.) It follows that the family dominion must be limited to a parental "privilege" coupled with duties—no rights—to direct the quotidian details of child-rearing. Meanwhile, in the school, the state must stand vigilant to rescue the child's mind from commitment to every fundamental moral or religious conception, for these tend to become permanent premises that only frustrate the march toward autonomy. Note also that neither author attaches particular value to diversity of ideas, cultures, or ways of life. When the liberal school has its day, it will honor only those versions that meet the standard of "public reason."

In my view, neither book makes enough of the poisonous effects of the present school monopoly upon the very values that liberals cherish. Nor does either author highlight the exploding reality of public charter schools; perhaps this new diversity only compounds the liberal fear.

Even talk of vouchers is brief: Levinson highlights criticisms from early studies of Milwaukee and neglects the now dominant success stories; Macedo thinks that parental choice depletes our moral capital, while monopoly "helps to advance values." But he is far from closed-minded, and—having whispered, "I will ne'er consent"—in the end consents to properly regulated vouchers even for religious schools that are not "pervasively sectarian" (that happy phrase).

Turning to Rosemary Salomone is, for this reader, something of an ideological jailbreak. Not that her book, *Visions of Schooling: Conscience, Community and Common Education*, is anything but liberal in spirit or content; indeed, she appreciates Macedo's earlier work, and she can recite the orthodoxies of the liberal sects. But she is not herself anxious to satisfy any litmus test or to privilege one authentic version of the creed. Indeed, *Visions* is more a story—even a pageant—than a unified theory. It is a well-tempered tale of ideas at war over the concept of a common school.

From the beginning, certain American educators wanted the state school "to be inclusive by being uncontroversial"; for others, public education was to practice straightforward "imposition and indoctrination." Yet a few others hoped the school might be diverse and inviting to all ideas. What was common to neutralists, inculcators, and eclectics was the impulse to disconnect the child from the lower-class family. We hear from Salomone how these contrasting and harmonizing aspirations played out in prolonged ideological struggle inside and outside (and for and against) the public monopoly.

This is an oft-told tale but includes new insight from two resources specific to the author. One is her professional grasp of the constitutional principles at stake. She is professor of law at St. John's (New York) and in full command of the legal sources as well as the many sub-isms of liberal philosophy. The other is her book's initial inspiration, which rises out of Salomone's earlier study of an outbreak of parental dissent in the 1990s in the patrician New York suburb of Bedford. A long chapter of "Visions" summarizes this story, and the five chapters preceding it are an artful Baedeker to the incubating theories of lawyers, philosophers, educators, and dissident families that were destined to meet head-on in the Bedford high school.

The objecting parents in this tale cooperate with central casting by being Christian, but with a twist. These are not Appalachian fundamentalists but a half dozen suburban Catholic professionals. I won't spoil the story. These parents think that weird cultic stuff is going on at the elegant state school their children attend. They are partly right but wind up with most citizens mad at them, including the trial judge who gives them only a partial victory in litigation, which is now on appeal.

The Bedford story confirms the inevitability of conflict and ideological oppression within the traditional regime. But there is something marginal about such occasional injustices to mobile middle-class families; the system imposes these insults almost as a harmless hobby. Its true vocation emerges only among its captive clientele in the inner city where, under state aegis, competing gospels offend a range of moral sensitivities that is much broader than that arising specifically from religion.

Such conflicts seem inevitable to Salomone, who tends to picture tax-supported schools as a unitary ideological system that must cope with a diverse clientele. She considers one remedy that might heal and justify the old monolith: the strategy of simple accommodation. Schools would excuse dissenters from the offending portions of the curriculum. To this reader her argument here seems (properly) half-hearted and even despairing; in any case, it ends in a near requiem for the "neighborhood school as [representative] of a functional community." She sees now that the United States has succeeded in creating ideological diversity even among the wealthy; one size can never fit all, and she lacks Levinson's stomach for universal coercion in the name of autonomy.

Or does she? In the end—as her preferred solution—Salomone would extend a more or less uniform state curriculum to the private sector, but now within a system of choice and with charters and vouchers. She would include only those religious schools "that agree to advance certain core political principles and comply with educational standards imposed by the state to assure . . . adequate education for democratic citizenship." This uniform civic curriculum is "a relatively modest" proposal, but one wonders. It appears that she would add materially to the regulations that now bind private schools, but it is not made clear how these new restrictions would enhance the learning and good citizenship of their graduates. The social science of today tells us that these youngsters are already distinctly civil, at least by state school standards.

On this very note enters Charles Glenn. En route from a rather different planet, Glenn brings us *The Ambiguous Embrace: Government and Faith-Based Schools and Social Agencies*. Glenn is an inner-city Episcopalian priest, a professor of comparative education (Boston University), and a father of seven. For many years he was chief designer and administrator of successful programs of public school racial integration that favor various mechanisms of choice. He is also our national guru on European systems of family empowerment. His new book is an invitation—enthusiastic and even (in some sense) liberal—to trust the family and its favored private institutions. But, it is also, and first of all, a warning. Glenn dons the role of sentry for those private religious schools that Salomone and Macedo are ready, well, to embrace. He plays Cassandra, not as a bureaucrat manqué (he is unrepentant), but as a prudent steward of precious but fragile institutions.

First of all, Glenn assembles and analyzes whatever social science has to tell us about the responses made by two sorts of religious institutions—schools and social agencies—to their experience of government regulation, or money, or both. To this he adds fresh historical accounts of two prominent Protestant agencies, the Salvation Army and Teen Challenge (a drug recovery program); carefully he assesses their adjustments to public threats and enticements. All this is further enriched by recurrent comparisons of these domestic American encounters to European patterns of interrelation between private religious agencies and governments.

The evidence strongly suggests that faith-based social agencies and schools serve certain governmental social goals better than can government itself. Our national project to "reinvent government" thus should seek out the genius of those "mediating institutions" that happen to be religious. They affirm in their nature the transcendent duty of the Christian to serve the common good through the church and thus, ceteris paribus, the duty to be open to service within government programs of contracting, grants, vouchers, and the like.

Glenn's caveat is this. The efficacy of religious agents appears to be a direct function of their maintaining their identity; they succeed at the secular task precisely when they conduct their work without suppressing their own beliefs, values, or confessional style. Liaison with government can threaten this religious identity through clumsy regulation. The federal "charitable choice" provisions currently assure some measure of religious freedom to the social agencies; strangely, however, there is no constitutional or statutory counterpart in education. Religious schools must beware the sirens of subsidized choice. Nor is government itself even the chief source of danger. Glenn shows that the identity of religious agencies and schools is vulnerable, first and foremost, to standards touted by private professionals. Their impulse to rationalize and regulate charitable work is plausible and hard to resist even inside the religious organization. It goes down hard with professionals (and their sometime government sponsors) to hear that, for many clients, therapeutic programs work precisely because they deploy the enthusiasm and spontaneity of amateurs. Glenn, of course, allows that professionalism must be respected; the trick is to regulate minimally and in a manner that preserves the religious identity of the provider.

Glenn makes his warning vivid, with a scattering of statistics and a few horror stories of virtual capitulation by certain religious providers. However, he never retracts or dilutes the imperative—itself religious— that these institutions be ready to serve the common good under the right conditions. Nor, on the other hand, is he fazed by the specter of "cults" and "sects" that haunts our liberal authors. Here our national experience with the regulation of hate groups and racists is relevant. In any school voucher scheme, Glenn would limit participation to schools that respect the norms of racial neutrality, civil order, and the rule of the law. Regarding curriculum, the standards now governing private schools are sufficient; as for the rest, little more is needed beyond certain protections for the poor, namely, admission and tuition rules plus transportation and information guarantees of the sort currently embodied and operating successfully in the school choice programs in Wisconsin, Ohio, and Florida. And private schools must be allowed to apply religious criteria in hiring; the point always is to maintain identity.

The reader will apply his or her own standard in assessing the individual merits of these very different books. But all four can be recommended for their relative candor and balance, qualities sometimes wanting in the literature of school reform. They deserve place with other recent works of singular quality by Stephen Sugarman and Frank Kemerer, Paul Peterson and Bryan Hassel, Carolyn Hoxby, John Witte, Joseph Viteritti, Cliff Cobb, and Jeff Henig. Choice has at last become an intelligible dialogue. As they say about fourth-quarter comebacks on Monday Night Football: We have a game!

GETTING DISTANCE ON CHOICE

Each of these books is a step—in Glenn's case a substantial and enthusiastic step—toward greater trust of ordinary people and their mediating institutions. Nevertheless, I am puzzled by two qualities of the writing (but I now spot them in my own). One is the apologetic air with which all but Glenn peck financially at state dominion over the child of the poor; every concession to parental choice raises some threat of an educational Munich. The other odd note, possibly related, is the relative neglect in books as professional as these of the more scholarly arguments for choice. When, as here, skeptics make concessions to choice, one would expect strong justifying reasons. But, apart from Glenn, the rationales are principally that the constitution allows it, that dissenters will be grateful, and that competition may improve test scores in the state schools. That choice would empower the nonrich is grudgingly agreed, but such freedom of parents is devalued with faint praise.

If choice comes, is it to be tolerated simply as an efficiency device and/or a concession to popular whim? Or are there strong positive arguments? Offhand, I can't think of more than two dozen. Most could be arrayed in categories such as these: *Practical* arguments about measurable elements, such as money and test scores; *vocational* considerations, such as the elevation of teaching to professional status; *intellectual* values that insist upon a free market for ideas held by the poor; *child welfare* claims about the best decider of the right school for this individual child; the *autonomy* argument that it is the empowered family not the state that best nourishes the independent self; *tolerance* theory, holding that social trust among groups is maximized when family identity is respected by government; arguments from *justice* that would end the system of conscriptive school assignment focused upon the poor; arguments for *racial integration* founded upon a new freedom of association across arbitrary government boundaries; and *family* theory, which understands the corrosive effect of losing responsibility for one's own children.

Why are these categories of justification largely ignored? I suspect that most of us who are not libertarians have come to the school question wearing an ideological blinker. Even good thinkers need good premises. But there is a diverting myth that remains a confounding premise for those who write about education. This is the widespread assumption that American state schools are functionally "public." For two reasons they do not merit the label, and this matters, for the false premise clouds all our judgments.

For a thing to be "public," the first requirement is that it be "open to all" in a manner of the park, the pool, the library, the museum, the street, the square (*O.E.D.*) But what Americans still call the "public" school is, in most cases, accessible only to its neighbors; to attend, one must first manage to live nearby. Stretching things, one could, perhaps, say that the schools of Watts are functionally "public," because most of us could afford to move there. But Beverly Hills we cannot save, for it is a legislated scheme of private choice that in effect peddles school vouchers in the housing market. The rich buy autonomy; the rest get conscripted. "Public"? To the contrary, the system is a balkanized plutocracy. Thus, the first abuse of this important word.

The second is subtler. It is the unexamined premise of universality that is inserted into virtually all discourse on state schools. The word "public" is deployed to imply some intellectual unity that is a quality of the system. The *Oxford English Dictionary* recognizes such a restraint upon the use of the word. Any conception offered as "public" must be "extended . . . or universal." Publicness entails a unity of informing spirit; in order to be truly "public" in the modern state, an educational policy must be the declared and coherent enterprise of a people.

Intellectual coherence can, of course, inform a conception that is not yet complete, a work in progress. Such, perhaps, was the idea of state education in its first century. Its literature, though discordant, was united in its confidence (as in Dewey) that the competing inspirations were all vectoring and that a common core could and would eventually be sculpted and realized as a truly public reality. If such a common vision still exists, it is a work in regress. What remains is a narrow core curriculum that pursues, first, the child's personal utility and, second, the barest kind of social contract. State schools do all claim to seek to raise test scores and teach the rule of law. Learn the skills, the sciences, and a little history; avoid committing crimes and torts. That much is coherent and universal and, thus, is still truly "public" (and, by the way, is part of the mission of every "private" school).

But, that is about it. Beyond these basics, each state school stands on its own moral bottom, for there is no cultural agreement—no public gnosis—about what it is to be a good person, or what such a person should seek to realize as the common good. This is not an observation about religion, its sects, or its enemies. It is a claim about human conduct. To make this plainer, consider the range of contested moral questions on which individual educators must take a side—or simply avoid. Animal rights, gender roles, obedience to parents, obedience to other adults, premarital chastity (and contraception), assisted suicide, pornography, economic justice, civil disobedience, the role of sports, ethnicity, abortion, environmental policy, gun control, cloning and genetic engineering, global capitalism, diet, hours, and free speech. Should PS 91 teach that homosexual conduct is good, bad, or a life-style option? Practical choices must be made concerning every such issue. And each question will be answered yes, no, or maybe, for even silence is a message. I have no advice on the right answers, but this I now see. Schools engage these questions differently from one another whether by a decision of the state, district, school, or teacher. Whose preference the individual child will encounter thus is determined more by chance than by any philosophy that could be called "public."

But add to these specific cases the grandest disagreement of them all. It concerns the very possibility of serious moral teaching. Is there a real good, or is social contract the only source of obligation? What sort of preinstitutional imperative, if any, is available to schools once they are forbidden to acknowledge religious foundations? Could natural law inform the curriculum of an Aristotle Charter High School? Perhaps, but even if enough of us could agree on the source of a natural law (fat chance), we would still divide over its specific applications. To render the debates on the schools coherent, we would need, first, to give correct names to the phenomena at issue, exercising self-restraint in the use of "public." Beyond the basic curriculum, no ideas currently qualify as such; what is taught is chosen according to the preferences of the individuals who happen to be in charge. Answers to contested questions always consist of somebody's private convictions. On such matters, the public square of education is not merely naked, it is not even public. Thus, it is the case that state schools such as Beverly Hills High that fail the criterion of free access also fail the test of universality; often they teach a variety of private moralities inside their own communities. In the rich suburbs, this is by consent of the individual families, who could, if they chose, flee to Santa Monica or St. Mary's. In Watts, by contrast, these private orthodoxies are simply imposed; whether the moral menu features sports, philanthropy, or Zen, it is a dish du jour. It has always been convenient to assume a vague state of neutral uniformity among state schools as a premise for our national conversation. In doing so myself, I have too often miscast the message of the state educator as the "Vanilla Curriculum." Many educators do serve vanilla, but clearly this is only one of several strategies. We need a more candid image of this uneven moral topography. My candidate is the Rocky Road curriculum; it may be laced with vanilla, but its soul is a particularity of hard chunks, marshmallows, and—for the connoisseur—nuts galore.

What exactly is the harm in such a government menagerie? The evil consists in the collaboration of this unprincipled diversity with a monopoly system of assignment for the ordinary citizen. Being choiceless, the nonrich family is conscripted for a moral lottery operating at its very unpublic local school. But seeing this is halfway to fixing it. And the poor and the worker now seem to grasp the reality; observing the curriculum wars in the media, they have come to understand their status as a captive audience for whatever gospel is delivered to their child. This populist insight could account for much of the huge shift of opinion toward subsidized choice among ordinary families, especially minorities. The poor do not fancy all the surprises their children now encounter in the Rocky Road curriculum. If my child is going to be taught somebody's pet ideas, that somebody might as well be me.

CHAPTER FIVE

Orphans of the Enlightenment

Belief and the Academy

The C. S. Lewis Foundation has invited my observations on the place of religious belief in the academy. The window through which I can view this important subject is relatively narrow, and I ask your sufferance of my inevitable oversights. Law school does not command a panoramic prospect of the university. Still, I suppose that this could be said of most disciplines, and law may not be the most cloistered among them.

To be fair to the truth and to myself, in my own academic work I have often strayed into the transcendental, and even the specifically religious — certainly in my writing, but even in my teaching. In schools and departments of several universities, I have taught material that either has assumed a human person who is free and responsible to a higher source or took this as an issue to be explored.

These courses were accredited in various disciplines that border law, in one case a school of theology. Generally, I taught them as the collaborator of some genuine professional of the other discipline; sharing the role of gadfly to each other's specialties, we could not help but learn something of the attitudes and beliefs of these distinctive professional cultures within the university.

I ask to be received only as a dedicated amateur. In any case, I suspect that my primary qualification is simply that I began teaching in 1955. Thus I not only can retrieve fossil evidence from that ancient

Previously unpublished remarks to the C. S. Lewis Foundation, February 2006 world but can myself serve as a specimen. I can claim depth in at least one dimension—time.

Since our discussion involves the place of religious creed in the university, I should confess my own and note my unremarkable history as a believer; this will allow you to discount my judgments as you think proper. Though my family was oddly split, I have from infancy traveled as a Catholic, and my orthodoxy no doubt contributes to my perception of just what it is that my colleagues believe, and seem encouraged to believe, by their environment. As I proceed, I will on occasion, by second nature, use the term "Catholic" when I could as well have said "Christian." I intend no offense or exclusion, and where I have assumed too much I invite correction. So, at last now I really begin, and I do so with four generalizations that I think sufficiently important to state, even if I lack the time or art properly to defend them. Here they are:

1. Over the last half century, as materialism (with its offspring subjectivism) has gradually become the academy's most fashionable premise, believers have experienced estrangement within the life of the university.
2. Believers within law faculties experience this alienation, but have come to it relatively late and in a distinctive manner that will be worth our noting.
3. This isolation of the academic believer (whether lawyer, economist, or biologist) is not all bad; much depends upon what one is estranged from. Paradoxically, it is the conventional materialist who today finds himself isolated in the most cruel way from both colleagues and society; his own premises narrow the opportunities for shared intellectual enterprise and tend to leave us strangers.
4. This state of affairs is unstable, and believers who keep their intellectual powder dry may yet play the role of the saving remnant, rescuing the academy from its self-imposed exile.

These four balloon judgments rest more than a little on personal observations over the fifty-nine years since I entered college, and there is no avoiding scraps of autobiography. I will report the changes in academic culture as I have observed them, beginning with the general academic outlook in the late 1940s and 50s, then gradually focusing more upon those law schools and their fostering universities—especially

Northwestern and Berkeley—that I know best. I will sprinkle a few conclusions along the way, then again at the end.

In the late 1940s, I attended an obscure but lovable public university in my hometown in Minnesota. I will try to reset its social-intellectual scene. The general atmosphere of town and gown was, I think, typical of the Midwest in those times. Except for an occasional Chippewa, the larger urban area of 125,000 was solidly Caucasian; the university almost so. Though religiously and ethnically mixed, the town of Duluth was overall a community of considerable social trust, not only within the resident population but also within the university itself, and between the university and the public. Whatever the professors were up to might have been over the heads of people like my largely unschooled parents, but the typical citizen assumed correctly that such brainwork was all intended in service of a permanent order of the True and the Good in whose reality few doubted.

The empirical content of that intellectual order—more specifically, the material insights of the physical sciences—was well understood by everybody to be in a state of constant and progressive change; the stuff of this world was to a point intelligible, and it was our calling to keep on probing its secrets day by day. But, just why anything—material or otherwise—had come to exist at all was something else again. Here there were eternal verities, including an ultimate source of the True and the Good and of our personal duty to represent them in our own lives. These were realities shared and settled, but, of course, in diverse ways. Like their supporting public constituencies (including my own parents), the professors quarreled among themselves over many important things, including religion. And, to be sure, there was what we so loosely call religious "discrimination"; in those days, relatively few Catholics or Jews were to be found as professors in my university, much less as deans or chancellors. But everyone agreed that there was a True and a Good, and, at some obscure level, they knew its author.

Within a decade or so this consensus was to splinter. The typical faculty attitude (as opposed to that of the public that supported it financially) underwent a great sea change. Whatever its immediate causes, this shift had been prepared by three centuries of Western philosophy that finally found its opportunity to flood the culture of higher education. The herd of academics whose belief drowned in that torrent is hard to characterize. By definition these were intelligent humans, but, equally plainly, they were pushovers for the invitation to disbelief.

Their nimble minds were strangely ready for plucking. Why were they so vulnerable? I would note that for all their cleverness and gifts, faculty members often had little sophistication outside their own arcane vocation. To the weary specialist, the news that Pan lives and God is dead might, for a while at least, be misunderstood as some sort of liberation. But, whatever the reason, they showed little defense against these ideological enthusiasms when they arrived on the scene as fashionable insights. Of course, many professors did maintain their settled and independent paths, but a critical mass at the center was to shift, more or less unconsciously, as a conforming bloc; a significant number of faculty simply lost their unreflective confidence that we live in an order of things that is supported by real authority, one that has a claim on our allegiance. For convenience, let me refer to these more pliant and representative professors as "modal academics." I will try in greater detail to describe their worldview before, and then after, their defection.

As I have said, until the 1960s, these minds, as a practical matter, had managed to accept the general conception of authority that was common to the various versions of Judeo-Christianity; they had done so while simultaneously affirming the great project of the Enlightenment. The two worldviews were assumed to be compatible. Insofar as the enterprise of the Enlightenment was conceived as a pure search for truth, I suppose they were. Western religion has had its occasional retreats into obscurity, but its own premises always drive it toward an ultimate intelligibility; indeed, much of seventeenth-century thought emerged from enthusiastically believing minds, such as Newton's.

In a second and crucial respect, however, the two inspirations were not compatible. From the seventeenth and eighteenth centuries, the spirit of modernity ever-more consciously delivered the individual not merely from ecclesiastical authority but from every burden grounded in belief. At first obscurely, but then more clearly, it became a liberation from all external claims whatsoever. Man's nature carried no imperative, and he was free to make himself according to his own private will. He was on his own, nor could we even say, "God help me."

As this reading of reality at last penetrated the consciousness of their world, the modal academics of the 1960s, who formed the plastic center of our universities, found it impossible any longer to sustain simultaneously these two visions that had shared their consciousness. At least one had to go, and often both. Many abandoned their religious heritage, but others, almost absentmindedly, proceeded to abandon the Enlightenment as well, raising or (more properly) lowering the ante for mankind beyond anything ever consciously intended by the eighteenth century.

Whether or not the logic of their premises allowed it, most of the great Enlightenment minds had tended to agree with Christianity to this extent: the factual and moral objects of human reason are real, and it is the free search for the truth about them that constitutes man's unique vocation. The new dispensation of the 1960s removed the vestiges of this premise. There are no real moral objects. Hume was right. What we can know is exhausted in the subjective perceptions that are generated by stimulations of our individual neural systems. Reason's role, then, is not to hunt the real, which is a phantasm, but only to discover new techniques that can satisfy individual preferences; we can either maximize these preferences for society as a whole or—to the contrary—manipulate them to serve some personal end of our own. The point of doing the one or the other was no longer clear. Indeed, the act of moral choice had lost its intelligibility. When I am my own authority, by what measure shall I command myself?

It remains a question why so many of my good-hearted fellow academics—many of them active in plausible social causes—took this slide into subjectivism. An autonomy so exaggerated is, in the end, self-canceling. If the True and the Good are merely the private deliverance of one's digestion, they cease altogether to be intelligible concepts. And so they have for many a good intellect that has taken curious comfort in denying whatever reality might lurk outside the lockbox of his or her own mind. It is common for children to experience anxiety about what might be out there, but intelligent adults too can resort to blankets and teddy bears. Our modal academic has lacked the healthy nerve to imitate the adventurous Pandora. Ever curious and hopeful—if a bit reckless—she was determined to confront whatever might be the actual state of things; she was the authentic realist. By contrast, cowering inside the box of his own consciousness, the materialist pulls the cover shut, taking refuge among the phantoms of the ego, those unruly goblins that believing generations had rejected as mankind's primordial intellectual and moral enemy. He prefers these demons of his own invention to the "Hound of Heaven" that might await him outside the box, confronting him with the responsibility of a real authority.

The general public has found this academic loss of nerve quite absurd, and its old confidence in the university has eroded. It is being replaced by two plausible convictions. First, the academic no longer merits special trust, except, perhaps, in the technical stuff of science and the professions (and even here we must worry). Second, it follows that, if society should support higher education, it should do so more for its direct practical benefits than for its inquiry into the good life. And here, whoever pays the bill for the college freshman—parent or voter—faces a considerable dilemma. We are rightly wary of the influence of the modal professor on the souls of the young, but kids still must learn something that will make them a living. Thus, higher education survives more and more as an economic mediary, and it should not surprise us that the free market now has its way within the halls of ivy; law professors and physicists fetch twice the salary of historians and philosophers. At the University of California, some medical specialists are paid fifteen times the wage of the average humanist—almost as much as the football coach. Meanwhile, the state's contribution to the total budget of its own university has declined to 25 percent. The point at which it should be deemed private enterprise is currently a subject of argument.

The flight from belief in an objective order of the good has had its inevitable effects upon the day-to-day culture of academe itself. For one thing, it has accelerated the retreat of the scientific part of the old community of scholars into its narrow, scattered, and uncommunicating specialties. As the fund of common human wisdom and uniting purpose shrinks, the cloistered professor of the laboratory more nearly approximates the norm, each doing his or her own lonesome windowless thing supported by whatever parochial outside source is interested in this specific work. Now, there is everything to be said in favor of an authentic diversity, but when diversity itself gets comfortably cabined in the skulls of intellectual hermits, its potential is reduced to litter. In the process we become strangers. I lose access to their worlds, and they to mine. These secular monks desperately need the fresh air of catholicity, if only with a small "c."

The Demoralization of Law

Lawyers love case studies, and I will now peek at the case I know best—the law school itself. The general academic rejection of responsibility to any authority that is external to one's own mind has had a distinctive effect upon law faculties, because of the peculiar nature of law and of the intellectual habits of the profession that serves it. The lawyers—at least we of the common law countries—were for very long heedless of the atomizing implications of advancing subjectivism. Paradoxically, the problem was in part our own relative sophistication. Unlike Continental jurisprudes, who still are puzzled at the relatively unsystematic character of common law justice, we were already smugly aware that the law we know and profess is to a considerable degree fortuitous in its content and vulnerable to change; we did not need to be told that such venerable doctrines as contributory negligence and the rule against perpetuities were accidental aspects of what was a very parochial social contract. This did not deny that judges usually stick to the rules, but we knew that, in the common law world—as in crucial parts of U.S. constitutional law—it is the judges who had invented the rules in the first place.

Thus, when secular prophets such as Justice Holmes taught us what they quaintly misnamed "legal realism," few of us were shocked. We saw that Holmes was right about most practical things, and if, in his ignorance, he had constructed a caricature of natural law, at least we could thank him for the laugh. Only a handful grasped what was at stake, namely, the virtual extinction of law's authority. When responsibility itself becomes a human invention, not only are the rules mere accidents (which, of course, many are), but there is no reason beyond personal convenience to obey any of them. No legal philosopher or social contract can obligate the citizen to respect a rule, unless that citizen is already answerable to the authority that gave him reason in the first place and invited him to use it. This vacuum of true authority is today perfectly evident to almost every legal academic I know. Unhappily, most seem either to have cast their lot with Holmes or dropped into silence, further eroding the remnant of belief in a grander order of things. I cannot explain this death wish.

Now, I will double back a bit and ask what all this has had to do with my own life in the legal academy. I'm not sure there are lessons here, but there are a few suggestive stories. My mind locates them in discrete times and locations. The first set comes from my twelve years at Northwestern. I joined the faculty of my alma mater in 1955, and, when I left in 1967, it was still the mid-century academic culture that I just described. Though the faculty was a lively and inquisitive bunch, the ultimate question about the source of authority was seldom asked; it was avoided, however, not as being irrelevant or in bad taste—as might be the case today—but only, I think, as being a diversion from our professional task. The necessary foundation for the authority of law, however one conceived it—natural or supernatural—was agreed to be there simply by implication; we all aimed at a good that was secured in something real. So, not to worry; we simply pressed on with Holmes's practical project of predicting what the courts would do given a particular set of facts. Such, I think, explains the surface indifference of those times.

I concede that, among my colleagues, I was myself a curiosity. Maybe one or two were churched; none was Catholic. Indeed, with few exceptions, their knowledge of things religious was surprisingly scant. And, of natural law theory they knew no more than the burlesque by Holmes. It would surprise me if the good minds that taught labor law had even heard of *Rerum novarum* (1891), the papal encyclical that had had rather considerable influence on the distinctive American system of labor relations. But, in any case, they turned out fine lawyers, and they were as generous and good to me as they were to one another, which was very good indeed. They sought a common practical objective with little discord, and they let the big questions ride. Only one of them ever pricked me for my belief. He is today in his nineties, the last survivor of that old academic gang, and we still keep in touch. Recently he reminded me once again that religion is bunk. It was a friendly observation.

My introduction to Berkeley was to be—as they say—something else. Considering what I just said, it will seem counterintuitive. Imagine this: just as most of the academy—with Berkeley itself at the front— was busy canonizing Timothy Leary, I walked into what could have passed for a papist conspiracy right there in the law school. I can't resist one story that suggests the spirit of the place. The great canon lawyer Stephan Kuttner had just left the chair of Catholic Studies at Yale to join the Berkeley law faculty. At my first faculty meeting in the spring of 1968, we agreed to invite the distinguished Talmudic scholar David Daube to leave his fancy chair at Oxford, luring him with the following elegant telegram:

Catholics are fine but so are Jews
Kuttner's coming, how about youse?

This vignette tells all I need say of the rich and open spirit of the place. By the way, though Jewish, Daube knew and greatly admired the Catholic Church. He was even known to visit Lourdes. His story allows me to flag one other of Berkeley's religious aberrations—the magnificent Robbins Collection, of which David became a sort of living organ. Possibly you don't know that Berkeley Law School has the largest collection of canon and religious law in the entire world. How we got it is a story for another time. In any case, its lush facilities are in great vogue among canonists and church historians on sabbatical.

These early years at Berkeley proved to be literally saturated in religious sophistication. It was an intellectual atmosphere of the most surprising sort, and one I think that was appreciated as much by Jewish and nonbelieving faculty members, who constituted the majority. In that era, no subject was politically incorrect simply by virtue of its transcendent implications. The believers learned from the skeptics, and they from us in a natural, uncalculating, and open-hearted forum. To be sure, on occasion it was noted that we were a bit short on Protestants, but in due course Phil Johnson rediscovered his Calvinist roots and to this day has managed, almost single-handedly, to keep the Reformation alive and well at Berkeley.

These are happy memories of a model of academic openness. I fear, however, that the Berkeley of those days was a fluke. Sadly, the box was about to close. The critical mass of believers was to shrink in numbers, in relative influence, and in its access to our colleagues' minds. Perhaps it was destined to do so as faculties exploded in size during the last quarter century. The explicit and implicit rules for recruitment have, I think, played some part in this decline. I do not here refer to race, or even to gender—though it may well be that relatively few practicing

Christian women appear in the applicant pools—at least of the law schools. I refer rather to two strictly intellectual protocols, now discernible in modified forms at all blue-ribbon institutions.

The Economist, the Equalizer, and the Equal

The first of these emergent protocols, one that threatens to become universal in the high academy, is the remarkable deference paid to economic interpretations of law and life and to the academic minds that promote them. Karl Marx has been turned on his head. Sometimes one gets the impression that no outcome is bad if only it is achieved by a truly free market. Now, economics is an indispensable servant but an utterly brutal master. This is a truth historically congenial to the Catholic mind; instinctively it deploys economics as a means but never the end. We are warned to be skeptical of every final solution for the affairs of this world. I would be curious to know what proportion of the true believers in law and economics are Catholics. My impression is that they are few. (Michael Novak is a distinguished exception.) If I am right, the number of such candidates who would make it into the academic hiring pool would be correspondingly diminished.

I come to the second modem academic protocol with somewhat less confidence that Christians can and will avoid assimilation into what seems the fashionable view. I refer to the current disposition of the university to define justice largely in terms of the elimination of differences. This tendency is complex and deserves a closer look. In the intellectual world, this hunger to equalize has tended to become an end in itself. Even believers often adopt it as a precept, and this is a profound mistake. No doubt differences can represent disadvantage, and some disadvantages are wrong and deserve fixing. But they are not unjust merely because they are differences, nor even because they are disadvantages.

Egalitarianism has, I fear, become the modal academic's substitute for those real goods that believers think humans are bound to seek by reason—the authentic order that the academy acknowledged until yesterday. Reason simply cannot function without smuggling in some conception of a truly correct way. Those who followed Hobbes in denying the real good have had to reinvent it in some proxy form; unfortunately, in settling upon equality for this purpose they have chosen the most formless and least perspicuous notion of justice available. Perhaps that was their point. But I cannot see that it is a Christian or even an intelligible point. There is nothing illuminating in the mere idea of the sameness of rights. Like cases should, of course, be treated alike by the courts, but the reason for this is not sameness but intellectual consistency and predictability. And the likeness of any two cases should not suggest that we make everybody else alike in this one way that is peculiar to the litigants.

Having said this, let me nonetheless recognize and emphasize the reality and importance of that one authentic equality—that unique relation among all humans that does deserve both Christian respect and an honored place in any vital curriculum. Here I could resort to Thomas Jefferson. For this equality is not some hypothetical sameness of station that we might contrive through law; it is the way we were created. Human equality is a descriptive term—a simple fact—and namely this fact: All rational humans have, in the same degree, the capacity to achieve personal goodness and salvation by freely doing the best they can to discover what is true and right. Ours is an equal opportunity God; neither law nor the academy can alter this.

I am not confident that even believing academics grasp the significance of this distinction between the created fact of our equality and those many contingent equalities of law that are promoted as social goals. But they should. It is crucial that they see this, and not because equality, when recognized as a fact, either enlarges or cancels their responsibility to oppose unjust discrimination. Of course not. Rather, the distinction between fact and value is here imperative, because, in their quest for justice, one thing that should not hypnotize the Christian mind—as often it seems to do—is the mere reality of difference among our worldly stations. The impulse toward sameness is a snare and a delusion, and it distracts us from the significance of equality as a central fact of our created nature.

I will take one strong example of this fixation as my focus from this point until my conclusion. It is a notion that hobbles the scholarly mind. I have watched sociologists—even Christian sociologists—fly into moral rage at research that reports IQ differences among human groups. Such reports may well be mistaken; I personally think that they are. But, what is even more mistaken—and quite un-Christian—is to attach a false importance to such an issue. We were never to suppose that brains are some sort of ultimate good—a *summum bonum*—of which justice demands uniform distribution among the Irish and the Chinese. There is great danger in any such notion. By demonizing the very possibility of such a difference, the righteous egalitarian risks enthroning a human feature that we should never idealize in the first place. Consider the stakes here. Even if brains are exactly equal by ethnicity, gender, and race, they are certainly not so among individuals. But, if a relative shortage of Einsteins has already been identified as a reproach to the human dignity of any group, it is all the more so for the individual—whatever his group—who must bear the stigma in his own person. We must never create an aristocracy of the smart. But it has been the permanent temptation of the intelligentsia to confuse the best with the brightest. To this I wish to dissent. We should certainly make our contributions to the just distribution of resources, but believers should never attach false significance to the uneven distribution of any contingent good, and especially to the fortuitous good of human intelligence. We must avoid what G. K. Chesterton called the "curious confusion whereby being great is supposed to have something to do with being clever."

That confusion is difficult to avoid once we exile God from serious human conversation. And, to the extent that the perfectibility of the human person comes to be judged by an intellectual standard, we will have re-created on the campus a form of that ancient idolatry known as gnosticism. The highest human achievement will consist in the grasp of a particular sort of truth, and it will be secular knowledge that will save us in the one, narrow, and exclusive way we can be saved. The elect will be limited to those who embody this vision of the educated.

We should be clear that the idolatry of knowledge is not a specialty of the campus or the unbeliever. It can be religious, secular, or something ambiguous between. The religious gnostic, as in antiquity, deems his particular theological insight essential to a self-perfection that, when achieved by or imputed to any person, entails justification and salvation. The secular gnostic perceives a different form of self-perfection, one to which belief in a God of any sort is a specific impediment. However, they agree on this. Getting wrong information and acting upon it are a barrier to the realization of the human ideal; the best among us, each supposes, are those who are brightest in their grasp of my own particular version of the truth.

For the consistent secular academic, the gnosis that saves requires, first, that one grasp intellectually the deterministic and subjectivist nature of reality. Perfection of the person then can consist in maximizing subjective neural satisfaction, or this can be supplemented by some specifically cognitive component. The ideal is the empirical enlightenment of the individual to the limit of his or her natural capacity. The victory occurs in the brain as portrayed in that fine film so oddly misnamed, *A Beautiful Mind*. Most gnostic unbelievers of my acquaintance are saddened that brainpower is not equally distributed; for them this disparity means that humans differ greatly in their access to "the highest form of moral worth." It was Bernard Williams who said this, then forlornly and famously added that we are the playthings of "moral luck." In Williams's bleak assessment, we witness the death of human equality exactly as a descriptive truth. Fortune has left us decisively different in our individual capacity to achieve the gnosis that is necessary to our own perfection.

Again, this calamity of ultimate and unavoidable inequality in our access to the highest perfection is not confined to the nonbeliever. The gallery of religious gnostic creeds is considerable, and each implies unequal access to the highest human possibility. My own confession has, on occasion, teetered in that direction. You will recall the stubbornness of the error "outside the Church there is no salvation." Even the gentle Aquinas could not excuse certain honest mistakes: "This error," he said, "arises from ignorance of the Divine Law, which [any person] is bound to know." And recall that Samuel Johnson supposed a hell that is paved with the good intentions of the misinformed. Such Christians were, according to my usage, agnostics.

I am persuaded that relatively few versions of Christianity could today be understood this way. For Catholics, Vatican II sealed the credal insight that humans come to God by doing the best they can to find the True and the Good with whatever gifts they have been given. Luck is officially dead as a determinant of personal goodness. I think that I detect roughly the same degree of inclusiveness among Protestants, even those from creeds that have officially included predestination. We are saved by saying yes to what is a universal divine invitation to seek the authentic good and to do so with diligence. There are exceptions to this version of our hope, but most of the Christianity that I observe takes divine friendship to be an equal opportunity for all.

By contrast, the *secular* version of self-perfection entails a stubborn and troubling paradox that lurks in the academy as an unmentionable and irresolvable embarrassment. There is no part of the American culture that is more committed to the verbal celebration of equality than is the university. Yet, to the degree that the academy—like Bernard Williams—supposes the bright among us to have a better chance at being the best, it must live in contradiction; for the idea of a meaningful equality has become incoherent. The university very much needs a description of the self that locates the possibility of goodness, hence of human dignity, not in the self's capacity to know all that is worth knowing, but simply in its freedom to commit, or not to commit to the search for that same truth. But such a description comes hard for the strictly secular mind. Why should one who honestly mistakes the truth be thought to be just as morally perfected as the one who finds it? In a purely material philosophy this is not easy. Equality needs some place to stand outside the empirical person.

Rediscovering that place may play a leading role in the moral politics of the impending world. The separation of hope for self-perfection from the luck of our individual access to correct knowledge could nourish the prospect for a world in which minds that are in conflict can treat one another with the dignity of moral equals. Consider the Muslim who today supposes, with some justification, that the gnostic unbeliever views Islam as an obstacle to man's perfection—an obstacle equal to Christianity in its power to obscure the real. The Muslim—especially if he is himself a religious gnostic—may return the compliment, adding his prediction of perdition for the secular, an outcome he may even be glad to facilitate.

My suggestion is that the nongnostic Christian may find it easier to engage the Muslim—or any other potential competitor in this world—as a fellow human being. Those who can recognize the other as sharing in full the capacity for self-perfection could well have the advantage in achieving that empathy toward the other that a red-blooded Christian might call love. He sees that the other (whatever his social or intellectual state), at least in his access to God, is in no way crippled by the "moral luck" of his rotten childhood or his bad education.

Rousseau got this practical problem just right: "It is impossible to live in peace with people one believes to be damned." This does not mean that those who do believe in equal access to God never sin against one another, but it does mean that they do not sin out of any misconception that they are superior in God's eyes simply by their own grasp of a certain knowledge that the other does not share. In its materialist form, that crucial mistake, I think, is the temptation of the secular academic. What I don't quite see is how he escapes this trap or even would wish to escape. If one is in fact intellectually superior, that's just the way it is. But, then, where will the academic anchor his ark of human equality? It will need a place somewhere outside his own subjectivity. But, that deliverance would require Professor Pandora to reopen the box of his own mind and take his chances in a larger and more dangerous world that he does not dominate.

Yet I think there is hope for just such an epiphany. The typical academic secular, I assume, wants to get it all right. I would predict that for many the flight from authority and objectivity will run its course—in your time, if not mine. It will die of its contradictions, but even more of its own boring dead weight. Of course, those inside academia but outside the narrow secular box are obliged to hasten that day as they can. We are patiently to anticipate and even encourage conversation with our colleagues—when they are ready. This is a responsibility we should prize and enjoy.

PART TWO

Education and Community

CHAPTER SIX

Can Education Create Community?

The title question calls for some conceptual apparatus. Only to the extent that we can define "community" could we hope to show its relation to the private and public and practice of the virtue of tolerance. "Community" is notoriously ambiguous, and only a partial definition may be possible. By contrast, "tolerance" can be clearer in concept, even if it remains very difficult in application. Along the way we shall also need definitions for both "human dignity" and "human equality." Together these four concepts—dignity, equality, tolerance, and community—may allow us to speak coherently of education's capacity to nourish community. Their definitions give no comprehensive answer to our question, but promise a good start.

Tolerating Real Evil

Let us begin with tolerance, an idea that is given contradictory meanings. Often in contemporary discourse it is said to consist in an attitude of moral "neutrality" that supposedly is required by philosophical skepticism. Tolerance is thought to flow from the Enlightenment premise that no authentic good exists apart from the personal preferences of individuals; therefore, so they say, we should never judge or interfere with personal or group behavior that does not "harm" others in some material way.

Originally published in *Revista Española de Pedagogía* 53, no. 201 (1995): 307–20

Now, were the skeptical premise true, neutrality would not be an inference but a contradiction; no duty to be natural—nor any other duty—could flow from the proposition that good and evil are arbitrary personal preferences. Neutrality would be simply one among an infinity of arbitrary preferences. But were we to accept neutrality as an authentic good, it could have little weight in the practical order; humans are highly interdependent actors, and neutrality among their conflicting preferences is seldom an option. Whether we interfere in these conflicts or stand aside, necessarily *someone's* preference is frustrated.

In reality we discover that not even the premise is taken seriously by the champions of neutrality. True philosophical skeptics are rare, and practicing neutralists even rarer. Those who like to wear these labels are as quick to recognize and resent misbehavior as are the rest of us. Ironically, it is this inconsistency that makes the skeptic bearable; for tolerance does not consist in abstract neutrality but in a well-tempered resistance to real evil. The only conceivable ground of tolerance is the belief in a good that binds us independently of our wills. I do not mean that the successful practitioners of tolerance always grasp the terms of the real good in particular cases; all of us make honest mistakes about its objective content. All that the practice of tolerance requires is that correct moral answers truly exist and that we are obliged to seek them. Only because every rational human recognizes this obligation to search for the content of the good can individuals and society ask coherently: When two goods are in conflict, which comes first and which ought to be sacrificed?

Tolerance is the diligent inquiry whether it is best to interfere with—or, instead, to allow—a particular evil (as one honestly perceives it) for the sake of preserving some (perceived) higher good that would be threatened by interference. When seriously engaged in that inquiry, persons and societies are by definition being tolerant, whatever we think of their answers. For our present purpose, perhaps the best example of tolerance in action is the careful application by Western societies of the constitutional presumption against official restraint upon written and oral expression. The state regularly permits the communication of bad ideas in order to preserve the fragile structure of open discourse, and the responsible legislator, judge, or citizen understands that the moral vocation of the human person is best conducted within such a free system. Our common experience tells us that everyone's freedom is gravely imperiled when the state chooses sides in the endless contest of ideas. On occasion, state intervention may be necessary, but this is the rare exception. Our judiciaries establish elaborate rules to give the process of decision the proper gravity and restraint, and censorship is imposed only in extremis.

Note that the tolerance of evil can be practiced in different forms and degrees. This is exemplified in the world of education. The evil can be simply *forbidden*: no school shall teach racial hatred or anarchy (zero toleration). It can be *allowed*: a private school may be permitted to teach the pernicious idea of double predestination. It can be *encouraged*: the same school can be subsidized (perhaps because parental freedom is perceived to be a very high order value). Finally, through honest political error, an evil may actually be *prescribed*: made compulsory. As we shall see, this occurs in state education today in the United States. The higher good that would justify this compulsion is undiscoverable, making the result—but only *objectively*—an act of *in*tolerance.

Tolerance, then, is the diligent effort to grasp and to realize true moral priorities; it is one aspect of the ordinary process of deciding moral issues in the objective order. This makes tolerance close cousin to the virtue of prudence; we cannot make everything exactly right, so we ask which goods come first. By definition, tolerance entails the sufferance of evil; it is in this respect a negative aspect of moral judgment.

COMMUNITY, DIGNITY, AND EQUALITY

If tolerance is negative, community is positive. It is good *as such*. In the effort to define it, one necessarily begins by asking what sort of beings are capable of community. Apart from a few hard-core determinists, the self-proclaimed *Communitarians* agree among themselves to this extent. To constitute a true community, its members—with rare exception—must possess rationality and free will. Clusters of nonrational or nonvolitional beings (e.g., fish or lemmings) could be communities only by the most remote analogy. Communitarianism, after all, is a self-conscious ideal; it is a movement. Infused with deliberateness and purpose, it pursues a certain state of affairs. It is only because community is a good requiring rational choice that we could be obligated to pursue it. Community is an imperative for free moral beings, hence, strictly a human enterprise.

This minimal criterion has been useful to the ongoing debate about community. It has allowed would-be communitarians who represent conflicting philosophies to criticize modern culture with something of a common front. It cannot, however, ground the sort of positive theory for which most of them ultimately hope. What theory would suffice for that purpose, I cannot say, but one necessary (if possibly insufficient) element is a descriptive human equality. Community entails Jefferson's factual claim of the fundamental equality of persons (at least as a belief shared by and about members within any *particular* community). Community will probably require more, but equality will be one inevitable part.

Thus any definition will also include a descriptive conception of equality. What I will now uncover is the only understanding of descriptive equality in which I have confidence. It begins with the assertion that human equality is both related to and importantly distinct from still another concept: dignity. Equality and dignity can be understood only together. Each is an identifying property of free moral beings. Dignity is familiar to us from the book of Genesis as the status bestowed upon *imago Dei*. By their created structure, men and women share finitely in God's infinite intellect and freedom. Our dignity consists specifically in having reason and will. And herein lies a problem. The analogy to the divine nature is naively intended to be ennobling but becomes problematic exactly to the extent that humans vary in their intellectual power, and so dignity is relativized. I do not mean that Christians actually talk this way. No hierarchy of dignity is suggested; the *sensus fidelium* would forbid it. Nonetheless, many theologians have clearly believed that the range of our individual intellect affects the quantum of our individual capacity for the good, a conclusion that necessarily implies relativity.

This moral gnosticism is an ancient misunderstanding. Thomas Aquinas was following Aristotle when he taught that self-perfection turns upon finding the correct answers to moral questions. Both men supposed that our intelligence, education, and sheer luck affect our capacity for moral fulfillment. In this view, dignity becomes a nasty paradox: the very human faculties in which it consists generate a gnostic hierarchy based upon accidental traits. Some of us are more dignified than others. Dignity begets indignity.

Happily, the escape from this is plain and leads straight to human equality. Socrates, Aristotle, Augustine, Aquinas, and Suarez were simply wrong about who qualifies as a good person. They were, of course, correct to conclude (as Pope John Paul II emphasizes) that we are bound by natural and revealed orders of authentic goods (or correct moral answers). However, it is not in the successful discovery of these correct answers that a person is morally perfected, but rather in the act of seeking them. The honest and diligent search that produces moral error may damage the social order, but simultaneously it perfects the fallible seeker who has tried as hard as he could to discover and serve that order. Persons become good and holy by doing the best they can. A possible example. In supporting the burning of heretics, Aquinas did an objectively bad thing. If he truly sought the correct answer, he advanced his own moral perfection.

This recognition that there can be disjunction between moral good of the actor and the good of acts in external order saves dignity from becoming a gnostic hierarchy and simultaneously provides the definition of human equality. Like every other instance of equality, it is a relation. It is the unique relation that holds among all rational persons by virtue of their capacity to achieve moral self-perfection by seeking the correct treatment of one another. This uniform potential for moral self-fulfillment was given its implicit *imprimatur* by Vatican II, which repeatedly stressed the primacy of conscience in seeking the authentic good. The roots of this idea are at least as old as Origen and—until Vatican II—were most evident in the work of St. Alfonsus Liguori. Unfortunately, it has yet to be taken seriously either by modern philosophy or natural law. Practitioners of the former deny that good can exist independently of human will. Conversely, natural law philosophers typically reject the proposition that a mistaken good intention not only excuses but perfects. Obviously this concept will also trouble those Christians who still hold for predestination and against human freedom. Nonetheless, it is not only orthodox but, in my judgment, the *sensus fidelium*. Shortly I will show that it is also a claim that has importance independent of religious belief.

Equality and Community

In rescuing dignity from the gnostics, the doctrine of equality satisfies the fundamental criterion of community noted earlier: to be a true community, its members must possess both rationality and free will. So far my grasp of this proposition is largely intuitive. I am confident that it can be defended, but for the time being I will only assert it as follows. If community is to hold, the most marginally rational person—the most wretched and disadvantaged member—must be perceived to have a capacity for moral and/or spiritual self-fulfillment (and, conversely, degradation) that is as plenary as that of the most gifted fortunate. In other words, the belief in human equality is requisite to community. Where, by contrast, humans are perceived to stand in a hierarchical order of moral perfectibility, the Brahmin and the outcast may achieve coexistence or even society, but true community will elude them.

I will not try to answer once and for all the additional question as to whether community, when properly defined, requires belief in the equality of *outsiders*. The members of some human clusters do in fact see nonmembers as deficient in moral potential. My present disposition is to include such self-defining moral elites within the definition but to demote them to a second-class status in the taxonomy of communities. It will be convenient simply to call them "elites," so long as that term is understood to be pejorative in our present context. My impression is that the gnostic beliefs that sustain elite groups have been on the decline in the twentieth century. Few Westerners, at least, suppose that those persons outside their own family, church, race, or other cluster are less capable of moral self-fulfillment. Whether this observation is correct, who can say? However, it remains true that members of self-perceiving elites are by definition incapable of belonging to any community in which perceived inferiors would be included. In specific practical matters, elites may, of course, either cooperate in or conflict with communities that contain moral inferiors as members.

By contrast, individuals who do accept the equality of all rational humans are capable of membership in an indefinite number of particular communities. And where this belief is shared by all members, a community is entitled to the label "authentic." This does not imply that all such communities share the same ultimate purposes, lifestyles, or rules of right behavior. Quite to the contrary, believers in human equality can cluster on the basis of disparate ideologies, religion, professions, or the like—differences that can set them in conflict with one another. Put another way, although they are authentic, communities by definition can be *exclusive* in important dimensions. The important point is that intercommunity conflict has a different meaning for those who do and those who do not accept *universal* human equality as a fact.

The world of Roman Catholicism is a useful example of the effect of this belief upon one's attitude toward ideological enemies. I will assume that the population of believing Catholics satisfies whatever other criteria might be thought necessary to constitute an authentic community (the reader may specify them). In that event, precisely as Catholics, their belief in human equality locates these individuals in two communities—one exclusive, one universal. Catholics are, first of all, a community to and among themselves; their church claims authoritative access to correct moral answers, and assent to that ecclesiastical authority is a criterion of membership. Exclusivity is no trivial matter to them. Their orthodoxy triggers meaningful obligation. In their own view, they are bound—and nonbelievers are not—to give the teaching authority of their community a presumption of correctness. When engaged in the quest for correct moral answers, observance of this presumption operates as the practical threshold of the good intent that does the work of personal, subjective moral self-perfection; the believer who would meet his moral responsibility for honest inquiry cannot reject an ordinance of the Church merely because he or she has reservations.

By the same token, even honest apostasy on a serious moral issue sets the individual outside this exclusive community. The dissenter emigrates from the cluster that upholds the authority of the Church. Because that authority is vaguely defined, there will be practical disputes about who is in and who is out. But the principle is clear enough. The doctrinal émigré asserts that the ecclesiastical authority can be wrong and, in this case, is wrong. In his eyes, the exclusive community that accepts that authority is deluded about its reliability. The act of emigration is thus the invitation to a new and more discerning community. It initiates a plurality of exclusive communities, even though each may aspire to the old name.

Finally, the exclusive community that consists of continuing believers also asserts the commission and duty of their church to teach *all* mankind whatever can be known of moral truth. But does mankind, then, have a reciprocal duty to give priority to these specific moral messages because of their source? I take it that, in the Catholic view, the answer is no. Every human is already obliged to seek the objective moral good wherever he or she can find it. The unbeliever or émigré thus has the duty, the natural duty, to consider Catholicism's moral answers along with the rest, but for him or her they can carry no special presumption of truth. Rome is for him or her one of the world's many representatives of the Tao. If there is some added element of community in this neutral didactic relation between the outsider and the Catholic believer, at first it seems very thin.

Nevertheless, note that in recognizing human equality, the Church has embraced a principle of community that renders its own particular moral answers irrelevant to the *goodness of the person*. Its commitment to equality thus entails the richly communal declaration to that outsider that, if he honestly concludes that the Church is wrong (on whatever issue), he is not only bound in conscience to *reject* the Church but, by doing so, he achieves the very end sought for him by the Church itself. Even in the midst of the most intense conflict, real human connection thereby remains possible. To the insider, the outsider becomes a full partner in the one essential community that consists of all moral pilgrims. And this occurs precisely when the outsider honestly refuses what purports to be the authoritative message of the exclusive community.

Nothing in this understanding of equality turns upon using Catholics as my example. This relation between their exclusive community and its ideological competitors is merely one very large and vivid instance of the subsurface harmony that is everywhere generated and sustained by the assent to universal human quality. At least in the West, this crucial belief is a cultural reality in most communities where they are families, nations, churches, or neighborhoods. The inevitable quarrels among such exclusive communities in their deepest meaning thus reduce to disputes within the human family. These convulsions, however destructive in the external order, never risk either the moral integrity of the individual or the community that is mankind.

Authentic community thus implies deep respect for the members of groups whose beliefs conflict either with accepted public values or with one's own. This is specifically a respect for *persons* and not for their ideas or practices when these are perceived as false or evil. Nevertheless, this very respect for the person is the primary guarantee that unpopular ideas will receive fair weight in the constant calculus of higher good that we call toleration. The common belief in universal human equality sets tolerance its specific mission. In the midst of their inevitable conflicts, exclusive but authentic community perceives the social order (domestic or international) as one in which persons — all linked in the relation of equality — constantly interact through the political process to determine exactly which concessions to evil will best sustain the highest good. There will always be political losers, but in such a moral culture the losers will be less often selected by raw majoritarian power, and they will themselves be the more willing to respect and to sustain the painful and unending process of judgment that is toleration.

Let's recapitulate. We now have comprehensive definitions for "tolerance," "dignity," and "human equality." For "community," we have only a split-level and partial definition. In order to restate it clearly, let us again assume that whatever group is to be tested satisfies whatever else the reader thinks necessary to the status of community. On that assumption, elite communities are those that accept the equality only of their own members; *authentic* communities are those that perceive all rational persons as equal in the sense that all have the same capacity for moral self-perfection. Conflict among authentic communities thus always prescinds from personal moral potential.

COMMUNITY, TOLERANCE, AND STATE SCHOOLS

The public decision to allow particular evils is more often art than science. However, the focus of our present concern is formal education, and here our conceptual framework actually yields some answers. The first of these involves the specific function of tolerance in regard to state schools.

When exercised in the public order, tolerance produces judgments that are embodied in a set of institutions, subsidies, duties, prohibitions, and freedoms. In the arena of education, a huge variety of arrangements is possible. Those institutions that teach children may or may not include schools that are owned and operated by the state, and tolerance plays a role in deciding that question. Schools necessarily teach *some* set of values. State schools are no exception, and, wherever consensus sustains a unitary culture, the state school has the capacity to deliver its homogeneous message. At the same time, out of respect for still higher values, even a unitary moral culture (Japan is an example) may—up to some point defined by law—*tolerate* contrary ideologies taught by private schools.

Because of the pluralism of their cultures, such toleration is not an option for the Western nations today. In these societies, a minimal consensus may exist regarding honesty, observance of law, caring, and (possibly) human equality. But, in respect to ultimate values, various important social practices, and the objective content of the good life, there is simply no agreement. By definition, above this minimum consensus, there is no *social* interpretation of the good for the state to teach. State schools that promulgate any set of ultimate values thus are affirming only some private good held by other individuals who happen to operate the machinery of government. This is just as true of those state schools purporting to teach neutrality. Even in this they did not succeed, but, if they did, they would affirm a good for which there is no supporting consensus.

In modern society, the wise political decision to encourage private schools often is paraded as an act of tolerance, but we now see that there is an abuse of language. Such a policy could be called "tolerance" only if there were consensus identifying some evil being taught by private schools that the state for some higher reason could choose not to suppress. But the modern pluralist state knows no such evil, at least so long as the private school satisfies the narrow and undemanding minimum consensus. Hence, any public critique of private teaching is impossible. To put it plainly in our own terms: There is nothing that private schools are doing that needs the state's toleration; there is no evil to be suffered in pursuit of a higher good.

This presents a lovely paradox. The only evil that needs toleration is the *compulsion practiced by the state school*. The very parochial and insular message of these schools—one that is favored by a monopoly of public resources and disseminated with the prestige of public officers to a largely conscripted audience—is a message that represents the values of almost no one at all. At its best, the public course of study tries to occupy the empty space between the substantive ideas that thrive in the private sector, vacuous and vanilla, and its highest aim is to avoid offense to mutually opposed ideological groups. At its worse, it constitutes the political triumph of influential advocacy or identity groups, including the educational establishment itself. In either case—whether it be pap or propaganda—what we are asked to tolerate is the ideological preference of *somebody* (teacher, administrator, lobbyist), who by art or luck wields the power of the state.

It is, then, the state school that must ask for our toleration. Happily there is a justification for this institution. A higher good is at stake: the authority and responsibility of individual families. So long as substantial numbers of parents would freely choose state schools for their children, tolerance would preserve that option.

But that toleration must be nuanced and qualified. At present, the most flagrant evil of the state school is its conscription of the ordinary family, which cannot afford to emigrate to the private sector. The existence of a state curriculum in a pluralist society is in itself merely absurd and of little consequence. It would easily be tolerated if every family— not merely the rich—could take it or leave it. Under conditions of freedom, in deference to those parents who want to use the state school, that institution could be endured. Unfortunately, this criterion of family freedom is not satisfied at present in many societies, most notably our own. The bureaucracies of the fifty U.S. states impose their own educational preferences upon all but the wealthy.

There is no technical reason that this narrow monopoly should continue. Many systems have been designed that would provide choice to the ordinary family. Some are now in operation. I personally prefer a system of family subsidies (vouchers) that are large enough to stimulate the formation of new providers for those families who are unable to add much tuition. In such a system, practical freedom would also require private schools to set aside some portion of new admissions for children of low-income families. And any tuition that a private school would charge above the voucher amount would have to be proportioned to the family's ability to pay.

Regarding curriculum, discipline, and teacher qualifications, private providers in such a system should remain as free as the private and religious schools are today in the United States. Racial discrimination and promotion of criminality would be forbidden (i.e., not tolerated);

instruction in the national tongue on traditional academic subjects would be required (i.e., supertolerated). The minimum popular consensus that exists in the West demands both of these policies, and no clear counsel of tolerance suggest otherwise. In all other respects, these private institutions should be allowed to be themselves. So long as they propagate no evil that is perceptible to the government of a pluralist democratic society, no issue of public toleration is presented.

One possible exception that could raise the issue is the private school that offends the consensus by rejecting the belief in human equality. If Jefferson's — self-evident — proposition is part of the consensus, the state will have to decide whether to *tolerate* schools that falsely propagate the moral superiority of some elite community. In the United States, the schools of certain churches that teach doctrines of an "Elect" might be examples, but the U.S. Constitution would probably forbid a separate legal rule for them.

Whether the state should tolerate such socially definable error is best decided by trying to predict the practical effect that official tolerance would have upon the reciprocal perceptions of all the ideological communities — elite and authentic — that constitute the larger society. If society publicly subsidizes the gnostic elitism of a Mormon school, will this injure or advance the general spirit of civic cooperation? To put the question this way emphasizes the particular definitions of authentic community that can demand a good deal more than mere belief in human equality. Some, indeed, would require as a minimum that the particular cluster seeking community status be one that shows respect for and participates in the democratic process, including active and positive relations with other groups that together constitute some larger order, such as the state. Because they identify a positive good or public value, definitions of this sort locate community somewhere in the hierarchy of goods that are to be considered in the decision of what (and how) to tolerate. In the context of schools, the teaching of bad ideas might, for example, come to be tolerated on the specifically communitarian ground that protection of free expression on the whole enhances both the belief in human equality and the acceptance of civic responsibility in all its familiar forms. These benign consequences would, in effect, become part of the definition of "community." And the sufferance of evil would be justified upon the positive values of community now understood as an activity and not merely as a shared belief about human nature and moral perfectibility.

COMMUNITY AND TOLERANCE AS THE PRIVATE HARVEST OF PUBLIC POLICY

Very probably, most Westerners see community vaguely in this more socially ambitious form. Indeed, they might have expected this sense of community to be the primary focus. They would ask: How might we, through publicly regulated education, encourage groups within a pluralist society to tolerate in *private* life most of the errors we all think we see in the thoughts of other, so that society together may better realize all its first-order goods under the banner of community? What system of schools is most likely to inspire an appropriate *private* tolerance of the perceived errors of others who are making decision about their own children? These remain burning questions in the United States, where the tide of melting-pot philosophy has crested and seems about to recede. Whatever the individual state has been doing has utterly failed to nourish community, in any sense. Nevertheless, it remains very hard for American public educators to face the obvious alternative solution that I have already noted and will now revisit as my conclusion.

A system of subsidized parental choice would enhance community, first of all by taking human equality seriously. It is precisely because it respects equality that the state would at last put ordinary and disadvantaged families in a position effectively to decide where their own child goes to school. Presumably, there would be schools teaching specific and diverse systems of ethnic and religious values; there would also be individual schools—private and public—that succeed as ideological melting pots. There would be home schools and schools for profit. The social arguments for family choice do not stand or fall upon a predication of the precise educational preference of social classes who have never before has a choice. Remember that above minimum requirements and prohibitions, society has no alternative but to trust the parent. This is not a counsel of toleration but of justice, for there is no socially definable evil needing toleration. So far as the state is concerned, these forms of education all stand on an equal footing.

Nevertheless, parental behavior may be thought important in regard to the achievement of community in the broader and positive sense that I just noted. If that is the question, we might start by remembering the actual historical effect of American schools upon intergroup perceptions. In the United States, the domination of state schools by nineteenth-century Protestantism and twentieth-century secularism has successfully ensured that only the rich have had choice; the rest have been regularly conscripted for the neutral state schools, many of which until recently were legally segregated by race. Just as forced segregation was unjust and socially demoralizing, forced association in government schools has proved to be nothing but sand in the gears of community. The ordinary family sees clearly that its children are social cannon fodder for those better off and whose own children study elsewhere. One could imagine no more effective stimulant to intergroup hostility.

However "community" is to be defined, its first operating rule must be this: Any society that would nourish trust in the common enterprise must first show trust in ordinary persons. Disadvantaged parents may not always make the choices that are preferred for them by skeptical educators, but—like the rich—they will at least be acting responsibly in pursuit of a good that is real and not merely a feigned neutrality. What we know historically of those American families who at great personal sacrifice have chosen private schools is that they tend to be strong supporters of the larger community. When children are sent by their families to schools run by adults who share the parents' worldview (whatever that view might be), those children are more likely to read well, vote, tolerate their neighbors' errors, and stay out of jail. This holds true independently of social class.

The conclusion that freedom of choice would be an investment in community—in every sense—seems plain in the United States to everyone except the operators of the education cartel. If society wants individuals, families, and groups to participate in the political process and to live in peace with their neighbors, forced assimilation of the poor is not the best answer. Mutual respect among citizens requires that the state itself show them respect, specifically in a system of choice. Of course, even then every individual would remain free to foment discord or to build social bridges. Far from being a static and finished thing, community is an unending and risky adventure shared by equals.

CHAPTER SEVEN

Education

Nature, Nurture, and Gnosis

Every natural law theory recognizes two distinct but related forms of goodness that can be realized by human choice. The first consists of behaviors: conduct is good if it satisfies principles and rules deriving from what it is to be human. The second good is the moral identity one can acquire as he or she chooses among possible behaviors. Most versions of natural law teach that the human actor must correctly grasp the good of the first sort in order to achieve that of the second. No one advances in moral self-perfection while mistaking bad acts for good. This view has the practical appeal that it identifies certain people as bad. It might also be true.

On a closely related point, natural lawyers are unanimous: rational actors are fallible. In making choices, humans can mistake either the facts or the rules that govern conduct, and they can do so without culpable self-delusion. The most diligent search for the objective good can turn up wrong answers. It might, for example, be truly wrong to withhold certain information from the police, but the most earnest pilgrim could conclude otherwise and act accordingly. The majority of natural moralists would think the pilgrim morally diminished by his good-faith error.

Originally published in *Natural Law and Contemporary Public Policy*, ed. David Forte (Washington, DC: Georgetown University Press 1998), 55–78

For all its venerability, this view of the good person is intellectually shaky. Natural law does, of course, entail the premise that behavior is good or bad apart from how we judge it. But that premise does not imply that bad actions make bad people. Such a conclusion would be consistent with the premise, but not required. An utterly different view, but one still consistent with the premise, would be that persons become morally good by doing their best to find the correct behavior, and that honest mistakes in no way diminish personal goodness. The diligent seeker perfects himself even as he makes a hash of the practical order that he tries to serve. Such disjunction between the good of acts and of actors is plausible. Nor does it risk the common good; the belief that moral self-perfection depends upon one's diligent pursuit of natural justice is an appropriate incentive for citizens.

I need names to distinguish these competing models of personal goodness. The view that requires correct knowledge of right answers I will call "natural gnosticism"; the one that is satisfied by diligent quest for those answers will be identified by various forms of the noun "obtension" (the *O.E.D.* allows us to enlist this old word). These two images of the good person are quite distinct; translated into policy, it would not be surprising if they should imply different regimes for education.[1]

NATURAL GNOSTICISM

Each view—the gnostic and the obtensional—claims to be the correct understanding of natural moral perfection, and it will be helpful to identify the place each holds among the various nature-based theories of the good person. A four-set breakdown of natural law theories serves this purpose (the confection is that of Patrick Brennan's and my making). Two types are clearly gnostic, each fusing the good of the act with the good of the actor: in order to fare well morally, one must discover and do the right external deeds. The third type of natural law is less perspicuous but probably agrees. The fourth rejects the gnostic fusion, allowing self-perfection by obtension.[2]

Aristotle and Aquinas personify the first of these natural traditions, which I will call "Common Sense." For Aristotle, the actualizing of the natural finality of the human person is an achievement of the intellect.

Indeed, it is the inferior mind of the "natural slave" that limits his moral horizon, denying him the free man's fuller access to *eudaemonia*. A millennium and a half later, Aquinas added a refinement: innocent ignorance concerning a fact can cancel the moral self-injury of an objective error. But its effect is merely to "excuse." The actor's futile effort to find and do the real good is never perfecting. If Oedipus strove for the best, his honest mistakes nonetheless left him a moral washout. This view finds contemporary expression in the language of "moral luck" that is preferred by philosophers such as Thomas Nagel and Bernard Williams.[3]

The Common Sense tradition was—and still is—widely criticized as lacking a ground of obligation. The scrutiny of natures may help to identify the act that would be proper, but who says that we should observe it? Responding to this criticism, Suarez and others identified God as the source of obligation and thereby solidified what Brennan and I call the "Classic Position." A discernible divine command gives natural law its obliging force, making it our task to realize the right relations (or matches) among created natures. These matches are disclosed by our reflection upon sense data and upon various self-evident propositions. Suarez and others concede, however, that only some of the correct behavior is self-evident. Under certain circumstances, actors can be invincibly ignorant of the right way. This is a pity, for again comes the gnostic turn: "such ignorance cannot exist without guilt." Indeed, "the existence of a precept obliges a man to know it." The Classic Position offers the misinformed no hope of moral fulfillment.[4]

The third school of natural law is a work of our times; its version of self-perfection is "integral human fulfillment," or, here, simply "Integration." The edifice of John Finnis, Germain Grisez, and others, it has deserved and received considerable academic attention. As a moral system, it is founded upon a set of seven or eight basic human goods (knowledge, friendship, play, religion, etc.). Integration is less plainly gnostic than the first two sets. Or, more accurately, Integration at first seems to recognize that all persons have knowledge sufficient for full self-perfection. True, our realization of the basic goods through the search for correct behaviors is a contingent intellectual achievement: fallibility is still in play even as, with "intelligent creativity and freedom," we act to achieve "practical reasonableness." But fallibility is consistent with the view that we achieve self-perfection by obtension.

Indeed, at one stage, the Integrationists make the prospects of the invincibly ignorant seem identical with those of the moral cognoscenti. Speaking of reason's proper attitude toward the basic goods, Finnis declares "the first principle of morality": "Insofar as it is in your power, allow nothing but the basic reasons for action to shape your practical thinking."[5] This might suggest that "reasonableness" is necessary to personal morality, but only insofar as it is in your power. Integration flirts with the obtensional conclusion that best effort is the efficient instrument of moral self-perfection.

This intimation, however, loses much of its promise in the succeeding description of "integral human fulfillment"—the achievement of natural personal goodness. Integration requires that the human actor avoid the neglect of any one good; "participating in all human goods well" is necessary to full moral development of the self. There is a certain harmony of the basic goods that must be achieved, and a person's intention to get it right is merely necessary and not sufficient. Unless I misread Finnis and Grisez, the interior commitment of the actor is not sufficient where he fails to achieve this state of objective concordance. My fear increases as they emphasize the role of religion in clarifying the terms of integral human fulfillment. Correct perceptions of the integrated good enhance personal moral perfection, and, alas, these are insights that some will have in abundance and others will lack through no fault of their own.[6]

Later I will speak of the consequences of believing in the one theory of personal goodness or the other. It will then be clear why I hope that my impression of the Integration school as gnostic is simply a misunderstanding. Meanwhile let me emphasize that belief in moral self-perfection by honest effort in no way impugns the value of nature as a guide to reason in the necessary and unending search for correct behavior. Indeed, where obtension proceeds without divine revelation, its typical methods of inquiry are those of natural law, and fulfillment of the natural good of correct actions is exactly what one must "put forward as a reason" to his or her own free and responsible will.

Moving Natural Law Inside

What Brennan and I had sought in the first three versions of natural law emerges without ambiguity in the work of Bernard Lonergan. To put it simply, Lonergan looks for moral perfection of the person inside the self. This is not, of course, a fall into solipsism. Like every other natural lawyer, Lonergan holds fast to the reality of the good that is to be realized by conduct; that reality is the very object of moral quest. The actor remains responsible to the external good. The question is, responsible *for what*?[7]

Not for correct answers, says Lonergan, who begins the vindication of honest error with a grudging concession of the fallibility of the moral self. This weakness of ours does not, of course, excuse or even diminish the cognitive burden of the moral pilgrim. Quite the opposite. To recognize that our minds typically fall short of full apprehension is only to intensify the duty to search. Because moral choice remains a step into the obscure, our hard-won, cognitive advances serve mostly to confirm the darkness that by nature we are commissioned to oppose. What is, however, clear to every person—and only this—is that we have been born free creatures who are made to say yes or no to the obligation to seek the real good. Putting it back into Aristotle's terms, it is precisely in saying yes to the imperative to search that we actualize our potential for moral self-perfection. Our natural finality lies in becoming one who is committed to the task. There is no higher natural perfection. The honest seeker reaches sufficient moral reality in the perceived content of his own committed subjectivity. He grasps whatever his mind can bring in from the cold to be judged. He may be wrong about the content of the moral truth of the extended world. His judgment, nevertheless, achieves full integrity by ardently affirming that elusive truth as its object. His moral grasp exceeds his cognitive reach. Lonergan calls this achievement "authenticity."[8]

I should emphasize that this effort of mine to squeeze the prodigy that is Lonergan into a nutshell is untrue to his own distinctively exhaustive method and is justified here only by necessity. Lonergan is his own best advertisement for the generative toil that is required of the successful (or unsuccessful) seeker of objective moral truth. I am content here to quote these few lines from *Insight*:

> Will is good . . . in the measure that antecedently and without persuasion it matches the pure desire both in its detachment from the sensitive subject and in its incessant dedication to complete intelligibility. A will less good than that is less than genuine; it is ready

for the obnubilation that takes flight from self-knowledge; it is inclined to the rationalization that makes out wrong to be right. . . .
In brief, as man's intelligence has to be developed, so also must his
will. But progress in willingness is effected by persuasion, persuasion rests upon intelligent grasp and reasonable judgment, and so
the failure of the intellect to develop entails the failure of the will.[9]

It is risky for a humdrum lawyer to declare that this move to the
inside is important to the future of natural law moral theory, but so I
see it. Natural law has been prodigal in its concentration on externals—
often on the most contestable particularities of behavior. Like waves
lapping the rocky shore, its progress in identifying clearly correct rules
is barely discernible. At the same time, its gnostic assessment of self-
perfection has caused natural law unconsciously to preach a moral
hierarchy of persons—a hierarchy that is foreign to the sensibilities of
many of its own faithful. Perhaps the flourishing of these several great
traditions might be restored by a turn to the one perspicuous law that
is both given and fulfilled inside us. I accept the need for and the truth
of rules of behavior. By all means keep telling us *what* is good, but
meanwhile reconsider *who* is good. On that question, there is territory
yet to be mapped by the moral psychologists of natural law.

LESSONS FOR EDUCATION

The Rescue of Dignity and Equality

My assignment is to reconsider the implications of natural law for the
political economy of schools. Specifically, then, what do our competing
natural theories of moral self-perfection have to say about the curriculum and the organization of schools? Presumably, the individual
natural law educator will teach children only that version of moral self-
perfection in which he believes and will debunk the one in which he
disbelieves. Thus, there will, in one respect, be agreement and, in another, conflict, about curriculum. The broad consensus that holds
among natural lawyers regarding the content of the external good (correct behaviors) will be represented in all schools. On the other hand,

regarding what suffices for moral selfperfection, there will be the sharpest division in their respective messages.

Consider the stakes in this schism. The division implicates core elements of the Western understanding of how humans stand in basic relation to one another. A teacher's choice between the obtensional and gnostic forms of moral self-perfection determines the coherence of several premises that are generally taken for granted in the classroom: these premises include human dignity, equality, and community. That choice will also affect the political design of a school system.

Dignity. I begin with the implications for the concepts of human dignity and equality. Most natural law pedagogues tend to be Universalist and inclusive in spirit; they would prefer that children learn a story of mankind in which natural moral perfection is an equal-opportunity enterprise. In pursuing this purpose, they very frequently resort to the concept of *dignity*, which they regard as both intensely positive and common to all human persons. Unfortunately, one primary victim of moral gnosis is human dignity.

Linked historically to the *imago Dei* of the book of Genesis, dignity is something lodged in the specific human faculties of reason and free will. Among the creatures, it is Man alone who through reason can seek the terms of his obligation to others and thereby realize himself. Dignity resides in this capacity for moral self-perfection through quest and choice. The problem with this idea is that, again, the grasp of correct answers to moral questions is plainly contingent upon circumstance. One person's apprehension of the relevant facts and rules (and his opportunity to reflect upon them) differs greatly from another's. Reason is ours, but differentially so, and, if reaching correct answers is the necessary entrée to personal moral perfection, dignity becomes relativized. It obtains only as a hierarchy of individual capacities. We all have dignity, but you have more. Dignity is transmogrified into the medium of indignity. This tendency of gnostic naturalism to relativize the human capacity for personal goodness is curiously confirmed in the current revivals of Aristotelian ethics. Happiness, we learn, consists in thriving intellectually, socially, and economically. Our natural finality can be had only by objective moral success. Humans are not perfected by struggle but by getting it right, an outcome that depends in great measure on brains and luck. We witness a surprising convergence of John Finnis and Martha Nussbaum.

When it is understood thus as a hierarchy, dignity also cancels any theory of a descriptive human equality, for equality requires a capacity for personal goodness that is uniform in degree. Mere possession of a capacity to advance morally by grasping aspects of the objective good will not serve. The problem is not that we are fallible but that we are fallible in degrees that vary by luck and native acumen. In order for our capacity for moral self-perfection to be uniform in degree, it would have to be purged of its gnostic elements and reconceptualized as the ability to be diligent in the search for the real good. That is a talent that might be evenly shared.

Bell Curve. Traditional natural lawyers recently confirmed their unconscious bent for moral aristocracy by participating in the spectacular overreaction to Herrnstein and Murray's *The Bell Curve.* Whether accurate or not in its empirical claims about the distribution of cognitive power, and on this I harbor serious doubts, the book was plainly received by many as a message about human worth; these critics misunderstood it as an implicit assertion of a natural hierarchy of moral capacity. The gnostic temptation was at work. How easy it is for the sophisticated to imagine that sophistication itself is the moral category! When this gnostic dogma cohabits a mind already committed to a putative belief in human equality, the effect is painful intellectual tension. It is not easy to serve both hierarchy and equality.[10]

I concede that the contribution of gnostic natural law to the relativizing of dignity and to the subversion of equality has been trivial compared to that wrought by Enlightenment theories. The most hierarchical of all moral conceptions is the notion that we invent our own morality; in such a world, it is the clever whose moral horizon is the most expansive. Sophistication multiplies the selves that any of us can choose to be. Nevertheless, gnostic natural law has unwittingly abetted this ideological tendency; celebrating the moral potency of the intellectual, it has paradoxically endorsed Nietzsche's catalogue of those qualified to be *Übermensch.* With him, the gnostic affirms the moral apotheosis of the smart. True, the natural law hero does not invent his own morality; nevertheless, it is he who has the right mental stuff for finding the authentic mother lode and thereby achieving greatness.[11]

If this be the truth of our world, then we are bound to teach it to our children, with its clear implication that the gifted child holds the key to a moral transcendence that is unavailable to the dull. The effect of this gnostic teaching upon the pupils' perception of one another is quite predictable. School (indeed, life) becomes a moral Calvinism in which the Elect are a subcategory of the Smart.[12]

Repicturing Community

The educator who would introduce natural law into her curriculum is, thus, forewarned. Delivered in its traditional intellectual modes, natural law provides its students a hierarchical moral perception of one another and of adults. Its gnostic criteria of moral fulfillment create an undertow of moral contempt for the stupid and the barbarian. Only by teaching obtension can natural law find a home in a democratic curriculum. As we continue to identify the benign implications of obtension, it may be hard for any friend of natural law to be indifferent to the choice between theories.

A few more examples of these implications can be sketched here, giving primary attention to the idea of human community, as it would be portrayed for the child. Regarding the definition of community, I am going to make an assumption that it is largely intuitive (and, of course, problematic). I am confident that this assumption can be defended as a truth both of human psychology and linguistic usage, but here I will simply assert it as follows. In order for the reality that is named "community" to hold, the most marginally rational person—the most wretched and disadvantaged member—must be perceived to have a capacity for moral and/or spiritual self-fulfillment (and, conversely, degradation) that is as plenary as that of the most gifted and fortunate.

In other words, the belief in human equality and the rejection of moral gnosticism are definitional to community. The original Hasidics may have taught something of the sort as a reaction to the elitism of the learned. Where humans are perceived to stand in a hierarchical order of moral perfectibility, the Brahmin and the outcast may achieve coexistence or even society, but community will elude them. I will not try to answer once and for all the additional question whether community, when properly defined, requires belief in the equality of outsiders.

The members of certain human clusters do in fact see nonmembers as deficient in moral potential. My present disposition is to include such self-defining moral elites within the definition but to demote them to a distinctly inferior status in the taxonomy of communities. It will be convenient simply to call them "elites," so long as that term is understood to be pejorative. Members of self-regarding moral elites are by definition incapable of belonging to any community that includes perceived inferiors. Of course, in specific practical matters, elites can cooperate with such communities.[13]

By contrast, individuals who do accept the descriptive equality of all rational humans are capable of membership in an indefinite number of particular communities. In addition, any community in which this belief is shared by all members is entitled to the label "genuine." This does not imply that genuine communities all share the same ultimate purposes, lifestyles, or rules of right behavior. Quite to the contrary, believers in universal human equality can cluster on the basis of disparate ideologies, religions, ethnicities, professions, or the like—differences that can set communities in practical conflict with one another. Put another way, although they are genuine, such communities can be exclusive in important social or ideological dimensions. Nevertheless, as we shall see, conflict between and among these groups has a meaning for their members that is crucially different from the meaning that is attached to such conflicts by members of gnostic elites.

Equality of Believers. It is my impression that the world of Roman Catholicism is one locus of the belief in universal equality. If I am correct about this, Catholics constitute a large and useful example of the effect and influence of the obtensional versus the gnostic interpretation of human nature upon group attitudes toward outsiders. Let us assume (this is not so audacious) that the population of believing Catholics also satisfies whatever other criteria a reasonable person might think necessary to constitute a genuine community. In that event, their belief in a natural human moral equality locates Catholics (*qua* Catholic) in two genuine communities—one exclusive, one universal.[14]

They are, first of all, a community to and among themselves; their church claims authoritative access to correct answers, and assent to that ecclesiastical authority is a criterion of membership. Exclusivity is no trivial matter for them. Their orthodoxy triggers meaningful obligation. In their own view, they are bound—and nonbelievers are not—to give the teaching authority of their community a presumption of correctness. When engaged in the quest for correct moral answers, assent to this presumption operates as the practical threshold of the good conscience that is necessary and sufficient to moral self-perfection; the obtending believer cannot reject an ordinance of the Catholic Church merely because he or she has vague reservations.

By the same token, even the most anguished and honest apostasy on a serious moral issue sets the individual outside this exclusive community. The dissenter emigrates from the cluster that upholds the authority of the Church. Because that authority is vaguely defined, there will be practical disputes about who is in and who is out. But the principle is clear enough. The doctrinal émigré asserts that the ecclesiastical authority is wrong; in his eyes, the exclusive community that accepts it is deluded about its reliability. The act of emigration is thus the invitation to a new and somehow more discerning community. It initiates a plurality of exclusive communities, even though each may aspire to the old name.

Finally, the exclusive community that consists of continuing believers also asserts a special commission and duty of their Church to teach all mankind whatever can be known of moral truth. But do believers then suppose that outsiders have a reciprocal duty to give priority to these specific moral messages because of their source? I take it that, in the Catholic view, the answer is no. Every human is already obliged by nature to seek the objective moral good wherever he or she can find it. The unbeliever or émigré thus has the duty, the natural duty, to consider Catholicism's moral answers on their merits along with whatever other wisdom is available, but for him or her they can carry no special presumption of truth. Rome is but one of the world's many representatives of the Tao. If there is some added element of community in the didactic relation between the outsider and the Catholic believer, at first it seems very thin.

Nevertheless, precisely in recognizing human equality, the Catholic Church has embraced a principle that makes its own moral answers about behavior irrelevant to the goodness of the person. Its commitment to moral self-perfection by obtension entails the richly communal message to the outsider that, if he honestly concludes that the Church is wrong (on whatever issue), he is not only bound in conscience to reject it but, rather, it is exactly by doing so in response to conscience that he achieves the fulfillment willed for him by the Church itself. Even in the midst of the most intense conflict, real human connection among enemies remains possible. To the eyes of the insider, the conscientious outsider remains a full partner in that ultimate natural community consisting of all moral pilgrims. And this vision of unity holds even as the outsider honestly refuses the authoritative message of the exclusive community.

Genuine Community. Nothing turns upon my using Catholics as the example. This relation between their exclusive but genuine community and its ideological competitors is merely one very large and vivid instance of the subsurface harmony that is everywhere generated and sustained by the assent to universal human equality. In their deepest meaning, the inevitable quarrels among genuine but exclusive communities thus reduce to disputes within the human family. These convulsions, however destructive in the economic and social order, never risk either the moral integrity of the individual or the community that is mankind.

Genuine community thus implies deep respect for the members of groups, however much their beliefs conflict with either accepted public values or one's own. This is specifically a respect for persons and not for their ideas or practices when these are perceived as false or evil, but, of course, this very respect for the person is a primary guarantee that the ideas themselves will receive fair consideration. In the midst of their inevitable conflicts, all exclusive—but genuine—communities understand the social order (domestic and international) to consist of persons of equal moral perfectibility and of inscrutable goodness who interact through social and political processes to determine exactly which concessions will best sustain the common good. There will always be political losers, but in such a moral culture, the losers will less often be selected by raw majoritarian power. Being respected themselves, they will be the more willing to respect and to sustain the painful and unending process of practical judgment. As it emerges from gnosticism, natural law prepares itself to teach genuine human community. It could have no more urgent mission to the children of the world.

Tolerance Reconsidered

The belief in moral self-perfection by obtension also presents the opportunity to reconceive the pedagogy of human tolerance within those schools that accept nature as authoritative. I do not pretend to see this matter whole and will suggest only the starting point. Again, it entails the severability of the two realms of the good—the world of behavior and that of the moral self as it chooses behavior.

I continue to assume the reality of good and evil in human conduct; the discussion here prescinds from all relativist versions of tolerance (e.g., "moral neutrality"). Whatever else tolerance implies, it means the sufferance of real evil—of bad behavior—for the sake of some good of a higher order than the one threatened by whatever is to be tolerated. When it willingly suffers pornography, the individual or the society does so for some high-minded reason, for example, that free expression is crucial to the quest for truth. We suffer the bad for the sake of the good. On this, our two versions of self-perfection agree.[15]

Note that tolerance so conceived is a behavioral good with an external and objective status. It is a state of affairs that occurs whenever one person or a set of collaborators achieves the correct ordering of two objective goods that are in mutual conflict. For example, by regulating the sport of boxing, the state might achieve the level of violence that is truly optimal.

Tolerance, however, also occurs as a moral state of the person. A moral actor can himself be tolerant. Whether or not he actually achieves this condition can depend upon whether one's theory of personal goodness is gnostic or obtensional. Given the gnostic premise, only the person who discovers and wills the correct priority among conflicting goods could deserve the label "tolerant." By contrast, obtensional natural law would identify the tolerant person as that man or woman who searches diligently for the correct behavioral ordering. By effort alone, the obtending person is already as morally enhanced as he could be by discovery of the right answer. As an aspect of the person, then, tolerance is a subspecies of obtension; it is generated by the free commitment to seek the external good in those specific cases that involve the correct ordering of two goods that are in conflict in the behavioral order.

Moralities of Persons and Nations. If it were simply one aspect of ob-tension, there would be nothing special to say about tolerance. It is in this respect no different from, say, justice, which also has its external and internal forms of perfection. What makes obtensional tolerance relevant to the pedagogy of natural law is its capacity to improve and clarify the rough analogy that educators often invoke between the mo-ralities of persons and nations. That analogy is rough precisely because political collectivities necessarily act by consensus and must consider many other factors besides the law of nature. Nonetheless, educators commonly evaluate nations by the same "human" criteria that they apply to individual actions. It is as if the teachers were natural lawyers and the nations were persons. Whole societies are judged for their tol-erance. Sweden tends to turn up at one end, China at the other.

Accepting this propensity of educators to personify societies as moral actors, the shift to an obtensional viewpoint offers a fresh per-spective upon which nations could qualify as tolerant. From the gnostic point of view, the answer emerges as a straightforward calculus of gov-ernment policies toward sex, drugs, cults, abortion, or what have you. If the policies of the society tend to be unusually proscriptive, the na-tion is intolerant. By contrast, viewed in obtensional terms, a nation's tolerance quotient would allow for disjunction between the correctness of the objective policy and the goodness of the (personified) society. The tolerant society would be the one that does its best to get a correct ordering of objective goods, given the way it is able collectively to dis-cern them. Singapore thus could be as tolerant as the United States.

Indeed, it could be more so. For tolerance, again, is the sufferance of a perceived evil. And here the evil is a collective perception. A con-sensus in the society sees certain behavior as bad and yet to some degree allows it. If, instead, it were simply a case of collective indifference, there would be nothing to tolerate. Take this hypothetical. Singaporeans become convinced that homosexual behavior is evil. For the sake of some other good, they nonetheless allow it. That would be a case of tol-erance. On that same issue, Americans might have no collective convic-tion; in allowing such behavior, the United States would not be tolerant but merely indifferent.

If an objectively repressive society can be tolerant, has the word lost meaning? One does have to be careful not to transmute the Nazis into tolerant folk on the ground that they took seriously the correct ordering of values. Perhaps it is enough to say that, far from trying to order objective goods correctly, their specialty was to deny their existence. Taking Nietzsche seriously, Nazis needed no moral judgment beyond their determination of the Führer's will. Still, I wish I saw a brighter line between the representative but tolerant society, on the one hand, and the totalitarian, on the other.

And there are other problems here. For the present, I only want to stress the heuristic payoff that comes from judging both individuals and societies not only by what they allow and proscribe but also by the quality of the effort that leads them to judgment. Strictly speaking, collectivities cannot obtend at all. However, natural lawyers who so often judge a society's deeds might well make the additional effort to judge the integrity of its search. By judging nations in their own terms and by objective universals, they could advance the insight of their own students, stirring an appreciation for the moral struggles of individual political actors.

Organizing Schools for a Nation of Natural Lawyers

I turn at last from these cosmic ideological concerns to the practical question that better explains my being invited to contribute to this symposium. How would natural lawyers go about organizing and financing formal systems of schooling? As to this, a good deal depends upon the sort of society natural law might be assigned to educate. Two social extremes will serve to illustrate my view of the matter. The first is a purely hypothetical society, one in which most adults believe in the moral authority of nature. They are—as it were—St. Paul's Gentiles, as yet uncorrupted by Thomas Hobbes and Richard Rorty. They are Poles, Eskimos, Ethiopians, and Celts; they are socialists, flat-taxers, free traders, and monarchists; they are of every religion and none; they even disagree about how to teach what every one of them agrees should be taught. And, like every community of natural lawyers, they divide into gnostic perfectionists, on the one hand, and obtensional perfectionists, on the other. In spite of all this diversity, what they agree on is (1) the behavioral good that is preached by Aristotle, Aquinas, Leo Strauss, and Henry Veatch, and (2) the capacity of at least some persons, using reason, to identify parts of that good.[16]

Call it a natural moral culture. How will this nation organize its schools, and will the gnostics and their obtensional opponents find something in this practical activity that they can agree on? In truth, regarding the regulation and structure of education, disagreement between them should be hard to find. At least on the central question of moral content, all natural systems (in whichever camp) seem to support principles—and even rules—of behavior that are roughly similar. And, in new and disputed cases, they conduct the search for the right answers in ways that, at least to my amateur eyes, seem compatible. This hypothetical society would prescribe schools that teach this moral content and this method of moral inquiry. In practical terms, there would be little in such a regime to dissatisfy even the gnostics.

In all other respects, the school system would be varied and dynamic. Having witnessed the consequences of state monopoly, no serious contemporary educator could still aspire to Plato's Republic on the ground that it is "natural." In regard to the form and content of schooling, outside the moral dimension, subsidiarity would be cherished, and the family would decide. Subsidized by society—and aided by professional advice—parents of every sort would exercise the kind of responsibility that nourishes the family relation and the civic virtues.

In such a regime, competition among pedagogical methods would enhance the mastery of the behavioral good. At the same time, it would nourish social unity amidst ideological diversity; encouraged by the trust of the community, parents typically would appropriate this expression of confidence and return it to the social level, affirming the bond among peoples of very different political, ethnic, and religious outlooks. On all these points, there would be no division between gnostic and obtensional natural law. Of course, if such a society has ever existed, it is long extinct.

Nurturing the Child's Personal Perfection in a Morally Pluralistic Society

The practical distinctions between gnostic and obtensional versions of education become more obvious once morality goes plural. To the natural gnostic, the present American moral scene is one great frustration. Every child in the public school incurs a direct and substantial injury exactly to the extent that he believes the school's message of indifferentism (or worse). In the gnostic view of things, the child cannot achieve a personal perfection that rises above the behavioral content of his moral beliefs. She is not actually doomed by moral misinformation (if smart or lucky, she may see through it), but heaven help the credulous child in the hands of the present school system. Of course, there are islands of authentic natural teaching in both the public and private sectors. But one encounters them by chance, or, if parents have the capacity to pay, they seek them in the market. The state could subsidize the choices of the poor, but even a general system of scholarships would not remedy the problem. For, in this society, the families themselves are in disagreement about the objective good. Given a subsidized freedom to educate, many parents would still corrupt their own children with false teaching. To the gnostic, this scene is one of hopeless moral derangement both of personal goodness and of the common good.

By contrast, the obtensional interpretation of pluralism is less tragic; indeed, a family-based system of education could be understood (for this society) as a reasonable approximation of the natural ideal. At first this difference between the competing theories is not so clear. Insofar as behavioral evil is taught in a pluralist system, the obtensional and gnostic camps agree that education is injuring the common good; all of us regret the damage to justice and the social order from teachers who portray real evil in positive terms. What is distinct about obtension is that it denies that teaching—bad or good—can affect the capacity of the child to reach moral self-perfection. Obtension has the advantage of the long view. It sees that unjust societies and false ideas do not make bad persons. The capacity of individuals to say yes or no to the quest for the real good is unaffected by exterior circumstances, including miseducation. Even if one fails to find the correct objective way, this in itself is no threat to personal moral achievement, so long as he fulfills the obligation to look for it. The world may be the worse for my works, but I can be morally fulfilled by having tried my best. This invulnerability of the moral person allows a more hopeful interpretation of the fate of children who are victimized by the schools. So far as I am concerned, it also presents a thoroughly realistic interpretation of the responsible self. The only tragedy for any human person is deliberately to reject the authority of the real good to demand our best.

If the personal moral prospects of children are morally invulnerable to wrong ideas about behavior, should we stop worrying about the ethical content of their education? Of course not, for obviously the common good is also at stake; we would all like to live among fellow citizens (whatever their personal goodness) whose education helps them to tell the difference between good and bad deeds. In a pluralist society, natural lawyers must keep looking for the system that will maximize the citizens' grasp of the common good. I will at the end return to the criteria of such a system.

The Child's Viewpoint. But stay a moment with the child. An important clarification remains to be made about the relation between the school system and the personal moral self-perfection of the student. Take the child's view of this issue. His or her ultimate moral invulnerability may console the rest of us, but it does not make the child indifferent to the form and content of the school's message. To the contrary, the child's natural capacity (and duty) to seek the good gives him or her a strong ethical claim to a legally protected right of a very specific sort. That claim is a clear implication of the obtensional premise, as I will now try to show.

Every rational child is aware both that good and evil are real and that his own grasp of correct behavior is inchoate and marginal. The child is also aware of the basic obligation to inform her conscience and to follow it. This two-sentence description of what in fact is a dense moral ontology serves my present purpose. The point is that the child is consciously responsible to obtend, and—as a beginner—her specific responsibility in her search for right acts is to will for herself the best adult source of moral advice.

The undirected child is not in every instance an efficient detector of the objective good. It is, however, his natural responsibility to try to become so; every child ought to want his moral education to commence in a relation of subordination that will aid his search for what he is by nature bound to seek. This involves no paradox. The child may remain morally invulnerable to anything except her own free abandonment of the quest for the good, but for the time being this means only that her own authenticity as a seeker depends upon her willing pupilage to the most reliable moral authority that is available.

Moral Dependency. Even a morally pluralistic society could understand this obligation of the child to will for herself the most efficient moral dependency. At least among ordinary people in the United States, the strong convention survives that all of us are obliged to search for answers that are correct, whether we like them or not. True philosophical skeptics are rare. Given this starting point, unless some countervailing reason appears, society owes every child a subordination to whichever adult sovereignty is most likely to encourage and assist the search for the content of the behavioral good that the child is obliged to will as the ideal.[17]

The obvious difficulty here is the moral pluralism of the potential sovereigns. Who among this menagerie of American adults is qualified as the leader by whom the child has a natural right to be formed? The state itself obviously is disqualified. Precisely to the extent that society lacks consensus regarding the good life, there can be no governmental candidate for the role of tutor. This, of course, is a primary reason that state schools fail; their moral curriculum can be little more than the private confection of professionals and lobbyists. Often, its highest objective is to avoid offense to any organized group.

But are not the parents even worse candidates for the role of moral sovereign? Here, again, the gnostic is torn by the prospect of twenty conflicting versions of sexual, economic, social, political, medical, religious, and intellectual good, all being thrust upon helpless infants in whatever school is chosen by their parent. Woe to the child and woe to the society the child will one day create!

Parental Authority. Obtension, by contrast, would separate these two questions about the child and the society. It concedes that parental authority over choice of school would result in the teaching of a smorgasbord of specific behavioral goods; some of these will conflict with every version of natural law, posing real risks to the social order and even to the individual child's material welfare. In such cases, woe, indeed, to society. None of this, however, poses the slightest risk to the child's capacity for moral perfection. Indeed, he is not only invulnerable; in one crucial respect he is positively benefited by the sovereignty of the parents, however misguided their leadership. For it is this relationship alone that guarantees to the obtending child a message that is responsive to his own moral impulse. Parents may differ about the content of the good; what they agree on is that there is in fact a good to be sought.

This is a trait that is specific to the role of parenthood. It may disappear temporarily, say, at the office, where economic actors can be driven to believe pro tempore in a Hobbesian world. It may disappear in the academy; professors—however correct their behavior—sometimes get promoted by talking like moral skeptics. In the home, by contrast, the reality of the good is indestructible. The most nihilistic parent is quite incapable of telling her child that there is no correct (or incorrect) way. Parenthood is the pulpit of objective morality, if only as the instrument of parental survival. Again, the actual content of parental notions about morality is protean, and many a child receives bad ideas. What he never hears is that the good is his to invent. Therefore, he is always invited to obtend—to seek the real good, just as his nature requires. A system of education could do worse for the child. Ours currently does. In a pluralist state, only monopoly schools with a captive clientele could survive preaching the bogus good of "moral neutrality."

Obtension, Parental Choice, and the Common Good

In this final section, I continue to assume a pluralistic moral order (such as the United States) and an obtensional—as opposed to a gnostic—view of natural self-perfection. Turning from the personal moral fulfillment of the child, I now consider aspects of the objective common good (including the child's material "welfare"). How should we think about and plan for formal systems of schooling that, amidst diversity, can still teach the commutative and distributive justice of natural law? In proposing an answer, I verge upon the very task I have often found so troublesome in natural moral inquiry. I admire the natural law method and the metaphysics but find them inconclusive. Although I'm often confident about the correctness of specific actions, all too seldom can I spot the illative connection of correct actions with the human nature that I claim as my premise. My own practical judgments often seem less an inference from nature than from revelation, and when the latter seems sufficient, on grounds of efficiency, I tend to abandon the natural side of the inquiry.

I say this, not to discourage anyone's pursuit of nature straight to the end; perhaps, for most people, obtension—the quest for the right conduct—can be managed in no other way. Henry Veatch is quite right:

"If morals and ethics are not based on nature or reality, then what else are or can they be based on?" I only want to warn that I am not very good at this sort of thing, nor am I always certain that I am talking the talk of natural law. A consolation here is that we need not get to the level of personal behaviors. Leave it to authentic natural moralists in schools of their own design to find and teach the specific objective good. My task is only to suggest a general system that is congenial to such schools and that could exist within a pluralistic society; it is an inquiry into the practical politics of natural law.

The Ideal System. The ideal system is suggested by substantive premises about nature, including the three already identified—descriptive human equality, equal human dignity, and genuine community. Each implies the other, and together they tell us something about the "natural" organization of schools in a morally pluralistic society. Specifically, the core responsibility of a nature-based ethic is to teach not only correct behavior but also—first of all—the complex truth of human unity. Elite gnostic communities must be shown the possibility that the rest of us enjoy the same capacity as they do for moral self-perfection. Individuals and groups who are ideological competitors of one another must grasp the intellectual structure of a descriptive human equality and appreciate its plausibility. Most of the churches will teach this sort of thing as revelation, but it is natural law that will make equality and its implications available to secular reason. In this project, the state is not a reliable ally, and moral relativists are the enemy.

It will be a proper work of the naturalists to evangelize the warring groups—by producing graduates who are able to distinguish the moral persons of their enemies from the evil of their policies. Success will depend upon the existence and example of a socially supported system of educational providers that in its own constitution affirms the message of human moral equality. Natural law thus has the vocation to persuade the larger society on practical grounds to adopt such an organic structure as public policy. The practical political objectives—peace, stability, liberty, and so on—will be wholly "natural" but will also appeal to persons of the most diverse philosophies, including moral relativists.

The political chance for establishment of such a system is suggested by the contemporary and very visible popular concern for the teaching of objective morality. Though the protagonists in this debate differ about the content of the objective good, their common affirmation of its existence provides a major pillar of human equality. The society must now express this deep agreement about human nature in an institutional way, and no technical or financial difficulty bars that end. The school system may be plural regarding the content of the external good while yet providing a unifying conception of the moral perfectibility of all persons. That is, the system can express the natural disjunction that obtains between the subjective and objective moral orders. Only such an economy of education could deserve the support of parents from incompatible moral communities.

The technical features of the system can be quite varied so long as parents of all income levels are assured practical access to the types of schools they prefer. This qualification is extremely important. The historic system of state schools in this country—contrary to its own mythology—has divided children by income class. Thus, any system of family choice that is not plainly tilted toward the poor will be regarded as business as usual. It will effectively contradict the hoped-for allegiance to human equality. Unnecessary limitations upon the choices of nonrich families will be interpreted as new instruments of gnostic hierarchy. Such a "reform" will simply reproduce the instabilities and group hostilities of the existing order. The natural lawyer's strategy, then, will include specific techniques that level the playing field for all income classes. Here I will simply assume the adoption of such protections.[18]

Social Stability. Earlier I noted that, in another society—one committed by consensus to a natural law ethic—such a system would contribute to social stability. We must now ask whether that would be true in the context of moral pluralism, and here we encounter dissent. The critic is located principally in the school establishment but deserves recognition. Though the particular issue is at a great remove from our starting point in nature, the spirit of natural law inquiry requires at least a skeleton response. I offer it as my conclusion.

In a pluralist society, does parental sovereignty bring us together or tear us apart? First, there is at least some insight available from those sometime friends of natural law—the empiricists. What they think they have learned from systematic study of private (i.e., family-chosen) schools that serve lower-class children is that educational choice correlates with tolerance and democratic behavior but also with academic success.

Controlling for class differences, separate studies headed respectively by Greeley, Coleman, and Bryk have over thirty years consistently found that low-budget religious schools graduate students who—along with the academic basics—have been taught to play by the rules in social and political affairs, to be tolerant and law-abiding, and to participate in civic life. The opponents of family choice have offered no data to rebut these claims. Hence, at worst, the reports of the experts are consistent with the conclusions I will now report as my own. These are propositions drawn from my professional and practical experience in the public and private sectors of education—here and abroad—since 1961.[19]

Family Choice. When the family is empowered by the larger society to choose the school and thus to monitor its own moral messages, its social connections are stabilized and enhanced in two ways: one internal, the other external. Internally, the child and parent, who have already spent five years together, see their special relationship extended painlessly into the formal world of large institutions. The settled function of the parental advocate and protector is maintained. At the same time, the strangers who operate the school never are forced into the role of sovereign. Instead, they remain free to act as the professional agents they were trained to be. As a consequence, they are able to relate to the parents as coordinating equals.

The child thus retains confidence in his or her only unconditional sponsor, and the message of the school remains consistent with that of the home. The parents avoid the indignity of being required by their poverty to yield the child up to an alien system of values. Authority and responsibility remain linked, and the parent gains the strongest incentive to learn about education and to monitor its course. The family members continue to function *qua* family in relation to one another. Education is transformed into a pro-family institution.

Meanwhile, viewed externally, this deliverance of the family from the moral randomness of public monopoly allows the parent and child to maintain an open and positive attitude to the school and to the other families who have chosen freely to be there. Perhaps, under special historical conditions, conscription to the moral melting pot actually once nourished social peace. If so, it has long since ceased to do so. The captive aspects of the existing state system have become the guarantee, not of mutual respect, but of conflict among the distinctive groups, and between all those groups and those who currently impose upon them the moral curriculum (neutral or otherwise). Conscription tends to close the eyes of both child and parent to the real good that it is the child's natural duty to seek in others. No doubt moral insight sometimes transcends incarceration, but its natural home is not the ideological barracks. For this purpose, the ideal is a free system in which children and families can follow their consciences to the school that teaches the moral truth, as they perceive it.

It is true that family choice does not fully liberate the child himself. In addition, his liberty remains important, whatever one's version of natural moral perfection. I will not revisit the details of our duty to honor the child's free nature, but only repeat the punch line: the child's best hope of practical moral freedom lies in a formal subordination to those who know and care for him and who will themselves be losers in the end if he does not achieve moral maturity. Paradoxically, children have their best hope of authentic liberty within the parental sovereignty.

I concede that, under a system of parental choice, at the margin of society there would be moral cadres—elite gnostic communities—who would continue to teach hatred and who would now be aided by tax dollars. Even if the new system strains to exclude such groups, the First, Fifth, and Fourteenth Amendments will very properly give them a strong de facto protection. One must assess the social risk posed by these surviving islands of rage and weigh it against the equivalent risk that is currently represented in the monopoly schools of the state. Family choice would not eradicate the freedom to hate, but it would eliminate a primary reason for doing so. The existing system is that reason; it is a hate-generating device. Parental fears of ideological submersion are a rich source of xenophobia. Families most willingly support the freedom of their ideological enemies when their own freedom is guaranteed in the same social bargain. As responsible moral beings, parents have by nature the best reason to wage social peace through choice, even as they conscientiously (and properly) wage cultural war through words. Even as they accomplish their own moral self-perfection, they would simultaneously honor the common good as their universal ideal. What could be more natural?

CHAPTER EIGHT

Magna Charter

The charter of thy worth gives thee releasing.
— William Shakespeare, Sonnet 87

The word "charter" has evoked a dozen meanings in a rich career of ambiguity, endearing it both to would-be designers of new institutions and to protectors of old. In 1745, Parliament voted a special tax to support the work of The Charter Society, a private organization founded to establish "charter schools" in Ireland, schools that would offer Protestant education to the Catholic poor. Such schools, I suppose, were touted as a contribution to parental freedom of choice, and no doubt in a sense they were. I would, though, prefer the Shakespearean usage, where the Bard longs for "liberty / Withal, as large a charter as the wind" (*As You Like It*, 2.7.48–49). Obviously there are charters—and then there are charters. Like the great one of 1215, they all share one property: an increase of private option. If in doubt, consult a legal dictionary.

I regret that Stephen Sugarman and I failed to grasp the political utility of this rubbery word as, in the late 1960s, we grappled with labels for schools that today would be dubbed "charters." Instead, in a ponderous 115-page article (then book), we contrived and explained a detailed model statute committing the entire California tax-supported system to parental choice. We gave our imaginary public schools the memorable titles "A through D," signifying four levels of subsidized

Unpublished manuscript

spending per pupil, each for the choosing (at income-adjusted cost to parents). A slightly different set of school budgets we proposed for participating private schools, which we styled "E through H." The latter were specifically termed "private," but supported in large part by public funds, and the parents also were to pay according to their capacity. The legal structures were very specific, pursuing two primary goals: (1) choice for the parent among all eight categories, public and private; (2) equality of sacrifice for families of all income classes. I wish we had called both forms "charters."

Scanning these proposals today, after a half century of wars over vouchers, tax credits, and charters, we still ask ourselves and our readers: Exactly whose liberty is at stake here, if anyone's? No system of assignment for school could, or should, locate the decision in the child herself. Thus the purchase of schooling for Susie cannot operate as a market in the strict sense in which a consumer satisfies his or her own need. Nor is the parent acting simply as a child's alternate ego or agent; the preferences of the two may differ radically. If the parent is deemed a consumer, this can only be in an oblique sense; his or her role is similar to that of the draft army, which might be considered the consumer of the food it purchases to feed its conscripts. But this is scarcely a bestowal of "freedom" upon the quartermaster: he doesn't get to enjoy his purchase as such. Army chow and school choice are better cast as the practical empowerment of one person over another. In the case of schooling, it is the financial empowerment of that person, the parent, who already enjoys whatever legal power anyone can have over a child. All he or she lacks is the wealth necessary to exercise that well-recognized power instead of surrendering to a blind determination of the child's school experience by a government agency.

To Sugarman and me, the emergence of the titular "charter" in the late 1980s represented one considerable technical step toward empowering those parents. Ted Kolderie had the aesthetic-political sense to give the new schools of choice in Minnesota a name that could take hold. "Charters" then soon spread like springtime in diverse but similar statutory form, all fumbling for a design prudent for their particular state. None of these schemes seems to us particularly artful or even adequate. The most regrettable feature, common to all but a few systems, is the gag on religious teaching; the Irish Charter Society would not be welcomed as founders of a Minnesota charter.

Some of the U.S. states, of course, consider themselves shackled by the state constitutional "Blaine Amendments" contrived by the nineteenth-century minds not entirely unlike Parliament's Irish Charter Society. Mr. Blaine's peculiar relic of prejudice has, in one important respect, helped cause today's charter movement actually to backfire as an agent of choice. The historic and heroic public role of Catholic schools in the inner city fades as the schools gradually disappear, in considerable part replaced by charters. To be sure, Catholic schools were already struggling as their religious orders declined in numbers and their white clientele headed for the suburbs. Many of them, however, had hung on in the inner city to serve poor non-Catholics at a modest tuition with no sectarian enchantments. But then came charters free for the choosing, and thus many families prudently went for the new tuition-free, faith-free, and better-funded choice. Half of the country's Catholic schools, and most in the inner city, no longer exist.

As we wrote in 1969, the very point of funding these new schools, later to be dubbed "charters," was to satisfy both the child's own right that the parent choose and the parent's authority to do the choosing among all schools—religious included—that meet the common minimum pedagogical standard of the state. The Blaine States, we blithely supposed, would in due course, through repeal or a judicial order, liberate themselves to empower the lower-income family with the private choices that the rest of us take for granted.

We had also in 1969 underestimated the resistance of the public school establishment to the prospect of diversity and choice. For a brief time in the 1970s, the unions—the AFT, NEA, CTA, and others—were to show genuine interest and seemed to listen, especially to our depictions of unions owning and running their own schools, perhaps for profit. Then, all of a sudden, my calendar of union appearances began suffering cancellations. Maybe I was boring. The number of union-funded and union-operated charter schools remained minimal.

Again I return to the army, which teaches a different possible response to compulsory institutions such as the public school, enrolling its draftees of diverse religious belief. I was drafted, just as in the five-year-old's prescriptive introduction to kindergarten. I arrived at Fort Jackson on a Sunday morning in time for Mass. I knew of nothing so profoundly social as taking an open-air view of the transcendental together with fellow conscripts.

A lawyer by then, I was next taken by chance to the Pentagon, there to discover that religious service was a routine every noon, and in many forms. I am still surprised at the military's corporate nonchalance about its own careful and efficient provision of faith experience to the GI. Of course, unlike the public school and the teachers' union, the military's respect for the realities of spirit entails no threat to anyone's job; there was no other army waiting to compete for my choice. In any case, it was a blessing for the boys.

Army support for religious experience continues, but today with a completely different foundation. The volunteer's contract guarantees access to government-supported religious devotion. It is part of the deal. The old days of selective service had done so on a wholly different justification, one more clearly relevant to the charter school: it was a matter of justice for the drafted GI. It is today as much a matter of justice for the drafted child and the indigent family. The child is ordered up. His charter will not teach the family faith. Throughout his or her thirteen-year government hitch—eight hours a day, 180 days a year—mind and soul are insulated from the most basic and utterly human question.

This offense to freedom of thought causes every sort of confusion. For example, many parents of this conscripted child object to Darwin in the curriculum. I suppose most of us would, to the contrary, insist on the school's explaining Darwin's picture of how we evolved. In any case, his story will be told in most schools. What will be omitted is this question: Who made Darwin—or anything else? In public school, one confronts all things good—except the source of good itself, and why it matters. Satan, I've heard, once told God that he could make a universe just like his. He was ready to prove it and asked God to lend him the necessary dirt. God replied: "Make your own." Darwin, of course, makes no effort to explain the original provenance of dirt or of anything else. The child deserves to see this, and reflect.

Why is it so painful for this polity, unlike most of Europe, to recognize the sheer justice of assuring all parents the capacity, so cherished by the middle class, of choosing among all schools, religious or not, that meet the legislated standard. And, to the point here: Why exclude would-be religious schools (charters), which are private in virtually all but their statutory misnomer?

To the serious observer—sophisticated or not—the most evident answer is the political power of government-sheltered teachers' unions. As I write, the California Teachers Association has its posse at several Los Angeles charters harassing mothers and their children who are trying to enter their chosen school. These vigilantes are tenured, protected members of a union who, unlike the charter teachers, are sheltered by law and by the union contract with the district. The public school teacher cannot, realistically, be fired for trying in this tortuous way to destroy competition from what the union regards (with good reason) as a "private school." The protesting teacher's own public school must welcome him or her back.

Imagine charter school teachers taking such hostile maneuvers against PS 109. The CTA would summon the police and every other legal weapon, up to and including the antitrust laws. Charter schools, being essentially private-sector institutions, live in a world of competition; government will not save the jobs of charter school teachers if they overreach and drive the charter school employer out of business. They must behave reasonably, simply as a strategy of survival. This, it seems to me, is a very telling factor in deciding whether charters are public or private for all purposes, including their status under both the free exercise and the establishment clauses of the First Amendment. If the charter school can discharge the unsatisfactory teacher according to the terms of his or her employment agreement—or if it can simply close up shop for economic reasons— in short, if the charter must behave like the very risky business that it is, it is at least as "private" as those religious schools of Cleveland whose children are now supported by government vouchers approved by the U.S. Supreme Court.

These are generalities, not a proper argument for religious charters ready for the Court. Happily, Sugarman is about to clarify in detail the role of the federal guarantees. The vehicle is a masterly article forthcoming in the *Journal of Law and Religion*.[1] He distinguishes the two central legal issues, and they will serve as my conclusion here: (1) Are charter schools sufficiently private in nature to permit the state to support religious charters directly or indirectly without affecting the establishment clause? (2) Does the free exercise clause secure the right of parent and child to such support, even in states with Blaine Amendments? Are religious charters not merely permissible but an entitlement?

PART THREE

Religion, Family, and Schools

CHAPTER NINE

Luck, Obedience, and the Vocation of the Child

Only the devil has an answer for our moral difficulties, and he says: "Keep on posing problems, and you will escape the necessity of obedience."

—Dietrich Bonhoeffer[1]

The first act of freedom is a moral act par excellence, and, at least implicitly, a religious act, since it can only be realized rightly if it is realized in divine charity.

—Jacques Maritain[2]

As a moralist, the late W. C. Fields occasionally lost focus. Still, one insight never failed him. Fields saw that children, even of tender years, could crave power over others and come to deserve moral judgment. He learned this the hard way from his nemesis, Baby Leroy, an urchin ever on the make at the great comedian's expense. In our own time, such imperious brats have secured adult allies who would by law annul the natural vulnerability of children, ordaining their "rights" and even their "liberation." They make Field's pedophobia seem vaguely prophetic.

Originally published in *The Vocation of the Child*, ed. Patrick McKinley Brennan (Grand Rapids, MI: William B. Eerdmans 2008), 75–103

Later I suggest why any liberation of Baby Leroy and his tribe that might be executed by civil rights lawyers will remain largely a work of the imagination, typically displacing one adult sovereign with another. For this reason, and others, I incline to the Fields school of pediatric morality, which is currently the ideological underdog, and given my occasional and unregretted encouragement of children's rights, it is time that I acknowledge their corresponding responsibility and concede the blessings for family, society, and the child himself that depend upon it. Here I focus upon one prominent aspect of that responsibility: obedience. I will ask what role the child's free submission to authority plays in achieving the two distinct forms of human good. I conclude that obedience serves the realization of each, but in appropriately different ways.

The distinction I intend between the two goods entails assumptions about human nature that are shared by many, but not all. Those who embrace them tend to stand in the tradition of either Aristotle or Judeo-Christianity, or both. I will assume specifically the following:

1.   An order of truth and correct conduct obtains and is authoritative apart from human will.
2.   The human person is not reducible to its contingent material parts but, rather, includes an indestructible self with a specific responsibility respecting the order of truth and correct conduct.

For the steadfast relativist/materialist, such premises, together with their moral and theological baggage, will appear to be nonsense, but, perhaps, nonsense with benign practical implications, even for the relativist. The specific significance of these ideas for children depends upon further considerations, and these will constitute the bulk of this chapter, once I have described the two types of human goods.

FIRST AND SECOND GOOD

First Good

Each good has its own form, which I will label respectively "first" and "second." First good is the unique perfection that every rational person either realizes or forgoes in his own self; I will use the conventional term "goodness" as its synonym. This perfectible (and corruptible) "self" I conceive to be an invulnerable and permanent capacity at the core of the person. Early in life, the self—this capacity—becomes activated by consciousness of its responsibility toward the order of truth and correct conduct (hereafter called "second good"). This consciousness is the calling or "vocation" of authentic authority that invites the self's free allegiance; the self accepts by setting every *other* resource of the person in search of the specific content of second good. These other resources, intellectual and material, I will shortly label the "persona." First good (or "goodness") is the fruit of a free commitment of the self to seek truth and right practice.

It is, then, the consciousness of the option to obey or flout authority that renders the child fully capable of either goodness or its opposite, thereby constituting the most consequential form of human freedom. So far as first good is correct, the manner in which this act of obedience to authority actually contributes to goodness is a question both fascinating and controversial, for the innocent child may misjudge the content of second good, or by trusting the wicked (or ignorant) adult, the child may cooperate in the promotion of error and bad behavior.

Second Good

Occupying the other box in the dichotomy are the endlessly varied examples of what I have just referred to as "second good." This set comprises all moral objects other than first good. It is literally *every human good other than goodness itself*. By a "human" good here, then, I mean any state of affairs that rational persons ought to seek and support because (if recognized and achieved) it would be what is right under the specific circumstances. The individual person might not grasp some specific answer, and therefore on occasion might act incorrectly out of ignorance. Nevertheless, whether he finds it or not, this right answer is the proper object of his free rational nature. Second goods are correct possibilities that the self is responsible to affirm and to seek.

Some instances of second good are realized in the actor himself, some in other individual persons, some in common; all represent outcomes worthy of our effort. By their nature, however, no matter how we try to identify and then realize them, none is guaranteed to occur, or, if it occurs, to continue. So it is, for example, with our occasional achievements of knowledge, friendship, justice, and all other states and relations that in specific cases carry positive moral content and are the gist of our daily experience. We are obligated by nature (and, if one is a believer, by revelation) to seek to make such goods concrete in this world for ourselves and for others, even though they are elusive and contingent. Some of our contemporaries would sort them into sub-categories that they label "basic human goods"—and surely they are that—but I will call all of them "second" in order to emphasize the primacy of simple goodness. This distinction in dignity holds, even though the search for second goods is authoritatively commanded and even though, in some subtle manner, that search is implicated in the realization of self-perfection. The priority of first good still follows from (1) the sufficiency of our created capacity to fulfill its condition and (2) its invulnerability so long as one wills to serve truth and correctness. It is goodness alone that stands as a potentially permanent state or prize that can be ours independent of fortune; on both grounds it is prior in dignity.[3]

"Second good" in its many forms is unequally accessible; whether by sheer luck or the effect of earlier choices, individuals acquire very different resources of intellect, wealth, and experience. We wield different sets of tools with which to discover what would be the correct outcome in a certain case and, then, to bring that outcome in a certain case and, then, to bring that outcome about. Put in negative terms, we bear different burdens of ignorance and impotence. I label our unique and constantly challenging individual packages of ways and means the "persona" (at this very moment you are dealing with mine). As I proceed, I will speak of the self and the persona as aspects of the whole *person*. It is the self that determines whether or not the persona's activity is directed to the quest for second good.[4]

It is my best judgment that, unlike second good—and from a very early age—access to first good, or the goodness of the self, is the same in kind and degree for every rational human, child or adult, who is capable of recognizing the calling to seek what is right. In this most crucial part of life, luck holds no sway. This is the most controversial part of the claim, depending, as I will show, upon a particular conception of the manner in which the self must cooperate in order to achieve its own perfection; in this conception the dramatic differences in the abilities of individual personas to discover correct conduct are irrelevant to the opportunity for personal goodness. It is our effort alone that secures or forfeits first good; this free effort bears the technical name "obtension." I repeat: this claim that obtension suffices is contested. Historically, the competing and more typical interpretation of human access to goodness has emphasized these very differences in the acumen of our individual personas. Diverse gifts and experiences produce errors in our beliefs, moral insights, and judgments, and these errors, even when inadvertent, are thought to prevent achievement of either form of the good—self-perfection or a rightly ordered world and persona. Because of their insistence upon correct knowledge and intending no disrespect, I call theories of this latter sort "gnostic." The gnostic criterion for goodness obviously bears upon my present inquiry. For children, though equipped to obtend—that is, to will second good—could vary markedly both from adults and from one another in their ability to understand moral rules and to apply them so as to get right answers in particular circumstances.[5]

In the gnostic view, it is also relevant that the range of each child's reason changes over time, making his or her ability to achieve either of the two forms of human good an unfolding story. At successive age levels, moral theories of this sort have tended to stop the film and declare—with Aristotle and Aquinas—that, here, or maybe there, begins the child's capacity to recognize correct answers and, thus by choice, to realize the good in both its forms. Taking snapshots of a young life at intervals in this manner has been a useful analytic device for moralists and theologians, but it has been most portentous—even ominous—when directed to the ultimate question: How are we to think about the child who dies or permanently loses rationality at some particular stage of his or her story? Is there a set of moral-theological terms that allows a nonsentimental assessment of a child's access to self-perfection? And is this opportunity of the child anything less than that enjoyed by adults?[6]

This puzzle has long worried all but the most relentless materialists. Any mind that is open to hope of an afterlife is left uneasy by the thought that—whatever may be the dead child's state—the poor thing had so little to say about it. Unless we are John Calvin, this unease about responsibility sets us scrambling for a fallback position that can assure at least a minimally happy state for the lost child, and here, many Christians can take consolation from baptism. Still, one cannot but feel anxious about those millions who die not only unbaptized but also too young for us to imagine even their "baptism by desire." We worry, too, about the fate of that older child who in life had seemed still uncommitted to responsibility and, perhaps, unconcerned for the good of others. I would never scoff at fears for dead children, and my own answers leave room for anxiety.[7]

C. S. Lewis was properly tortured by questions such as these, addressing them in a romantic fashion in his novel *The Great Divorce*. Lewis supposed that, after death, all of us pass through a sort of parentheses in which even those who were prerational (or postrational) at the moment of death are empowered freely to say yes or no to what is God's final invitation. Lewis's flight of fancy represents his—and, I fear, my own—deep concern to maintain the goodness of God by confirming the liberty of every man. Since it is not credible that God is arbitrary, theodicy must provide all of us—including children—the opportunity for real guilt and real goodness.[8]

I will not here attempt such postmortem rescues, nor do I address the mystery of the status of the child prior to his consciousness of duty to seek the content of an authoritative order of truth and goods. However, like Lewis, I do suppose that human freedom is the critical element in the child's relation to that order. This raises the familiar "Pelagian" threat. Here, without argument, is my position on that issue: divine omnipotence can create beings who are free to say no or yes to God's invitation. To reject this as a possibility would constrain God's own liberty. The question about an efficacious human will thus is not whether creation would be within the divine power, it is rather an issue of act about how that power has been exercised. The evidence, including revelation, allows us to disagree without any way challenging God. I would not stand with Pelagius, but I do assert my belief in a real human agency that God fashions and maintains in each of us; he seems to prefer that we compose our own RSVPs to his external invitation. This is what he wants, and he gets it.[9]

This problem about human freedom is certainly not confined to children. However, it becomes most strongly focused when posed for those young beings whose consciousness has only recently experienced responsibility. I take that experience to be prior in time to the grasp of the correctness of particular behaviors. The awakening child finds himself invited—ordered, if you prefer—to cooperate in an enterprise whose content he cannot possibly imagine but whose reality and authority are unmistakable. Although still unable to grasp the terms of specific duty, the child is aware of the possibility of good and of a personal obligation toward it. Here is the opportunity for what I will call "primary obedience." The expression identifies the child's free choice to cooperate with this nonspecific "vocation"—this consciousness of a general state of responsibility. The child's affirmation of authority coupled with his or her readiness for specification of duty, satisfies the condition of the self's highest possibility; at the same time, this commitment—this act of primary obedience—sets the child on the quest for second good in that other sphere of life that is affected by contingency. Later I will identify other and more mundane forms of obedience that function in that world of second good, forms that help the child to discover and realize the specific correct outcomes that he or she has already willed to seek.[10]

THE PIOUS PREDATOR

All these species of obedience—primary and the rest—are illustrated in a cunning way by what I consider one of the finest short pieces in the moral theology of childhood. It is Phyllis McGinley's "The Giveaway." The poem describes St. Bridget, the less well-known female patron saint of Ireland, as a "problem child." Her problem, McGinley explains, was her insatiable generosity. She gave away "to any soul whose luck was out," not only her own belongings but also her relatives' belongings. She would "give everything away," including "her father's gold, her granshire's dinner," and even "the mattress of her aunt." As a result,[11]

Saint Bridget drove
The family mad . . .
. . . .
She could not quit.
She had to share;
She gave so much
And grew so holy
. . . one must love her.
Nonetheless,
There's no denial She must have been
A sort of trial . . .

McGinley concludes by asking, "Who had the patience of a saint? Saint Bridget or her near and dear?"

Saint Bridget seems the embodiment—or, better perhaps, the ensoulment—of my problem. To realize her own understanding of correct behavior, Bridget committed several apparent wrongs. These giveaways of others' property seem both a material mistake about the content of second good and a violation of two prominent commandments from the Decalogue. And what was the sequel of all this theft and disobedience? Bridget was canonized.

GNOSTIC NICETIES

If that outcome seems to threaten contradiction, the worry may be credited in considerable part to the deep and continuing influence in Christian, certainly in Catholic, moral philosophy of what I have already called gnostic versions of natural law. Their relevant common themes often are traced to Aquinas and ultimately to Aristotle; their concept of the good bears on our assessment of Bridget's bungles. For convenience I will focus upon one of this school's distinguished contemporary representatives, John Finnis of Oxford and Notre Dame.

Like their Greek and medieval predecessors, Finnis and company profess a version of first good, or personal goodness, which is strongly "intellectualist," sufficiently so to justify my label "gnostic." Goodness is for them, first of all, an affair of right reason. In the gnostic's interpretation of Bridget's enterprises, there is no way that she could improve the state of her own self while ignorantly performing these well-intended acts of larceny. True, a certain material form of *second* good would have been accomplished; for the poor, after all, did get fed. But the circumstances—including her own noble ends—failed to justify the means; these things were not hers to give. Bridget has done what are unreasoned and incorrect deeds, and to that extent her goodness is compromised. If she, nonetheless, is good, this can be true only in spite of it all. In his later book *Aquinas*, Finnis asserts that such acts of misconduct "are essentially self-determining—i.e. internal to and constitutive of an individual's character." But if her acts are "self-determining," Bridget remains at best a paradox of good and evil. She is simultaneously a corruption and a very holy person.[12]

The gnostic version of our moral nature clearly has strong implications concerning authority and obedience. The act of obedience in itself can never be effectual in advancing the goodness of a child or anyone else. If Bridget resolves from this day to follow the insights of her mother and father, she remains unsafe; not only may they be wrong in particular cases, but it is she whose reason must, in any case, be correct, and as yet she may have none of her own that she can trust. Finnis here allows Aquinas to speak for the gnostic tradition about children: "Before they reach the age of reason . . . children cannot make free choices . . . and when one does reach it, one is immediately confronted with the rational necessity of deliberating."[13]

In fairness, Finnis does as well with this moral conundrum as can anyone who is committed to these plausible and traditional premises. But here the gnostic settlement pinches and binds, and especially as it disposes of children. Cannot the dignity both of reason and of second good be honored without making correctness a condition of first good—of personal goodness? They can, and sometimes have. Specifically, that view can be found in, or at least teased from, other moral masters—some of them natural lawyers, some not. I think here of Maritain, Barth, Lonergan, Liguori, Balthasar, and, of course, Phyllis McGinley directly or indirectly—they and perhaps their churches support the insight that earlier I adopted as my own, namely, that rational persons are so constituted by nature that they achieve each form of human good in its own distinctive way. The first form—goodness—comes to the person independently of correct works actually realized. It is the effect simply of commitment by the self to the quest for those same correct works; thus, it flourishes irrespective of all the errors that are made unavoidable by the feeble state of our personas. Bridget, in her ignorance, did bad deeds—acts that did not and could not make her a good person. What, nevertheless, did make her so was her earnest pursuit of good deeds, using whatever reason and experience were hers.[14]

The "Obtending" Reasoner

Note well that, even in this nongnostic view, reason remains both relevant and necessary. Just as the gnostics insist, Bridget's salvific commitment cannot be a pure act of the will, for there is no such thing.

Commitment is by its nature a response to the cognition of something, in this case of an insistent message of obligation with which we are all wired. Commitment is an act based upon knowledge. What Bridget knew—and all she needed to know—was that she had been invited to embark upon her personal search for second good. She had received a calling. She could have answered no, but in fact she answered yes and promptly began her benevolent campaign, which is where and when her behavioral blunders began. These errors made hash of the contingent order of "basic human goods," but the intelligent choice that preceded them had already made a saint of her.

Bridget's commitment honored a sufficient reason that was itself the experience of real obligation. It is this specific cognitive experience that moved Patrick Brennan and me occasionally to adopt the strange English word "obtension" to identify Bridget's choice to seek her response to vocation. The *Oxford English Dictionary* defines the verb "to obtend" as "to act for a reason." And so has it been for all of us adult humans, just as for Bridget. At the threshold of our rational life, we encountered the insistent and permanent fact of responsibility. It was a form of knowledge, and we all faced the free necessity of giving it a conscious response.[15]

Finnis might ask, "How can obligation arise from . . . just one more fact?" But, in this case of the awakened self, it happens to be the unique fact of an inescapable invitation (or command). This message is itself the content of the experience of obligation. Now, Finnis properly dreads the "naturalistic fallacy," but here, I think, he can safely drop his guard. In the case of human actors, the point is not to prove responsibility from some other fact—incautiously to infer an ought from an is. For the experience of responsibility is itself the fact. No inference of an ought is necessary, for, in this case, the *is* happens to be an *ought*.[16]

And the specific imperative that merges in the self is this: to seek the content of second good. *To seek it*. That is our vocation—and the whole of it. Which means that we have the opportunity to canonize not only infants and amnesiacs but also all those feeblest of minds who know only this most elementary of calls. I could not possibly be certain, but I do conclude—with some support from modern psychology—that children experience something like this vocation at a very early age. In their otherwise indeterminate world of what must seem weird and shifting images, they grasp at least this: there is truth and there is correct conduct that one day I might be able to recognize and honor, and I am called right now to look for them. Shall I say yes or no to this vocation? As the child considers her choice, the better of these two possible responses is not self-evident (nor shall it ever be). For the vocation comes with the insight that there will be costs in either answer; to seek second good is to surrender so many other alluring possibilities. And so the self-perfecting yes, when and if it comes, does so as a responsible act, initiating the child's free dedication to the quest—a mission that in the ideal case remains uninterrupted for a lifetime.[17]

PRIMARY AND SECONDARY OBEDIENCE

Now, back to my theme. If one believes all this, two distinct roles for childhood obedience become reasonably clear. The first is simply the child's embrace of this duty that is borne by every human of the most marginal rationality—the duty to commit to the search with whatever resources lodge in his or her persona. In this radical obtension or commitment—in this act of "primary obedience"—the child chooses to do the best he or she can for second good. This elemental and non-specific vocation of the moral tenderfoot can be understood as natural, as religious, or, for my part, as both (but I confess that the idea of a purely natural calling is for me elusive for want of any caller with authority to bind). Primary obedience, then, is the necessary and sufficient condition of the child's first good; it is, if you prefer, his or her first act of cooperation with grace.

But, if we accept this piece of very good news, it is not the end to the practical question about obedience, even in respect of first good. For, any child who offers primary obedience—who truly wills the quest for second good—must now proceed in practice to do his or her best to discover and realize it. And, if we return with this in mind to reassess young Bridget, we discover her in a rather awkward mode. Assuming that she has made the fateful act of primary obedience, this now drives her to seek correct conduct. But just how does an obtending child proceed in this world of which she knows so little?

Here—up to a point—we can join forces with the gnostic. The child, obviously, must seek the path of correctness by engaging her reason to consult whatever knowledge of human affairs is already available in her own persona. But, among the things she knows is the fact that she is only a beginner on this voyage of discovery and her resources are thin. These weaknesses make it her first practical task to seek the experience and information that might disclose the right answer to whatever moral question next faces her. Here reason itself insists that she look for the best older navigators available and follow their authority so long as her own ignorance persists. This submission to a specific adult or elder child is distinct in kind from her prior act of primary obedience to ultimate authority. It is obedience of an expedient and very practical form that addresses specific moral cases. For convenience I will call it "secondary" or "artless" obedience. It is the act of a pilgrim who puts confidence in a more experienced and discerning fellow human; one thinks of Dante and Virgil.

Finnis is reluctant to bless this prudential submission of one's judgment to that of another; for him any use of the minds of others is merely instrumental and, in the end, must issue in a reasoned and independent judgment by the actor himself. One must reach an autonomous conclusion that *this specific act* is the very one that is required or justified by reason. I think that the case of young children really puts this idea to the test. For the beginner, this pure and pragmatic obedience to a particular adult may in specific cases be the *only* act of reason that is available. The child's intellectual resource consists in whatever experience justifies his or her trust in the other's mind. Given the vacuum of personal insight, the child's submission to the elder's view is an artless, but not a blind, obedience. It is an act founded upon the reasonable consideration that the judgment of this other is better in this particular matter than is my own. Just which substitute decider represents the ideal locus of authority for the individual child is a question that I will address in due course. To no one's surprise, except in extraordinary circumstances, it will turn out to be the parent. Of course, roles can be reversed; even the younger child will sometimes see some specific correct answer that eludes the parent. I would not argue that the child's duty in such a case would be satisfied by a purely passive obedience that abandons reason. The child cannot in good conscience elude or shift responsibility by retreat to a comforting self-delusion of vicarious correctness (but this must be a sore temptation in cases of conflict). This problem of the child who faces an erring adult authority deserves more reflection than I can manage. For the moment I take practical refuge in an analogy to the way presumptions are used in the law. Acting as a reasonable person, the child should accord the parental judgment a rebuttable presumption of correctness. Its strength should correlate inversely with the child's age and experience (plus the parent's track record) and eventually shrink to an honorific deference; its basic justification correspondingly shifts over time from the child's relative intellectual imperfection to an ultimately symbolic role of the parents as "ambassadors" of the good.[18]

Holy Innocents?

To this point I have said only a little about the "Religions of the Book" and the various confessional views of the issue. The question of the goodness — and the salvation — of the child is, of course, a matter of historic theological conflict that I am competent to penetrate only so far. After several millennia, the main issues seem to remain unsettled. There is, however, for our edification, a contemporary religious literature about children that increasingly seeks its conceptual anchor in philosophy as well as in revelation. Various fine essays in Marcia Bunge's collection, *The Child in Christian Thought*, are a good illustration. *Theology Today* has recently published a number of insightful articles displaying a range of interpretations of childhood.[19]

I find this literature elevating in spirit but analytically wanting on my specific question. Indeed, as a whole it seems almost to shy away from any serious apology for obedience. Few modern writers want to make company with what they take to be classic interpretations of childhood; some of these traditions have portrayed the child as a locus of evil who becomes only a bit less obnoxious when obedient. Michael Wigglesworth and even Augustine are definitely passé. Today, instead, in terms drawn from Mark and Matthew, children are typically portrayed as exemplars of the kingdom of heaven. They have become not the absence of moral perfection but its one clear example. Perhaps we adults should be obeying them. It is easy to see how Christians tease this tender attitude out of the New Testament. And, of course, the apparent natural humility of most children is a thing well worth imitating; it suggests their uncorrupted intuition of an ineradicable human hope.[20]

This contemporary vision of childhood innocence and excellence needs to make its analytic encounter with the more traditional constructions. The infatuation with simplicity does not by itself rescue any child from the effect of moral errors arising either out of sheer ignorance or from mistakes of some authority whom the child artlessly obeys. If one happens to share the gnostic view that honest errors in belief and conduct stand in the way of the child's self-perfection, the mere rejection of Wigglesworth will be insufficient.

Happily, as I have argued, there is help available to spare us the gnostic conclusion. The alternative interpretation of goodness as the fruit of the act of primary obedience (obtension) could interest modern theologians of childhood. To be sure, this leaves a three-stage model of childhood consisting of (1) a prerational period, followed now by (2) a stage of conscious responsibility to make the effort to think and choose and (3) a time of ripened "reason," but at least the possibility of self-perfection comes much earlier in time. The barest awareness of responsibility empowers the child to commit to the search. At the same time, for the child, just as for any minimally rational adult, this responsibility to think and to seek implies freedom and thus the possibility that the child will reject the vocation. In short, responsibility always introduces the possibility of tragedy. Children must be free to corrupt themselves in what is the primal act of disobedience. One remembers Baby Leroy's despotic moments.

RESCUE DECLINED

In the present climate of religious opinion, such a view of childhood responsibility may appear a bit upstream. This impression could be tempered by recalling that, in respect of his or her access to first good, the child who is invited does not differ in opportunity from the sophisticated adult. Each has plenary capacity for the gift of goodness. Each has been given the same commission: do your best with whatever tools you have been given. This capacity of the self to commit is unvarying in degree. Like an on/off switch, it is binary; one can say yes or no in the primary act of obedience that constitutes our calling and our access to goodness.

What could vary in degree is not the capacity to obtend, but individual effort. A person's commitment to seek the good may be carried out with varying degrees of devotion, hence of goodness. Among good people, some may be better than others, because they try harder. The diversity of our personas—our individual gifts and burdens—probably does make the exercise of "best effort" a thing different in many respects from person to person. But effort can properly be conceived as the activation by the self of some *proportion* of that sum of gifts, whatever that sum may be in the individual case. And so would I understand it. Now, just who is exercising which proportion of his or her gifts is a thing opaque to all but God. Constantly we are tempted to judge goodness, perhaps because we have to make practical decisions based upon our experience of individuals. But neither the reality nor the degree of anyone's goodness is transparent, and perhaps least of all in our observation of moral beginners. Baby Leroy himself must remain a mystery.

This obtensional view of childhood leaves the fate of the preresponsible child still unexplained. I see no reason to doubt that the child's first consciousness of the responsibility to seek the good is a postnatal event. But what, then, if anything, have we gained by taking the obtensional turn? At least this: the act of primary obedience becomes recognized as fully consequential for the achievement of first good. Though the child does not yet see the correct way, his obedience is the endorsement of the hope to find it. It is this act of cooperation with grace and nature that perfects the self; it constitutes the free human moment in the miracle of justification. And at some point very early in life the child shares this dignity in fullest measure.

Secondary Obedience

The focus now shifts from first to second good. This plenary capacity of the child for goodness may have implications, benign or otherwise, for that other world consisting of true ideas and right conduct. These implications deserve their separate accounting, and I turn now to consider the significance that the obtensional view of childhood and primary obedience might hold for the role of the child in society, the family, and civic life. At the start here I reemphasize that the very act of primary obedience wills the perfection of this contingent world (including the child's own persona); in the language of economics, we should "maximize" second good. Even though these trail in the order of dignity, the fundamental imperative for all of us is to seek them here and now. Thy will be done on earth.[21]

Primary obedience thus commits us to secondary obedience, that is, to human authority, to the extent that (on the evidence available) this deference will enhance correct outcomes. Finnis's perfectly free submission to another's judgment is not a good in itself. It is merely an instrument. This is nowhere more obvious than in the artless submission of children to adult direction. As Yves Simon well observed, children are the archetype of that peculiar form of obedience in which authority is necessary as a *substitute* for the judgment of one whose own judgment is *deficient*. Substitutional authority may be temporary or permanent, depending upon the nature of the deficiency in the subject person. In the case of the child, the deficiency ordinarily is temporary, and it is the role of the adult authority to hasten is disappearance; maturity ends the occasion for artless obedience, but not necessarily for obedience justified on other practical grounds.[22]

If secondary obedience is directly instrumental for second good, it is reflexively so for the self-perfection (first good) of the child. It fulfills the terms of the invitation to seek. To be completely specific, the regime of substantial adult authority and artless obedience by the child has three objects: (1) to reaffirm for the child the reality and authority of the order of second good that the child is invited to seek as a condition of goodness; (2) to reaffirm the child's fundamental responsibility or vocation to seek it; and (3) to identify the specific content of truth and correct conduct for the child when occasions of obedience arise in the practical order. The adult authority reinforces the general imperative of primary obedience while giving specific content to the immediate objects of artless or secondary obedience. What is common to the child and adult in this regime is the hope to serve both first and second good.

PRACTICE: THE PARENT AS PREVALENT AUTHORITY

All these abstractions eventually take practical forms. In daily life, one evident and consequential example is the framework of civil law as it recognizes and supports those adult authorities who substitute for the child's own judgment. The parent's general authority is conceded, but distinctive limited species of authority over the child are recognized in government. One of these provides legal guarantees of *minimums*, such as education and medical care; the other forbids *abuse*. Taken together, these familiar regimes constitute a system of child welfare. Little Rodney shall be inoculated and sent to a licensed school for 180 days a year; he shall not be physically abused. This authority to intervene is narrow in principle and—with one exception—in practice. The de facto exception is the school system that conscripts children of ordinary and low-income families for education by the government. Otherwise, the legal norms of child welfare are few in number and modest in reach.

Indeed, apart from schools, all but last-ditch authority over children lies in their parents. For better or worse—outside the government's narrow authority to rescue—the parent makes the rules for the child and enforces his or her will in ways and for purposes about which the state is not entitled even to express an opinion. Thus, Bridget, you shall be in bed by nine, you shall not play with Marcia, and you shall attend this church service and say your prayers. Virtually every act of the child, from nutrition to worship, is subject in theory, and typically, in fact, to the mandate or veto of the parent. Quite literally, the father and/or mother will govern this young person. The power of the state itself may be enlisted as an instrument to support the authority of these millions of unique family dominions. Absent severe abuse, the sheriff will return the runaway to confront his brussels sprouts, to mow the lawn, and to attend his parents' church at their command.

Here, then, is the great practical domain of childhood obedience—the family. Yet, this fundamental authority to ordain the content of childhood could have been centered elsewhere, as Plato and Rousseau advised. This is a possibility that still lures at least a few of our contemporaries. Some of these would completely decommission parents; children, they say, ought to be liberated altogether from adult sovereignty and either left to their own devices or allowed to enjoy the parent as their indentured servant. Meanwhile, at an equally ambitious but opposite pole of reform, their opponents plausibly observe that the child will in any case be dominated by some adult, the only question being which one; critics of this latter sort tend to be professionals who remind us that the law might wisely commission them to replace the parent. If some adult will in fact be running the show, it is best that it be someone competent. These professionals at least get this question right: Who is the best decider for this individual child? Would it be better for Rodney and Bridget to live under the dominion of their parents or under that of the Department of Children's Welfare?[23]

Justifying the radical authority that historically and currently has been recognized to lie in the parents is no great task, at least for basic day-to-day choices. Here the best interest of the child ordinarily is served by a comprehensive domestic dominion, and this for at least three reasons. First, it is the parent who *knows* the child (including the child's own view of things). A professional may have superior knowledge regarding some specific need or gift of Bridget's, but (as with lawyers or engineers) at decision time the expert should act as auxiliary to the clients. The ideal is to infuse the more intimate (if amateur) insight of the parent with the information of the professional. Second, it is parents who *care* for the child in a manner unique to the relation. Not always, but generally, this attachment helps assure that the decision will be made for the child's own sake and not to serve someone else's ideal of policy. Third, and most important, it is the parent who is *accountable* for errors in the use of authority; it is she who will suffer if the child turns out to be a disordered and dependent adult. Accountability makes for better decisions. I suppose I should add here a fourth reason: the parent is cheap labor, and no society could afford a comprehensive regime of child professionals.[24]

But if the presumptive parental authority well serves the child's own "best interest," it seems at first to be coupled only very loosely to the child's moral quest for second good and, even more importantly, for goodness. Assume that Bridget's original act of primary obedience has put her in search of the particular adult authority that will best teach her a specific set of authentic duties. Is her mother really up to this? Bridget is willing at her mother's direction to eat the spinach, but where in all this is the moral beef? How good is mother at leading me beyond mere health and security into the more challenging quest for truth and correct behavior that affects not only my selfish interest but my virtue and the common good. As Plato and the political sages of every age remind us, obedience is a question for the society and for the child. In some manner, we—the collective—must seek a harmony between the terms of a real common good and those versions of it that gain acceptance in the minds of obtending individuals, such as Bridget and her mother.

Enter Luck

What are these versions of truth and correct behavior that are delivered to the individual child? They are legion. Children are born to adults who have rather different ideas about the good, and it is the ideas of particular parents that the child will hear. Call this providence. Call it luck.

Nor are the differences among parents confined to the virtues of spinach. In diverse ways they identify for the child the roles that are correct for men and for women, the proper relation of humans to the natural aspects of their environment, the meaning and uses of our sexual powers, the significance of law, respect for life, assisted suicide, war and peace, contemplation versus striving, the duty to vote, attitudes and obligations toward the poor, lying for specific reasons, tax evasion, the authority of teachers, the value of book learning, the dignity of work, the idea and authority of God, claims about primary obedience, and the proper treatment of animals. To all these issues parents give explicit or implicit answers; among other things they say yes, no, maybe, I don't know, it doesn't matter, or ask your father.

Where does this jungle of contraries leave the rationale for parental sovereignty? Is there anything positive to be said for our historical regime of secondary obedience in a world where parents enforce the belief and practice of contradictory and often simply wrong ideas? The answer is a resounding yes. Even in an incoherent moral environment, obedience to parents is efficacious to both first and second good. But this takes a bit of seeing.

Luck and First Good Reconciled

With regard to first good—the child's own self-perfection or goodness—the principal justification for the historic parental authority is this: the spectacular diversity of parental worldviews paradoxically presupposes a universality that holds at the deepest level of moral conviction. That is, virtually all parents plainly share the imperative to pass these peculiar private convictions to their own children; whatever they believe they would transmit in ways effective or ineffective. They acknowledge a real order of second goods that their child is obliged both to seek and attempt to realize. Few mothers indoctrinate their infants in theories of moral anarchy. And the father who plays the moral skeptic for his buddies at work rediscovers the rule of virtue whenever he enters the nursery. The office of parent reconfirms every child's experience of his or her own responsibility to the authority of a real order of correct behavior. There is a good; here are its specific contents; believe it; do it. And, by contrast, outside the home this elemental ratification of the child's basic vocation to a real good is nowhere guaranteed.[25]

Observe, however, that even though the parents' affirmation of responsibility may encourage the child's own goodness, in respect to second good it is problematic and, again, paradoxical. For, by its nature, this shared imperative of parents to indoctrinate their own children tends to preserve the overall riot of human opinion and belief. And this could be consequential for the common good. For, as my litany of difference was intended to show, parental convictions can conflict on matters of great moral and social significance.

LUCK, COMMON GOOD, AND UNCOMMON CURRICULUMS

Plato warned us of the social threat posed by parental pluralism. He would have addressed it by relocating authority in professional guardians who would determine the specific beliefs and conduct for which children's obedience would be the important instrument. This policy retains its allure for certain confident Americans who discern those correct ideas we must all accept in order to be a true community. In our own time, techniques of persuasion and organization that were unavailable to the Greeks have encouraged these intellectual descendants of Plato to hope for better luck at imposing uniformity.

To that end they have made the shared civics curriculum a central justification for a school system that is the Platonic exception to the rule of parents—at least for the lives of have-not families. In the face of parental discord, the common message of our public schools provides the United States its social glue. Obedience of lower-class children to the disparate values of their parents is the social problem; the constant message of the public schools is the solution. Should we credit this broad challenge to the regime of parental authority?[26]

First of all, I take this picture of intellectual accord among government teachers to be a claim of fact, and their curriculum is indeed common to the following extent: all government schools aim to teach reading, writing, and arithmetic, science, computers, and obedience to positive law. Those students who actually master the ideas should wind up knowing roughly the same things about these specific subjects that consist mostly of uncontroversial skills taught also in every nongovernment school.[27]

By contrast, the "civic" part of the curriculums of public schools is anything but common. It's rather a great patchwork of ideological retreats, each dominated by adults who are at least as fractious as the parents. They address children's minds in various ways as textbook writers, school board members, union leaders, administrators, or simply as teachers who rule within very private domains. The subject may be same-sex marriage, evolution, economics, abortion, marijuana, multiculturalism, affirmative action, contraception, witchcraft, or vegetarianism, and the take on each issue will vary from teacher to teacher. Scholars as diverse as Rosemary Salomone, Katherine Simon, Christopher Barnes, and Kenneth Karst have confirmed the reality of this great smorgasbord. Among these moral pedagogies of our public schools, the only one that might claim to be the mode is that of avoidance; many an educator ducks all civic questions. Who needs controversy?[28]

Of course, the more primary and eternal question for the civics educator concerns the authoritative *source* (if any) of every human duty. Is a child in fact subject to any responsibility that precedes and transcends society and that itself makes citizenship an authentic calling? It is not clear under prevailing law that government schools are entitled to get serious about such a question. In any case, on all these basic civic issues, by definition there can be no public answer, for that would require an American consensus, and there is none. There are only private answers delivered by teachers, whether these teachers hold forth in government or private schools.[29]

BABEL, OBEDIENCE, AND THE SUBURBS

But if government teaching on civic subjects is such a Tower of Babel, is that so bad? I have not yet said so, and my answer is — not necessarily.

So far, I have meant to be critical only of the public school masquerade of a common curriculum; for it is a thing that, in our present state, simply cannot be. Hence, I see nothing intrinsically wrong in the fact that diverse teachers do the best they can to transmit their own private versions of truth in the marketplace of ideas. Just as it is with parents, what else can these teachers give but what they think they know?

But recall that my subject is obedience and its place in the child's vocation. Now, it is not the children who choose these teachers; thus, what we seem to witness in government schools in the United States are very provincial regimes of authority in which adult strangers promote their parochial philosophies simply because the state has given them the opportunity to do so. Viewing the resulting hodgepodge, we are bound to ask, by what justification? One might defend a common curriculum democratically derived. But what argument could support this intellectual litter?

I can think of one, but it requires a premise. Let us suppose that these petty intellectual sovereignties were not in fact imposed by chance assignment but, rather, were freely chosen by parents. Suppose, that is, that these variant educations were all on offer in a functioning market. Insofar as that were true, the regime of secondary obedience of the child to the parent would be intact. And in many cases in the United States, this is the social reality: many parents are able to make choices of schools that tolerably reproduce their own regimes of obedience. These parents rule because they can afford to. They exercise their "freedom" (their authority over the child) by buying a home in Beverly Hills or by paying tuition at St. Mary's or College Prep. Their chosen school—public or private—is not merely, as lawyers say, *in loco parentis.* It is the very embodiment of the parental will concerning the moral regimen of the child. The school is their agent.

ELUDING THE CURRICULUM LOTTERY

The five-year-old of the middle class understands that this new thing they call school is just another expression of my parents' authority. It confirms the established order, teaching me the content of second good. I will attend to its voice as to the word of my father and mother.

The parent who decided for this same middle-class kindergartner has consciously exercised at least two distinct, if related, functions. The first, borrowing from Yves Simon, is the parental *substitution* for the *deficient* judgment and experience of the young person; the parent is the proxy for the child's untutored will, working toward an eventual state of autonomy that will include access to this parent's version of correct ideas.

This parent also carries out a second function of authority and obedience that is quite distinct. It is one that Simon identifies as a general justification for government itself, but which by analogy also explains the regime of the family. Simon specifies what he calls authority's "essential" function in establishing law and government. Essential authority is that of the decision-maker who is empowered to decide questions that competent and equal—but conflicted—people need to have settled. This same legitimating function must be served in that other lawlike system that is the family. When there is division among its members regarding alternative paths, decisions must nevertheless be made for the common good. Parents hold the authority to make them, and this continues even when the children have reached an age where they have their own distinctive and plausible views of what is the best course. On some issues, this group of people needs a corporate answer, or it ceases to be a family, which, for various reasons, it is important for it to be.[30]

Both of these functions—the substitutional and the essential—are served when middle-class parents exercise authority to choose the school. They affirm their version of correct ideas, and, at the same time, preserve family integrity. It is not at all surprising that middle-class parents put such stock in their own authority and are willing to bear substantial burdens, both financial and personal, to exercise it effectively.

LOSING THE CURRICULUM LOTTERY

The very young child from the poor or working family also tends at first to see his or her parent as an authority figure, and much in the manner of the middle class. The parent is protector, teacher, and advocate, mediating every challenge and change in the child's environment. The child knows where the parent stands, and the parent governs. Furthermore, this authority is the very glue of the family; in Simon's terms, it is the essential vehicle of decision for all those cases needing a decision for the collective good.[31]

This application of Simon's insight to the family invites a second borrowing, this time from James Coleman, who compared the effects of Catholic, private, and public schools that enroll children from various social backgrounds. My application of his conclusion will be a bit of an extension; his own focus was more upon the school and less upon the authority that selected the school. Coleman concluded that, for children from low-income families, the Catholic schools were the most successful, an outcome he attributed to a school's capacity to build "social capital." Later studies have confirmed this claim. What I strongly suspect is that, though choice does generate a fair harvest of social capital in the school, an even greater bounty is experienced within the family itself; it is embodied in the child and in the parent who has managed to make the school an instrument of her authority. The critical mass of cooperating humans that became a particular Catholic school was assembled by specific acts of parental responsibility—personal choices made among moral options. Such commitments do tend to make any school cohesive and effective, just as the champions of school choice claim. But in the final social calculus, that may be the lesser of their contributions.[32]

In a freely chosen relationship, the family and the school obviously influence each other, and that is all to the good, but the real payoff here could consist in the confirmation of the family as the locus of childhood authority. It is precisely in this act of self-affirmation through choice that parents generate the derivative authority of the school, making it ready to serve them in the values to be taught, and to serve the child in his or her impulse to obey. Studies of the psychosocial effects of school assignment have to date neglected this relationship between these distinctive authorities, a relation that looms more ultimate—and, I fear, even more ominous—than the spectacle of the schools separately considered. If our nation is at risk, the danger may lie less in the academic failure of particular schools than in the baneful effect of the system of assignment upon the ordinary family. How does the social capital of the family itself fare where the parent is unable to choose?[33]

Start with the perspective of the child within such a family. One September morning, she discovers herself at PS 27. She may at first mistake the school as mother's own choice, and mother may for a time encourage this impression. Inevitably, however, it dawns on the child that this was a decision made by no one at all. Worse, even if she would, the child's mother could do nothing about it; the child is here by the judgment of no human mind, and she will be so for the prime hours of the week for the next thirteen years.

The child soon grasps that her understanding of the idea of family was wrong; parents really are quite undependable as authorities and advocates. And the school has impeached not only their power but their judgment. Your mother, says the state, does not know best. What reason has our kindergartner now to credit the judgment of this adult whose ideas count for so little in the eyes of the world? I am not here suggesting that any child (or even any adult) ever ceases to experience the responsibility to search for the right way to give primary obedience and to keep on looking. This is a given in our nature. But she may well cease to check the content of second good with that specific adult who, until now, has been its only consistent cheerleader.

The child's teacher cannot become her substitute authority. Teachers are soon gone, and in any case, they must fail for all the reasons that prevent government schools — at least in this society — from delivering a coherent account of either first or second good. There can be no government version of either the practical content of the good life or even of a source of the responsibility to seek it. Nevertheless, with family now decommissioned, the child may well transfer her emotional allegiance to the school and its culture; in that event she may cease to know intelligible authority altogether. The American school can function morally as servant, but as master it can be nothing but arbitrary.

But if the child is threatened with moral anomie, consider the plight of the parent. School people sometimes picture ordinary parents as feckless, uncaring nincompoops who will not stir themselves to help their child. Since it is the educator who has stripped parents of their authority, this comes as a nice piece of irony. Still, I cannot assert that ordinary parents are today in fact responsible. In respect of school, they cannot be; they have been rendered irresponsible by definition. They have nothing to say, and they are quite sensible to save their breath. Sadly, what they cannot save is their self-respect. They watch the middle class carefully planning every move for their children with the approval and collusion of the state and the free market, and they grasp all too well where have-not parents like themselves stand in this society. No message could be more poisonous. If mothers and fathers are passive to the point of pathology, it may be that we reap what the schools have sown.

The solution obviously is not to fix someone's right answer to be imposed exclusively upon the poor—an answer that this society does not and could not possess. It is, rather, to respect and empower the ordinary parent as we have the parent of the middle class. And, please notice, I have said nothing about raising test scores, nor shall I. The point here is not one of technical mastery. It is, rather, the soul of the child and, simultaneously, of the nation. In the United States, practical support for the authority of ordinary parents and the obedience of their children would be a crucial affirmation of the dignity of families, and a positive and healing statement from this society, a bit of good news preached to the poor.

Would the poor respond with choices that intensify racial and religious hatred? Is that what empowerment does to people? My own experience is the opposite. People who are trusted tend to return that trust. A policy of parental choice would give parents and their distinctive schools every incentive to participate as equals in the unending social and moral debate. No longer forced to stand silent—compelled to be "tolerant" in the face of error—they would be invited authentically to tolerate the erring *person* and to offer him the compliment of a good argument. That is the constitutive meaning of a system of subsided parental authority—respect for persons and strong challenge among competing views of the world.

My friend the gnostic might have preferred a more uniform and compulsory school policy. For that, however, he would need a world in which more of us see the same correct answers. Meanwhile, perhaps, he can hope for the sort of transformed pluralism in which, for the first time, children of all social classes would experience the conventional rule of the parent, because that authority has finally been extended in a practical way over the school. This most truly civic response to pluralism would secure to every five-year-old the dignity of a free and saving obedience to the one coherent authority that a young child can know. It is the parent alone whose judgments can simultaneously affirm both our moral diversity and the universality of the child's responsibility to seek what is true and good.

CHAPTER TEN

The Religious Rights of Children

The law protects children outside the family much as it protects adults. In addition, children have special rights appropriate to their age: the state forbids their neglect and guarantees them education, medical care, and the like. The crucial right that society denies to children is that of autonomy—the right to decide for oneself. The exceptions to this are few.

Normally, the adult is sovereign and, absent abuse or neglect, that adult is usually the parent. Society makes the parent into legislature, court, and sheriff for the child. Parents set the rules and may use reasonable coercion to enforce them. The case of religious behavior is no exception. As Justice Douglas complained in the Amish education cases, the religious freedoms recognized by the Supreme Court have been those of adults. No child has yet invoked the free exercise clause to challenge a parental decision to require or forbid specific religious activity.

Nonetheless, this autocratic rule can properly be understood as a regime of children's rights, including religious liberty. Indeed, this adult regime constitutes an entitlement unique to children—the right to a parental sovereign. It is aggressively paradoxical in nature, for it is a "right" to be dominated by another.

This assertion, however, implies no contradiction, because adult dominion is inevitable. Children are not born with the capacity for

Originally published in *Religious Human Rights in Global Perspectives*, ed. John Witte Jr. and Johan D. van der Vyver (The Hague: Kluwer Law International, 1996), 157–74 authentic autonomy. In their early teens, some acquire a maturity that might allow self-determination. Even for the precocious, however, the requirements of the adult world—physical, intellectual, economic—make autonomy an unrealistic ideal.

The practical question is which adult should define the good life—the bureaucrat, the teacher, or the parent? Someone big will decide whether tiny Alice goes to work, to bed, or to Sunday school. Radical liberationists reject this premise, insisting that children *could* be self-determining; it is precisely for want of autonomy that they are vulnerable. Yet what use can a nine-year-old make of a freedom to quit school, to take a job, to "divorce" her parents, and live an independent life? I will go this far with the Kiddie Libbers: *the liberty of children is worth protecting.* But this protection will not come by allowing the child to dump the parents. Just *how* to secure optimal self-determination and just how this might affect religious liberty are difficult questions.

The child has an interest in exercising personal judgment and control in particular matters, and these multiply over time. The specific opportunities come to the child in the form of licenses granted by some adult. Parents or the state select those matters about which the child may decide. Today a girl is given the option to play, read, or watch television; she may take the car, but only to the game; and, if she goes, she must be home by 10:30 p.m. These "petty liberties" are limited and revocable.

This tempered but authentic self-determination is a thoroughly Christian notion. Children become moral beings from the age of reason. And, no matter which adult sovereign may dominate daily life, in the crucial matter of conscience the rational child remains a truly free agent. Even though, from inexperience or adult misinformation, the child may mistake the objective good in a given situation, he remains responsible to look for correct answers and to pursue them. This obligation is identical to that of the adult, for all of us are wholly capable of *seeking* the authentic good. It is by this diligent quest that moral self-perfection is achieved.

Every rational agent, of every age, is a full-fledged participant in the economy of salvation. Christians express this idea in different ways, but recognition of the adult-like responsibility of the child is at least as old as St. Augustine. Any theory of childhood that would diminish moral responsibility would be problematic to most Christians.

This premise of practical accountability justifies widening the zones of petty liberty as the child becomes more competent. To be sure, limited self-determination regarding sports, hours, diet, and the like may not directly raise issues of conscience, and the exercise of personal freedom, even in trivial matters, inevitably raises a moral challenge. But to inject a child into moral conflict beyond his grasp will seldom advance his general capacity for the social exercise of liberty. The key is to subordinate the child to that adult who will select and ration petty liberties in a manner that best nourishes the capacity of *this child* for moral autonomy. What sort of person is best equipped to regulate this mix of freedom and dominion?

Three general criteria help to identify the adult who decides for the child: knowledge, caring, and accountability. Adult responsibility for children requires both personal knowledge of *this* child and professional knowledge of children as a class. Ordinarily these two forms of insight are held by different adults. In general, the parental form of knowledge best equips the adults to choose the appropriate course of action. Professional opinion is important, but it is the adult with direct empathic insight who—by uniting both forms of knowledge in himself—becomes the best person to choose. Parents assimilate the opinions of others and best select among the possibilities they identify, drawing upon professional wisdom for their own purposes. Parental insight, by contrast, is not easily transferable to the professional. The parent, like the client of the lawyer or architect, may be in a weaker position originally to identify the options, but in a superior position to decide among those given. Professionals are more helpful as servants than as masters.

"Caring" is the concern of the adult for *this* child as distinguished from children as a class. Caring improves decisions by keeping the adult's attention focused over a period of time. Caring flourishes in permanent and intimate relations, but professionals cannot afford such a continuing relation with each client, nor would it be appropriate.

Though professionals who serve children are marginally affected for good or for ill by the fates of their clients, making the right decision is most important to the person who must live with the child. Thus parents are also the most accountable.

The parent best satisfies these three criteria in the vast run of cases, at least with respect to the child's liberty. The social, economic, and moral interests of parents require that the child grow toward autonomy, and most parents will strive to dispense liberty accordingly.

Parental sovereignty is the principal generator of civic virtue. Children best learn the importance of commutative and distributive justice in an environment in which adults whom they know and trust are in command. In a pluralistic society, there can be no collective vision of the good life, and hence no clear moral teaching function for government. Outside math and the physical sciences, the course of study in government schools will and must be confined to a narrow set of political ideas. The really interesting ideas about human happiness must be politically censored to avoid offense. The resulting message is that the good citizen can do whatever he or she pleases "so long as no one gets hurt"—the object of the good life is to invent one's own self-satisfying morality.

This vacuous narcissism may be politically unavoidable, but it makes no contribution to the common good. At least in a pluralistic society, public values are best secured by a vigorous market in contrasting moral ideas taught in free institutions by adults who believe in them. Children who conclude that morality is a matter of private taste are the least likely to embrace civic responsibility. It is the child imbued with strong ideas who will best contribute to social dialogue about the common good.

The reverse side of this truth is that the adult authorities that produce specific commitments simultaneously nourish the individual child's autonomy. *For it is only the belief in a real order of value that can liberate us from moral impotence.* And here we confirm the harmony of parental sovereignty with the Christian understanding of moral liberty. Western religion has for centuries accepted the rule of thumb that things run better when authority is lodged in the social unit nearest to the problem. The state needs competition and direction from labor unions, fraternal societies, trade associations, churches, and voluntary groups. But the quintessential locus of decision, the only one besides the state that is armed with legal dominion over the person, has been the family. Building upon Hebrew and Roman foundations, Christianity gradually came to prize and to nourish parental authority. It rejected categorically the systematically regimented childhood offered in Plato's *Republic.* The family had become the paradigm of subsidiarity long before the word itself was coined.

In promoting parental sovereignty, Christianity acted from its own creedal imperatives, including a theology that harmonizes authentic liberty with objective morality. It was a theology in which personal decision contributes to our justification. Fifteen hundred years of debate have convinced most Christians that God made human consent a necessary, if insufficient, element of personal salvation. The new *Catechism of the Catholic Church* puts it that "every man who . . . seeks the truth and does the will of God *in accordance with his understanding of it*, can be saved" (para. 1260; emphasis added).

In that case, it is not only the pagans who are moral peers of the believer. The child's prospects too are identical; for anyone who reaches the threshold of rationality fully recognizes this personal responsibility to seek and attempt the authentic good. And, if self-perfection is achieved, in part, by this honest quest for the correct answers, here is a vocation for which children at the age of reason are as fully equipped as any moral philosopher. St. Augustine got that part right; when he stole his neighbor's pears for the sake of evil, he freely rejected the divine invitation. The capacity to choose between self-perfection and self-corruption is democratically distributed. Children receive an adult share.

Personal salvation thus turns not upon getting the correct answers about that objective good but upon the effort to do so. Our actual choices can have different effects in the subjective and external realms. The recent papal encyclical *Veritatis splendor* allows this conclusion: Good intention and invincible ignorance cannot make an evil act good, but they can make the agent good.

The capacity for moral self-perfection thus is invulnerable to circumstance, but this does not justify social indifference to the form of the adult regime. The child is entitled to systematic subordination to that personal sovereignty that in the long run is most likely to yield a true picture of the objective moral order. For to will such subjection is the condition of his own perfection; absent good reason, it would be unjust to deny the child this arrangement. Hence society must seek and secure it—whatever it is.

Not all families agree about the details of the authentic good, nor do all children agree with their parents. Soon enough the child perceives that the parent is fallible. In due course some reject the parental code either in detail or altogether—temporarily or forever.

Still, this smorgasbord of opinion about right behavior is merely inevitable. What is contingent but worth guaranteeing is the child's experience of a sovereign who insists that our choices have moral significance and are worth arguing about. And there is no parent, however jaded, who tells her own child that he or she is entitled to invent the rules.

What no child can escape while remaining within the jurisdiction of the family is the direct and constant experience of an adult who believes that *there is a good to be grasped* and who demonstrates this belief even in the course of conflict with the child. Simply by insisting upon his own vision of the good, the parent furnishes the child with the day-to-day reminder of the basic human duty to look outside our own selves. It is in this inescapable encounter that the child constantly sees justice as an issue and experiences the personal imperative to seek its content. In accepting or rejecting that basic human vocation, the child moves toward or away from perfection.

So, in the end, what qualifies as a child's religious right? At least for Christians, I think it would consist in the social guarantee of membership in a family or family-like environment, including adults to whom the child is both close and subordinate. This very subordination is the child's best hope of experiencing the real, if petty, liberties that come coupled with the affirmation of an authentic good. Both liberty and obligation will thus be presented to the child in personal decisions made by an adult sovereign who has a profound interest in this particular child's ultimate moral autonomy.

Finally, I want to clarify the extent to which the adult sovereignty represents a practical risk of an unjust moral and religious subjugation of the child. Justice Douglas is still correct. Society has not yet recognized for the child any state-protected religious autonomy. Thus, the child who dissents from his family's religious convictions is, indeed, at risk of having his conscience violated. I see no clean escape from this, but at least three imperfect responses make this outcome tolerable.

First, the child's obligation to obey minimizes the range of moral and religious conflict. I concede that the duty is conditional. Plainly, as a free moral agent, a child is bound to apply his own reason to moral issues and to reach a personal decision; the duty to obey thus does not license servile assent to what the child perceives as wrongful acts ordered by adults. A parental command to despise your neighbor ought to be resisted by any child who recognizes this as evil. Hence, real conflict is possible. On the other hand, while embracing his primary obligation as a moral seeker, a child can be honestly unclear about the objective good in a given case. In that event he should give the parental command the benefit of a strong presumption. So long as there is *bona fide* doubt, the conscience of the obedient child is clear. Hence cases of authentic moral conflict are few.

The second imperfect justification for overriding the moral or religious dissent of children is the relative flexibility of the family, compared to the courts, in accommodating conflicting views. A child may feel a religious imperative to attend a racially integrated school; if the parent prefers the more convenient neighborhood school, something has to give. But a clean-cut rejection of conscience may be avoidable. For example, some alternative experience of racial diversity may substantially satisfy the child's concern. The family is not a civil court that must utter a simple yes or no. It can temporize, adjust, and compromise; children sometimes change their minds; so do parents. We learn from each other by joining together even when we feel momentarily and mutually oppressed.

This suggests a third and related justification. In a system of rights that makes the parent hostage to the religious preferences of children, the identity of the family is deeply compromised. It is one thing for the state to raise barriers against physical abuse and to protect the child when the family is already moribund. It would be quite another to strip ordinary parents of their authority to make the family into a representation of their own values. The family is for most of us *the* primary medium of moral expression. The parent experiences the child both as an audience and as a message to the world. In a faint echo of the divine, children are the most important *word* most of us will utter. I am willing to preserve that medium for adults at the cost of an occasional and temporary injustice to a particular child. For most children, the family—autocratic and even arbitrary—remains on balance the best hope of authentic religious liberty.

CHAPTER ELEVEN

The Sovereign Parent

How very small the very great are!
> —Thackeray, *Vanitas Vanitatum*

Does the word "law" in the United States identify anything besides the rules and commands of our federal and state governments? I will call this combination of fifty-one formal lawmakers "The State." Does it monopolize things legal? Or are there regimes that create and enforce law outside and beyond the hand of The State?

The question begs a definition of "law," and these abound. Some give the final word in human affairs to various loci of "higher" law, divine or natural. Such a view disposes of the finality and monopoly claimed for formal government. If we hope here to address any audience beyond the choir, the simplest course will be to hear and accept The State monopolist's own definition then set it against our experience. If we discover independent actors who meet his criteria, this would be interesting for its own semantic sake—and might have constitutional implication.

A common description of The State monopoly concept has law as "a general rule of external human action enforced by a sovereign political authority." Henry Maine refined this as "mentally uniting all forms of government conceiving them as stripped of every attribute except coercive force." This offers The State monopoly its best chance, and I adopt it here.

Adapted from "In Defense of the Sovereign Family," *First Things*, December 2008, 39–43

Are there, then, effective systems of command that no formal government can preempt or forbid?

Common experience is quite sufficient to address the de facto existence of such non-State entities that independently and successfully issue, then enforce, commands.

But first note the clarifying distinction between two forms of legal relation here relevant: "right" and "power." The former is the broader term declaring that a person, group, or everyone may freely engage in, or avoid, some specific activity, such as to speak, drive a car, marry. Note well that the exercise of any such right does not impinge on those of another. Let us call such rights "pure."

The term "power" identifies a subcategory of rights whose exercise does affect the rights of another. Consider this view of "power" from a current legal dictionary: "The ability . . . to alter by an act of will, the rights, duties, liabilities, or other legal relations . . . of another." Recalling our definition of "law" as "the consistently successful command," the affinity is obvious and will be central to this essay.

SOVEREIGNS GALORE?

Various religions flourishing in the United States have rules for clergy and believers that are assumed by many to constitute "law." In some Christian versions, they are entitled "canon law"; Jews and Muslims often invoke similar rules of their own. Do these private organizations then qualify as specimens of independent lawmakers in the positivist sense here assumed? I think not; such organizations have no capacity to use force on offenders; they must resort to civil authority. Where there is irresolvable conflict, the enforcement of the organization's right depends on The State. True, the U.S. Supreme Court has decided that a church's control of property may be according to interpretation of rules set by their own authorities, but the *enforcement* that will be necessary will be the work of civil authority—The State. Consider, then, the notion of individual self-imposed legislation. I find it totally unconvincing. The extreme individualist—Thoreau or Ayn Rand, for example—might give him- or herself "law" in some poetic sense, but the positivist cannot accept law as a command purely self-initiated and imposed. He needs

Jones acting as a practical sovereign, successfully ordering Swanson to do his will. For the secular modernist, a discrete human authority plus reasonably consistent obedience by the subject are necessary elements.

International law is more plausible. The individual State is limited in its choices of what can appear an extrinsic hovering order of nations. The State monopolist here dissents, urging that the law of nations today exists only by The State's free agreement. I'm not so sure. For centuries, nations, quite without agreement, have recognized themselves as bound to refrain from certain forms of violence and/or even to rescue the victims of "lawless" states and punish the offenders. True, such "natural" or "divine" rules could be, and have been, domesticated by formal government adoption. I'm not convinced that such adoption cancels the existential reality of the original source, but, again, God and Nature are outside this inquiry. Perhaps others will find some clearer picture. I have not, and international law will not be our focus.

More plausible are Native American tribes — at least some of them. The more likely could be those described by treaty as "nation" and, perhaps, "sovereign." The words vary widely, but the concept of lawmaker seems as well satisfied for some tribes as for The State. This apparent dominion, however, can seem subject to review by federal courts. Twenty years ago, the Supreme Court held that a certain tribe lacked the authority to pluck a "native-born" infant from a nontribal adoptive home far removed in culture from the origin she had scarcely known. Still, this decision can be understood as no more than the inescapable act of identifying the "real" parents, then stepping aside to let these adults exercise authority. Next time this could be the tribal parents. In any case, the effect of such contests seems largely "academic" in contrast to such non-State powers as we witness in daily life.

LAW'S LITTLE ACRES

We are looking for instances in which Smith holds his place among lawmakers by being the law for Jones — his subject. Initially this two-party relation can seem an odd and uncomfortable example of law.

Instinctively, we shun historical specimens of personal dominance; the end to human slavery in the United States might even appear a happy effect of State monopoly. But, imagine instead the case where Smith is not the owner but the parent of Jones, a person below the "age of emancipation." By our chosen definition, could the parent be an authentic lawmaker for the child? Are there insular systems of real law operating behind domestic doors?

It would seem exactly so. As the Supreme Court has consistently decided since 1925, the parent decrees, commands, and enforces without interference. This domestic jurisdiction extends even to the child's mind and body; the parent chooses freely from a broad universe of commands and permissions, all outside the scope of The State. I emphasize the parent as distinguished from the cluster we call "family." The family, as such, does not make law. The locus of command is the individual adult; the subject person is the son or daughter. That is how it is with things legal.

Consider Alice, who has two boys, five and fifteen. The younger, Leroy, she rouses at 6:30 a.m., presenting the clothes he will wear. He is ordered (if nicely) to fetch the paper. She decides on breakfast, lunch, and dinner, and, when she chooses, makes him sit until he finishes his portion. She cuts his hair, or doesn't, as she decides. He must listen to her music, watch her choices on television, recite the alphabet, attend church, and sing the hymns. She sends him to kindergarten at the church school and to bed at nine. When she deems it morally necessary, she spanks his bottom. Leroy may not play with a certain boy next door.

Her fifteen-year-old she tells to do his homework, wash the car, eat his spinach, and come along with the rest to church. When he balks, she reminds him that he will soon be eligible to try for a driver's license—with her permission. He'd like to try out for football; here too she will say yes or no. On rare occasions she even makes The State the agent of her will; last week, when the teen ran away, the police had to find and deliver him to home.

If Alice has a daughter, the latter's surprise pregnancy may or may not present an exception. But, if abortion is the child's own legal choice, it is her only one until emancipation. And, do note that this specific act of dominion over the fetus (child?) will, for many Americans, make the teenager herself a sovereign locus of law—of power over another.

Parents are an embodied unity of those three powers that our fifty-one constitutions otherwise keep separate from one another. The parent is, to his and/or her child, a government more empowered than a legislature, executive, or judiciary. Alice is what we might call a *parentarchy* or *parentocracy*. She is legislator, executive, and judge. She makes and administers rules, adjudicates infractions, and executes corrections. The parent constitutes a uniquely integrated system of law.

Too often this reality escapes the mind of the monopolist, who takes refuge in an increasingly common slogan. Parental rule, he tells us, is merely a borrowing or "delegation" from The State. Though the law recognizes that The State itself lacks authority even to define (much less impose) any specific version of the good life upon the child, somehow for the monopolist it is only by the implied permission of Arkansas or Maine that the parent herself may do so. In his eyes, The State anoints the parent its agent to make and enforce decisions for which it is itself incompetent.

This confidence in a non sequitur is vexing enough, but is compounded as the same statist at day's end returns to a suburban world where he exercises a jealous and exclusive dominion over the minds and bodies of his own children. The State has no power to replace him in defining the good life. I applaud and have practiced this private hegemony. I only wonder how the next morning the same mind resumes its conviction that other parents received their portfolios from Alabama or Utah. There is nothing in U.S. history, law, or even logic to support this.

The domestic sovereignty is, of course, a hodgepodge. Individual parents legislate strongly conflicting visions of truth and the good life and impose their own regimen to encourage the child's endorsement of their adult project. Every such package of rules will offend somebody, but this only sharpens the point. Our question here is not who is the best decider for Susie, but who is the final decider. And no post hoc claim of a delegation from Leviathan to Susie can establish in The State those powers it never enjoyed in the first place. The definition of law as pure command cannot, either in theory or practice, dethrone the American parent, who, in respect of minor children, starts and remains the locus of authority. Thus perishes any hope for a State monopoly of law. But so what? We have here merely recognized the existence of 80 million diverse American parentocracies, each unique. But does their disparate and independent jurisdiction bear upon anything practical?

DOES IT MATTER?

This radical domestic pluralism holds, in part, because the U.S. Constitution does not refer to parent, child, or family. The Declaration of

Independence and the *Federalist Papers* are equally barren. The California state constitution (perhaps typical) refers to children but once, and then only to encourage legislative aid for orphans, abandoned children, and "children of a father who is incapacitated."

Why were our Founders laconic about so fundamental a legal reality as parental authority? So far as 1787 is concerned, the answer seems clear enough. Americans saw no need to express the obvious. The federal constitution was expressly a grant of limited jurisdiction: as for the original states, restraint in their drafting of their own basic texts would, I suspect, confirm this universal assumption. For the common mind of the late colonial American, it was not the parent but The State itself whose jurisdiction would need to be justified by any new and specific social contracts. That any such artifice could, if it chose, redesign the legal relation of parents to their children is a notion that could never have occurred to such people. Even where adoption has occurred, the child is the legal subject of his or her new parent. The State chooses to whom the child best becomes subordinate, acting only as agent of the child's own right.

It would in fact take a good deal of nineteenth- and twentieth-century incubation before anyone could suggest that Plato might have been correct about a general threat to civil order posed by parental law-making autonomy. Even in 1850, Tocqueville could remark the chummy informality of the American family only after he had stressed that "the father then does without opposition, exercise the domestic dictatorship which his sons' weakness makes necessary." To be sure, the various cults of social absolutism were soon abroad, and John Dewey would have his day. He might be having it yet but for enthusiasts in Oregon who, in 1920, took The State monopoly of compulsory schooling so seriously as to try to depose the parent altogether. That was a miscalculation, as even Oliver Wendell Holmes Jr. would concur in the *Pierce* decision in 1925 (quaintly confirming his own sire as *Autocrat of the Breakfast Table*). The agitated court reeled off half a dozen slogans ever dear to parent-champions and still much in play. The American child may be on his way to ultimate personal autonomy, but so long as he is technically an infant, it is parents who "direct his destiny."

Pierce is famously uneasy in its constitutional foundation. The Court at the time was deep in its campaign to rescue the individual from State regulation in both commerce and culture. The judicial weapon of preference was the due process clause tucked in to the Fourteenth Amendment, which specifically limited the states after 1868.

The free market aspect of this judicial tilt was soon to evaporate, but today, as the seed of the *Pierce* insight continues to flower, the Fourteenth Amendment very gradually recognizes more of the guarantees discoverable in the first ten Amendments to the U.S. Constitution (Bill of Rights). Only rarely is there a cautionary judicial word for *Pierce* and its broad view of parental authority (as we shall see, Justice Scalia was a distinguished exception).

To be sure, many a modern "child welfare" case rests upon public authority to correct particular wrongful acts of the parent—all forbidden also to The State itself. The significance of this child welfare aspect of law is threefold. First, it is a picture of minimalism. The child will by right be fed, housed, medicated, and educated, but, beyond the bare essentials, the parent decides where and how—and how much more. In this universe of child welfare, The State's zone of intervention—its "police power"—is a fragment.

Second, judicial rhetoric that distinguishes parent and State roles is always suggestive of the domestic sovereignty. Opinions, majority and dissenting, recognize The State's emergency role as being "in loco parentis," often coupled with reminders of "the private realm of family life that The State cannot enter" and that has its own order of authority.

Third, the emergence of more specific "children's rights" entails no corresponding expansion of State power. Again, these are rights of the child himself: The State becomes the child's steward, and its intervention can only be characterized not as a power but as *duty*. The child is entitled to The State's protection; The State is encumbered with a responsibility. Of course, these rights of the child run against parents also; as with The State, the parent here is not the commander. Where some right of the child is violated, there is symmetry between the legal impotence of the parent and the legal responsibility of The State.

But no right of the child is an occasion of his own authority. Parents may in fact cease to command, but there is no trace of an infantocracy. When a claim is made on his behalf, whatever his own wishes, the child receives the welfare due him as determined by some adult. He will, perhaps, be consulted, but he does not decide. And, if neither State, parent, nor child commands in these cases, whence come these duties for State and parent? Here it becomes difficult to avoid ideas forbidden by any command theory of law—ideas about a more ultimate commander. But I promised not to go there and settle here for this existential picture.

Once we grasp that The State's role is limited to the duty to rescue the child, conceptual difficulties diminish. The parent remains the general authority, but the child's right does make certain commands and neglect forbidden; in such cases, the parent and The State both bear important responsibilities. In the argot of contemporary law, The State has only *duties*, the child has only *rights*, and the parent has species of both plus those rights that are also *powers* of his or her unique office. Put in terms of force and command, with the exception of certain children's rights, the parent is law.

BEING STRUCK BY THE RIGHT NOTE

What the parent, then, claims is the power during childhood to enforce rules of his or her own broad choice. This power is limited only at the physical, intellectual, and moral extremes. The boundaries that distinguish the parental from the government zone do deserve continuing attention in the interest of child protection, but this project is one of clarification and never of domination by artificial government. The effect is a symmetry that can elude us only so long as we focus only upon the multiplication of specific rights of children. Whatever these minimal guarantees prove to be, their significance is dwarfed by the great menagerie of autonomous commands available to parents. In the diverse cultures of American childhood, the parentocracy is perfectly at home and, I think, secure.

It will be a civic blessing to begin stressing and believing this. It is a confirmation the public deserves to hear more often. And, if lawyers say it well enough, judges may discover new resources in their endless dialogue about jurisdiction. Courts will be asked on occasion to reexamine the limits of the parentocracy; in the child's interest these will expand here and contract there. I predict an overall expansion of parent's choice. Wealth and technology will constantly present new options for parents of various circumstance and opinion. All but the extreme will lie within their zone of command. For example, the constitutional boundaries of home schooling should expand as the indirect consequence of the educational versatility of the internet; the current multiplication of home schools is an intimation. Conversely, by 2030 some state's antispanking statute may have a chance of approval by the Supreme Court.

Imagine this scenario. A ban on spanking in Pennsyltucky raises the Fourteenth Amendment issues of free expression, religious liberty, and the whole treasure trove now resting on *Pierce*. Its constitutional challenge is plausible. However, the primary significance of any such litigation will depend less on who wins, or even which provisions of the U.S. Constitution are featured, than upon which of the two master images of parent and State come to dominate the consciousness and discourse of the justices. The choice is between the myth of "delegation" of powers to parents from The State and the preexisting reality of a parentocracy limited only by a passel of children's rights. Delegation theory would have the justices picture the spanking ban as The State's partial withdrawal of its previous license (delegation) to the parent. Whoever wins the particular case, adoption of such a legal worldview would essentially cancel the separation of parent and State that is central to the *Pierce* inheritance.

The alternative is to reaffirm the Founders' apparent assumption that any rights of children constitute exceptions to what is an extant and general parental dominion. So long as such a primary legal authority is distinct and assured, one could accept a no-spank zone in good humor. Of course, rich political theater would follow such an outcome—reformers chanting that parents may no longer take the law into their own hands, parents lamenting that here their hands are the law. The idea of The State's policing parents in such matters conjures the delights of Prohibition. De facto parental "violence" would quietly shift to more subtle and calculated techniques of persuasion—all equally painful to the child. Counteradaptation by State legislators would then begin to specify more and more details of what constitutes cruelty. Eventually, a dutiful officer would arrest Alice for instructively squeezing some accessible part of Leroy. We would all revisit Dickens's assessment of the law as an "ass."

This sparing of the rod and similar crises will invite collective focus upon the parent's historical claim to be a distinctive species of power—

of law itself. The judicial denouement will come in an epic clash over the teaching of the good life by The State to the school child. In this public educator's tale, The State requires and provides universal education, but an older story lingers in which the parents and their chosen teacher were the child's educators, and The State, when needed, their invaluable aide. School is, of course, a right of the child himself; at the same time its character is within the choice of the parent, or in the rare case of necessity, of The State as substitute—again "in loco parentis." All may agree that schooling is "compulsory," but in our jurisprudence, the parent retains her legal dominion and delegates the child's schooling to a teacher she chooses—or does it herself at home. She has, then, both powers and duties; the State has duty only; the child has simply rights. Alice remains the active source and enforcer of her child's law.

"Substance," Scalia, and School

However, for lower-income parents who cannot afford their own best choices, The State is tempted to frustrate and simply preempt their exercise of power. It has done so in its design of compulsory education. It holds the common purse and locates its "public" schools in or near clusters of family residence. In theory it concedes (as it must) the parents' constitutional authority to decide on the teacher, but this power can be exercised only with wealth sufficient either to take up the necessary residence that is served by their preferred State school or to pay tuition. Beverly Hills High is "public" to your child—if you can afford the house.

By instituting this very efficient mechanism of social, economic, and often racial, division, The State enhances the wealth and isolation of the suburb while beguiling our civil conscience with the misnomer "public." Meanwhile, the sovereignty of the nonrich parent is simultaneously affirmed and frustrated; the parent is hailed and her child conscripted. In effect, *The State has revived for parental choice the property qualification once attached to the citizen's right to vote.*

Public schooling was designed in the nineteenth century to cloister the children of unadmired low-income immigrants, thus to shield the student from un-American ideas, civil and religious. Such parents were deemed a social and civic problem, close cousin to the freed slaves; the nation needed to repair the mental and civic damage they had wrought upon their own children. Today we can recognize the systemic effect of this indenture upon the parent herself as an independent and personal locus of responsibility and power. Any general awakening to this intellectual and civic catastrophe should help twenty-first-century courts, federal and state, to address the reality that is our school system.

The judiciary could begin by resolving what has been a puzzle for a passel of good judicial minds, and, in the process aid the rescue of the authority of the lower-income parent. The late Justice Antonin Scalia is the obvious example of our doubter. Although he recognized parental sovereignty, he could not allow that the words "due process" are sufficient to justify its protection by federal courts. For him this phase was sufficient only to secure a hearing; the plaintiff must then show that the right/power asserted is grounded, not in mere process but in specific constitutional "substance." The *Pierce* decision protecting the parents' choice of private school was, for Scalia, merely an odd and feeble survivor of the notion—dead since the 1930s—that these two words by themselves protected business from excessive government regulation.

In 2000, in *Troxel v. Granville*—a case invoking *Pierce* and the Fourteenth Amendment—the Court disapproved of the application of a Washington State statute that gave its courts the authority to order visitation of a child living in the family home by a person not approved by the parent. More specifically, the Court recognized and enforced the parents' power to exclude a person whose visit the state court had considered to be in the child's best interest.

Scalia dissented, even though he still recognized and applauded independent parental authority. His stance in *Troxel* can appear puzzling, even contradictory. It had two aspects, the first was his blasting the use of due process to protect an interest not shown protected by some "substantive" constitutional guarantee. Next, however, he argued that, in any case, protection of parental power should, by wise judicial discretion, be left to political (nonjudicial) discourse and decision. Yes, "the state has no power to interfere with parents' authority over their children," but courts are not the place to correct bureaucratic invasion of such complex, disputed, and unenumerated powers. Leave it all to the legislatures and politics.

Satisfying Scalia's concern for "substance" would not cure this second worry about the Court's inaptness for such disputes with the risk of judicial overreach. But, I rather suppose that members of the "new" Supreme Court could find it encouraging to be reminded of the truly substantive and final parental power whose disregard Scalia deemed unjusticiable. State courts frequently decide such claims, recognizing and protecting parental choices that are beyond the powers of formal government.

Finally, there are other constitutional resources apart from due process that encourage judges to protect the parent's role. One yet untried is the apparent relation between the Ninth and Tenth Amendments. The former reads:

> The enumeration . . . of certain rights, shall not be construed to deny or disparage others retained by the people.

A few justices have found these words a resource for the defense of unstated but—to them—discernible and protected individual choices, for example, that of abortion. This has been frequently criticized but remains plausible. And note that with scant linguistic strain these words could be found to protect those "rights" that are also *powers*. Such an insight might seem supported by the Tenth Amendment, which speaks of protected powers "reserved . . . to the People." True, most scholars have seen this expression as a mere political gesture without practical application. But, powers, as noted, are a breed of rights and could, with no linguistic strain, be seen as protected by the Ninth. The idea seems worth pursuit, and would be encouraged by skillful presentation to the justices of the empirical and historical reality of parental lawmaking and sovereignty. In any event, this genuineness of parental supremacy could seem sufficient to identify the substance of the *Pierce* right/power and give it the full protection of the process due it under the Fourteenth Amendment.

Conclusion

Exit, with Spirit

With firmness in the right as God
gives us to see the right.
— Abraham Lincoln, Second Inaugural Address

For four centuries, beginning with the Reformation, the laws of individual European nations and the American colonies tended to maintain either a love or hate relationship with specific and conflicting religious belief and (in some nations) with religion itself as a subject appropriate to the mind of the school child. Even recently, the European picture was a hodgepodge. Unlike Imperial Russia, the Soviet Union and its satellites were to encourage atheism in their schools for seventy years with evident effect. In other nations, religion was publicly cherished and its study mandatory, but often only the particular faith of an established church, excluding conflicting ideas from the curriculum and even denigrating others creeds and their believers.

In the last century, with the Netherlands in the lead, European governments have, in considerable part, withdrawn from the role of sectarian patriarch and censor. Their law has impressively transferred more decisions about the school to the family, financially supporting the parental preference. In various EU countries and Great Britain, parents can choose the school representing the belief—religious, nonreligious, even antireligious—that matches their own.

Historically in the United States, unfortunately, such reform regressed. In my own time, the First Amendment was reread to close off, in public schools, all that vaguely Protestant teaching that, since public

education began in mid-nineteenth century, had been the de facto reality in most states. This policy had become standard, even in spite of
constitutional ("Blaine") amendments that, as the law of half the states,
in so many words, forbade public assistance to any school teaching religion (and, in recent years, have been commonly used as a weapon in
litigation challenging such aid). Today, despite the positive trends favoring increasing parental choice, in both education policy and the law,
most families who cannot afford private schools will have their children
educated in schools that foreclose any discussion of the God their parents worship or reject.

What can we say to the comfortable suburbanite who responds,
"Go talk to the Supreme Court," or, perhaps, "Consider the balancing
advantage of the city child on whom more is spent than on the kids here
in the suburbs"? The latter point is sometimes factually true, and today
there is no case to be made that large urban districts are today systematically victims of dollar discrimination: some are, some are not. The
primary victim of public education is not the occasional underfunded
school, district, or its students. It is the poor and working family and its
child, the latter drafted and locked up for an experience designed by
"the public" simply for lack of parents' access to the dollars about to be
spent on the child in PS 99, often an amount that might have paid for
two desks in St. Aloysius or John Dewey.

It would be no extravagance or injustice to label this "public" system an invasion of the parents' (and child's) right of custody, a charge
that in all other cases of outside interference with that right is resolved
by the courts in favor of "the child's best interest." After all, the school
child is in effect seized by a stranger who has no legal right to determine
where or with whom she lives, or even where she goes to school—that
is, if the parent is not in fact too poor to exercise that responsibility
and authority. It is the *parent's economic status*—not "the child's best
interest"—that determines the custody, control, and ideological diet of
Suzie for a very large and crucial portion of her life. It would be quite
rational and fair, whenever the parentally preferred school appears to
the social worker to be subminimal in quality, to ask the family court
whether this choice is in the best interest of Johnny. But it is absurd to
assume that choices made by the poor will be systematically harmful.
And this is even more true when the alternative and dominating (but
silent) assumption then must be that his best interest is served by the

accident of an assignment to some school determined by his family's address on the east side of Fifty-First Street.

Of course, historically, society has rather consistently doubted the good judgment of the poor. To a degree this is understandable. The "successful" among us—we with station or wealth—can easily suppose that we deserve especially to be trusted. When functioning at its best, this nation has resisted this inclination. Over the course of two centuries, the United States has, bit by bit (with important bungles), devised legal structures that are at least intended to smooth the playing field for all citizens. I accept the general sincerity of those who profess a vision of "equality" while instinctively viewing the well-off as especially trustworthy, but I am intensely puzzled by the manner of government's mindless adoption and implementation of that assumption. And I cringe at the scene of a school system that remains radically and systematically unjust in so many ways that could be reexamined and fixed in the best interest of all—with the possible exceptions of the teachers' unions and the public school bureaucracies.

Over the years, my work on law and education has focused on alternate remedies for various of these inequalities—each such model designed to subsidize the choice for all lower-income parents among *all* lawful schools, public and private, religious and otherwise that wish to participate. My trust of parents' batting average in governance of the child over the assignment by the chance of address will be mistaken by some as another liberal plug for "equality" of social class to be imposed through government. Let us be clear that our present system is exactly that in theory—all children getting the advantage of public schools—that is, of some particular "standard" school, designed to elevate all children alike to a state of national equality. But "equality before the law" is an especially tricky notion. It is doubtless an important concept, but one that can be made to mean no more than "like cases deserve like treatment." The present regime is defensible in these terms: the wealthy are treated like the poor; they go to their local school. And Beverly Hills has a mission and tools identical to those of Compton. Okay, but now we see that the problem with treating all like cases alike is that minds disagree about what "fact" is the one that will satisfy the test of sameness. I suppose the slaveowner of 1850 could have invoked such equality: "All slave owners have equal right to direct their slaves."

The word "equality" cannot itself answer the core question: Which similarities should count as categories of legal right? Often the answer is in dispute whenever society struggles to build a structure of formal propositions of law that preserve its identity as it prepares to face the challenges of the future. In the case of school choice, I am unclear what equality would mean beyond the need to finance the decisions of working-class and poor parents. The ultimate "equality" relevant here, I suggest, is that of human dignity and truly equal opportunity to have a conversation about God and about the appropriateness (or inappropriateness or even irrelevance) of religious consciousness and perspective as a fulcrum for intellectual development, and as a foundation for ethical, philosophic, and civic maturation.

In any case, thirteen school years of subordination of the parent and child to the state hardly seems good medicine to nourish the parent's will and capacity to exercise authority over the child. Having no role in society's compulsory experience for their own kids, parents' sense of responsibility atrophies; the temptation to leave the hard stuff in life to the government gradually triumphs. This moral decline affects the child as well. He sees the impotence and distance of the adult and wonders:

> What is the point of marriage and family? In fact, what is the point of seeking the good itself, at least so far as the school is able to describe it? Yes, I might become a scientist or an athlete—maybe a Wall Street broker; I could get rich and famous. Being "good" is an interesting idea, but what has it to do with my own plans? My teacher tells me we should act fairly toward others—but why?—what is my fairness anyway? And "love thy neighbor"? Who sez? You should meet my neighbor!

Children—all humans—need a serious encounter with the idea of a divine authority and the underived provenance of all matter and energy, plus an encounter with their own freedom either to honor that authority as the best they can discern it, to reject it as a false idea, or, even as free actors, to simply stake out some nonconfronting distance. They need something intelligible that they can embrace or refuse in their own lives, something more than their unchosen state school can give them. For the child of the poor, the consistent and intelligible sources of these ideas outside school can be slim. Hence the challenge of religious learning and belief are foreign and their importance misunderstood; education has not prepared the child to reflect on the transcendental and to act with a sense of responsibility to higher authority — or even thoughtfully to reject the idea. May I say it? We leave them to be religiously stupid, and to remain so in ways quite beyond repair by the occasional Sunday morning.

One may be confident that a just God would ensure a final justice that takes a loving account of invincible ignorance, but I also suppose that he would reward the best efforts of his lambs — and of their earthly adult shepherds. Parent and child alike might rise to the occasion, if we but take the trouble to recognize the civic hope invested in their freedom.

APPENDIX

Editors' note: Over the past decade, Jack Coons has continued to contribute to education policy debates (and to advocate for parental-choice policy) through more than two hundred blog posts, which are now available at reimaginEd.org. Several of these posts are included here as an appendix.

SOLDIERS AND SCHOOL CHOICE
September 2, 2014

Long, long ago I spent two years stationed at the Pentagon as a JAG officer. Early on I discovered that, daily at noon, a cadre of my fellows attended Mass down the hall, where a proper room had been set aside for the purpose. I was not surprised; even as a draftee in 1953, I had learned the U.S. Army provided opportunity, not only to visit the various chaplains, but for communal worship according to individual religious commitment. This was not just "released time"; the army paid for it all. In 1985, a federal court of appeals held this to be a constitutional duty of government.

So far as I can see, little of this policy has changed in the military, but its justification today is supported as much by the free contract that constitutes enlistment; access to religious practice is a promise of the government that is a basic tool of recruitment. In my day, the military draft made this policy of the army imperative, not only as a First Amendment responsibility but simply as a matter of justice. No Western nation would pluck a person from his home and family to serve any civic imperative without assuring that—as the requirements of his particular task allowed—he could pursue and perfect his own religious commitment through counsel, study, and communal devotion.

Or would it? Consider the American system of state-imposed education and specifically the "public" school. Schooling is compulsory; the child is drafted to serve a civic imperative. It may not be full-time duty, but for the most receptive hours of the child's days, for twelve years, the experience of being educated by unchosen strangers is intellectually and emotionally preemptive—and even dominant. Nor is there any lack of homework to conscript what remains of the day—and all of this for twelve years, a tour of duty three times that of all but a few soldiers. Schooling in this environment approaches a conscription of the mind; indeed, that is its point. Paradoxically, the experience can eventually be liberating, but within state schools it can be so only within a vision of life's purpose narrowed by the absence of transcendence. Many Americans do not regard this as liberation.

By contrast to the army—both that of 1953 and now—these state schools provide their intellectual draftees neither chaplains nor invitations to pray together in the manner of their parents (or even of their own manner). Nor do they receive instruction in the content of their own family's beliefs. If the parents can afford it, the opportunity for a more inclusive curriculum is available in a less conscriptive private school. But for the rest of American families, there is only the daily seven hours absorbing the wisdom of the intellectual descendants of John Dewey.

The charter school, though a salutary reform, is no exception; the mind of the child is still to be carefully insulated from any suggestion that the good life implicates the transcendental or even that there is such a dimension to human existence. The school may teach that some people believe such things, but it may not prefer any such idea even in the ways so familiar to the soldier. It lacks even foxholes.

The public-school draft could end its undemocratic and class separative effect with the most simple adjustment—the option for the charter school to teach religion.

As charters continue to proliferate, the recognition of their freedom to teach and practice a religious (or antireligious) faith would become the most effective liberation of the underclass in half a century. It would complete and confirm the promise of government to extend authentic school choice to every level of income—affirming that the assignment to a particular school is essentially a private decision to be unencumbered by any remnant of historical religious bias. Charters are today already largely private in their operation and completely so in their selection by families. Can government continue this crude exception to the general rule of free religious choice without confronting the First Amendment? Where is the accommodation for the transcendental that any buck private would expect and experience during compulsory attendance at his assigned post?

There are a half dozen cogent legal arguments supporting the constitutional right of conscripted school children to expect faith-based content congenial to the parent. My only purpose here has been to emphasize the relevance of the sometimes neglected reality of compulsion by government. Few among us would object to the basic requirement of schooling. But, unless some major practical impediment makes faith-based schooling inordinately costly, difficult, or dangerous, it is hard to justify the existing empire of secular compulsion except as a relic of prejudice.

It Takes a Village? No, When It Comes to Schooling, It Takes Parents
April 16, 2012

Blog editor's note: As momentum builds across the United States for expanded school choice, it is important to understand the movement's legal and philosophical foundations. For more than forty years, John E. Coons, redefinED cohost and professor of law, emeritus, University of California at Berkeley, has argued that parents — and not government — have the primary legal and moral responsibility and authority to educate their children. Coons is a powerful thinker whose reflections are best consumed slowly and with respect. Enjoy this special post.

It takes a village to raise a child — or so they say, and perhaps it's true. Humans are interdependent, and every particular village, whatever that word means, has influence, for good or ill.

But the phrase is murky and subject to many interpretations. It can be read as the quirky proposition that the village is what logicians call a "sufficient condition" of some outcome; alone, it determines the bundle of effects that will be the person called Andrew or Susie.

An equally strange interpretation converts the term into a moral proposition. The thing called "village" actually ought to raise the child, displacing all competing influence; whatever its peculiar norms and culture, the village itself is the official moral standard for child-raising. If there is strong variety among villages, this proposition would be hard to swallow. At some point one begins to grasp that — in minds that love the metaphor — the word "village" has come to imply more than the old neighborhood.

As we watch these enthusiasts, we gradually understand that this transcendence of the village is a twofold concept. First, the all-good village has morphed into an idealized version of the nation itself, but, second, the corporate mind of this perfected nation mirrors the preferences of whichever speaker is using the expression. "Village" means what he wants it to mean.

I remain thoroughly puzzled by this modern mystique so often introduced to justify our coercive assignment of children from have-not families to schools of the state. The claim seems to be that, for such a kid, it takes a village, therefore . . . Therefore what? One awaits today's favorite battle cry inviting us all to go out and occupy something, in this case the mind of the child. Let us occupy Jimmy!

In all these village slogans it seems forgotten that, in the first place, it took families to create the village. Although the village may be important, it is not the concept of village, but that of parent (as part of family) that will allow us to disentangle the intellectual mess we have made of the various relations of the child to village, to state, to parent, and to family.

This state of our culture and its favorite metaphors bears upon educational choice. We can and should celebrate "family," but in thinking about the ways in which the United States disposes of its children, we must distinguish family not only from village, but from parent. "Family" is a word useful in social science, politics, and religion, and it has diverse meanings among cultures. Only one of these meanings expresses the specific legal relation that holds between the child and one particular adult (or, at most, two) who holds the power to decide where and how the child is to be schooled. Parental authority is precisely that legal attribute lodged in the adult person who, together with the child — and generally others — constitutes the family in this society.

Here, then, is my quick take on the parent–child relation as the unique system of law that it is. By "law" here I will adopt the meaning of the most up-to-date positivist: law is "a rule of external human action enforced by a sovereign authority." The parent is exactly that sovereign authority for eighteen years in respect of her own child. This is true whether this custodial parent is single, a drop-out, homosexual, or adoptive. She alone decides that little John shall rise at 6:30 a.m., and then determines what he shall wear to the school she has chosen. She makes countless rules, and then enforces them with physical duress, including spanking. Yes, there are limits; John is born with rights. But these are few indeed, and exist only at the extreme.

And her authority is more than a delegation from that Great Village we call "the state." The state does not, and did not, delegate this authority that it never held in the first place. Simply put, in 1787 sovereign parental authority existed as a relation recognized by the common law to preexist the state. The U.S. Constitution and its "powers reserved to the people" explicitly recognize and respect such primordial authority. Recall the Tenth Amendment.

As we have seen in the history of the *Pierce* (1925) decision, the parent was and remains the practical sovereign over what will be taught the child apart from basic skills. She may choose any school or none, as the success of home and virtual schooling make plain today. As Tocqueville put it, in America the parent–child relationship is a "domestic dictatorship."

The real question for us here is how to get practical support for such authority. When we argue for choice, we can, of course, wave the flag of freedom. We should be clear, however, that this is the freedom not of the child—or even the family—but of the parent. And this parental freedom to indoctrinate the child is clearly a part of the constitutional armory of what lawyers call "speech rights." It constitutes true speech, not only in its message to the audience that is the child, but to that other audience that is the world. To choose a school is to deliver a message and exercise free speech.

The specific benefits of choice, both for the individual and the village, are too many even to name here. In our discourse, none must be lost, even as we properly praise competition and markets. My only specific example today will be the reform of the family itself and in turn, reform of the village. The empowered parent is the most promising agent of broad reform in society through restoration of the responsible American family.

Suppose that one day social psychologists at last dare to study systematically the differences it makes in family life to have or to lack practical choice in your child's schooling. Today our wealthier families cherish choice as an encouragement to family integrity and personal responsibility. To make and, then, to enforce, law for one's own child is seen as an experience good for the adult commander, the maturing child, the family, and the village. Suppose such serious academic inquiry also shows conversely that conscription of the child by the state correlates with the enveloping passivity of all parties concerned and with a general withdrawal from personal responsibility.

Will the state conscripter still argue that some great purpose is nonetheless served? What purpose?

Public Schools and the Bingo Curriculum
September 5, 2012

Among my vices is the collection of reports of conflicts between public schools and their parents over the moral and civic content of the curriculum at every level, from kindergarten through high school. These battles seldom challenge directly the reality or authority of human good. And although we disagree on which are which, we do agree that particular actions can be really right or wrong. The bitter local fights concern two sorts of issues.

The first is at the very general level. Citizens disagree about the source of the good. What is it that makes an act wrong or right? Just why is male supremacy or greed or lying evil? Who is entitled to say so, to impose duties, and then to ask government to enforce rules through law? What or who is it that makes same-sex marriage, drugs, gold mining, guns, or gossip something that the school should either encourage or censure? The answers given include scripture, natural law, and various forms of hedonism. There is a God, and he simply has willed it so, or this activity tends either to frustrate or fulfill something called human nature, or it maximizes the sum of individual pleasure.

As a moral authority, God is a subject forbidden to the school, and the claims for nature are difficult even for adults to understand. The pleasure concept by contrast is easy; it is unfortunately circular. It holds that it is our moral duty to maximize pleasure and thus minimize duty; in this escapist theme, our schools can stick to a superficial utilitarianism, but call it civic duty or the pursuit of happiness. It is an idea with no identifiable content, offensive to those parents who believe in concrete forms of the real good. It is especially galling to parent-objectors whose income leaves them no other choice of school.

The second and more frequent subject of citizen conflict is the state schools' teaching about specific behaviors, either to approve or to condemn. We witness this daily in the schools' diverse treatment of the environment, sex, animals, marriage, abortion, and national defense. If you live in a mining town, the classroom message about the environment may differ from the take in Chicago. My morning paper today tells of a seven-person school board, five of whose members are ultra-conservative Jews. Good, but in that district's schools, what is likely to be said in class about modern Israel? Many a public school (or its individual classes) simply clams up on the hot issues of life; many others take sides—if only by the wink and the nod. It depends on the teacher. This form of relentless unpredictability I call the "Bingo Curriculum."

As our national bingo dealer, America's public school is a crucial reality in the debate about school choice. The unpredictability of any specific moral curriculum plus the imposition of this random ethic upon the lower-income family, which can't escape, requires some specific and ingenious defense. I can think of none beyond that of settled habit plus the self-interest of the school establishment and the teachers' union.

SCHOOL CHOICE RESTORES PARENTAL RESPONSIBILITY
July 8, 2013

The American school system was, from its inception, a product of intolerance for human difference. Grounded in nineteenth-century religious and cultural prejudice, it was artfully designed to assure no government resource would end up supporting the teaching of religious or cultural notions that were uncongenial to the Protestant majority. Carefully limited by the constitutions of various U.S. states, the curriculum was centralized and sanitized in each of the states to favor the beliefs and values of the dominant group. Further, students were confined to their own school districts — indeed to their own neighborhoods — assuring (at least in the cities) that children of different social classes and races would see little of each other within government schools.

One overall effect was and is a quasi-market for the affluent: well-to-do families choose admission to the government school of their preference. By contrast, for the ordinary family, government schools are a compulsory monopoly. There are, of course, private schools, and we know from survey research and direct experience that they are very attractive to the poor. Nevertheless, though most such schools are relatively inexpensive, they can scarcely compete with the "free" government alternative. It is, therefore, remarkable that the private sector is still able to attract nearly 10 percent of the total student population; equally impressive is the proportion of these students who come from poor families who make enormous sacrifice to pay tuition. I suppose Justice Sotomayor's story suggests this reality.

The tragedy is that nineteenth-century America, a new country exploding with creativity, decided to hobble the minds and souls of its children with a system of finance and assignment that for ordinary families was, and remains, oppressive. Americans spend $800 billion each year in state-owned schools; I suspect they constitute the largest socialist enterprise outside of China.

The effects of this government monopoly upon the ordinary family have been what one would predict. The family is put under the most destructive pressures. At age five, the child is taken from the parent, who has been both friend and advocate. The child now discovers the parent is impotent to intervene. The parent learns self-contempt and withdraws from responsibility.

Whatever one's philosophical starting point, schools in the United States pose a moral issue of crisis proportions. Intellectual monopoly by the state is especially peculiar in a culture as diverse as ours. Where there is no consensus about values, it is on its face ludicrous for an ephemeral regime of bureaucrats to impose its own favorite curriculum upon everyone. The case against monopoly, however, need not rest upon pluralism. Monopoly control over value content is unjust and, in the end, will be destabilizing even in a society with a common culture. The idea of a social consensus itself rests upon an underlying conception of human freedom. That is, consensus is a clustering of beliefs that are *voluntarily held*. We value these ideas not simply for the numbers who profess them, but out of respect for the individual human persons who freely believe them. Consensus can, of course, be one among other principles of policy, but it is a very weak principle. A just government never opposes value diversity as such, but only those rare forms of diversity that threaten social order. To say diversity itself is socially destructive is merely to beg the question. It may be quite the opposite. That very issue seems to me at the heart of the problem.

In the end it boils down to this question: *Whom* do we trust to choose the ideas the child of the ordinary family will study—the family or the government? Society needs a theory of the best decider, the one who decides best for the good of individual children and for the common good.

Let us straightaway dispose of any suggestion that there are liberty rights of children that are violated by recognizing parental sovereignty. There are, to be sure, liberty *interests* of children; that is, children have an interest, first, in achieving here and now some practical autonomy in particular matters, and second, in emerging later from childhood prepared to function as an autonomous adult. Liberty is a *value* that is relevant in childhood. Children's *rights* to autonomous choice, are, nonetheless, irrelevant (at least until the teen years); that is so simply because children will in fact be dominated by adults who have the size, strength, money, and experience to do so. Thus the only useful question about liberty is which adult is most likely to exercise dominion in a manner that will effectively respect the child's interest in limited autonomy now and full emancipation later. Is the parent or the bureaucrat a more effective liberator?

I will come to the answer after noting the child obviously has other interests in addition to liberty; let us call them simply "welfare." Furthermore, society itself has a number of important interests in education that we can summarize loosely as the "common good." The question thus becomes a more general one: Who is the best decider for all the interests of the child and of society?

Focusing first upon the child's liberty interest, I suppose it is self-evident that the parent is, in general, the most likely to make a good judgment about when the individual child is ready to choose his own television programs, diet, and sports. As for the question of ultimate autonomy, I would simply ask, who is it that most wants the child to be economically, politically, and socially functioning as an independent adult? The answer is that few sane parents want to have their children permanently dependent upon them, either financially or emotionally. In theory, government should seek this same end; unfortunately, it is often in the interest of the educational and welfare professionals to keep children in continuing need of government services as often and as long as possible. Most professionals, I assume, resist this temptation, but our question here concerns not individual behavior but the design of the overall system of incentives. With all due respect for professionals, my own conclusion is the parent is in general the most likely agent of the child's "autonomy." It may seem paradoxical, but the most patriarchal of our institutions—the family—is also the most likely to serve the child's interest in liberty.

Next we should look for the decider who maximizes the child's *welfare* interest. Here I would ask three questions: Who knows the child best? Who cares the most? Who is most accountable for bad decisions? Only the first question presents any difficulty. Obviously, the parent in general knows the individual child best—his or her hopes, preferences, strengths, weaknesses, and so forth. Still, any parent is capable of self-delusion, and often the more neutral professional can be helpful and even crucial to the welfare of an individual child. The real point, however, is that the parent has one kind of valuable information, the professional has another. There is in fact no conflict between them; at least this is true so long as the professional child worker or teacher—like the architect or attorney—relates to the parent in freedom and equality through the voluntary bond of contract. The professional gives advice; the parent benefits by that advice and incorporates it into his or her own personal knowledge. If the parent can be provided such professional support, then, who in the end is the best decider? I cannot believe the superior sophistication of professionals justifies their imposing school assignments.

I pass only briefly over the importance of adult *caring* for the individual child. I do not doubt most professionals care, nor that some parents either don't care or actually care too much to be rational. On the whole, nonetheless, the emotional bond between parent and child is obviously a healthy and positive aid to decision-making. Finally, with respect to *accountability*, it is the parent who must suffer the long-range effects of bad decisions; the effect upon the school or even the teacher is by comparison both trivial and transient. In my experience, such accountability helps in the long run to produce better decisions. The parent can correct her own mistakes; last year's school teacher cannot.

The sum of it is that parents—except in rare cases—are the best judge of their own child's liberty and welfare interests. Any objections then must stem from a belief that these parental decisions that are good for the children are somehow bad for society. The critic of choice must urge us to sacrifice the child's welfare for the common good by empowering government to force the school and its curriculum upon the family. Is this a contribution to social welfare?

Such an essentially totalitarian view of education simply misunderstands where the real threat to the common good is coming from. I would ask educators to take a close look at the actual social effects of the American decision to impose "the one best system" upon children. Let them compare the public consequences of this regime to those of systems based upon the dignity and autonomy of the family. For my part, parental choice in schooling is a matter of the common good even apart from the interest of the child.

No mini-essay of this sort could spell out all the blessings of parental choice. Not only is choice a mechanism of efficiency in learning, but it also represents the only practical way of eliminating failing and destructive schools. It is the hope of introducing fresh and creative ideas in society. By encouraging different views to compete, choice protects society against its own "grand mistake." For teachers it represents the possibility at last for teaching to become an authentic profession in which client and professional relate to one another voluntarily as equals;

in this regard teachers should remember that a system that honors parents encourages parents to honor teachers and to give their political support to the proper financing of education.

For me, the decisive argument for school choice is its restoration of the ordinary family relationship. In the United States, the schools were selected originally as the instrument to drive a wedge between child and parent. They have served this divisive function all too well. In our society, it is parental choice alone that could make the family once again responsible and justify the child's confidence that, indeed, the parent is an effective friend and advocate. The family needs the chance to regain the muscle that atrophied when the state plucked its authority.

MLK and God's Schools
On August 26, 2013

I grew up in a Minnesota city of 100,000 with—in my time—one Black family. My introduction to the reality of public school segregation came in 1962 as—now at Northwestern in Chicago—I agreed to probe the public schools of the district on behalf of the U.S. Commissioner of Education. The racial separation was there as expected, but there was one big surprise; I was astonished to find enormous disparities, not only in taxable local wealth—hence spending—among the hundreds of Illinois districts, but even in individual school-by-school spending within the Chicago district itself. I wrote about both problems, sprinkling research with "action," including marches and demonstration both in Chicago and in Selma (prior to the main event there).

My interest in desegregation politics had already provoked a law review article on the risks of antitrust liability for those who were planning boycotts of private discriminators. On the strength of that essay, Jack Greenberg, then director of the NAACP Inc. Fund, invited me to meet with Dr. Martin Luther King Jr. and his lieutenants at dinner in Chicago to discuss the question. We spoke at length—mostly about boycotts but also about schools. By that time, I was already into the prospects for increasing desegregation in Chicago, partly through well-designed school choice.

I won't pretend that I recall the details of that evening. What I can say is King's mind was at the very least open to and interested in subsidies for the exercise of parental authority, which clearly he valued as a primary religious instrument. I took my older boys next evening to hear him at a South Side church and, possibly, to follow up on our conversation, but he had to cancel his appearance. We heard sermons from his colleagues, some to become and remain famous. I did not meet King again.

King's "Dream" speech does not engage specific public policy issues—on schools or anything else. Essentially a sermon, it is a condemnation of the sins of segregation and an appeal to the believer to hear scripture, with its call for indiscriminate love of neighbor, as the life-task of all who recognize the reality of divine love for us—God's image and likeness. It is purely and simply a religious appeal that declares the good society to be one that rests upon benign principles that we humans did not invent but that bind us. I don't know King's specific understanding of or attitude toward nonbelievers, but the "Dream" speech clearly rests the realization of the good society upon its recognition of our divine source and its implication of the full equality of all persons.

Given that premise and the Supreme Court's insistence upon the "wall of segregation" in the public schools, plus — on the other hand — the right of parents to choose a private religious education, the logic is rather plain.

Private schools live on tuition, and many American families couldn't afford to employ them, then or now. If low-income families were to exercise this basic human right and parental responsibility enjoyed by the rest of us, government would have to restructure schooling to ensure access to an education grounded upon, and suffused with, an authority higher than the state. Given the economic plight of so many Black parents, the only question would be how to design the system to secure parental choice without racial segregation by private educators.

And that possibility was to be the principal crutch of "civil rights" organizations in hesitating about subsidized choice.

Of course, many of their members were public school teachers who wondered about their jobs. Still, in the early 1970s, both the NAACP and the Urban League were sufficiently interested in parental choice to engage the usual suspects, including myself, to describe solutions to the apparent problem. In 1971, Steve Sugarman and I published a book that was a first crack at designing a structure that would preserve the integrity of the private school while assuring nondiscriminatory access. Others made similar proposals. The civil rights groups still dallied.

One political difficulty was media domination of the argument for choice by free-market libertarians who fretted at — and opposed — every suggestion that would in the least diminish private school control of admissions. Their narrow focus forfeited a good deal of centrist support. But the more fundamental problem was the teachers' unions, which froze at the prospect of competition and gave the civil rights groups plausible (and tangible) reason to balk. One example: in a long private conversation, Cesar Chavez expressed to me his regret that the United

Farm Workers (UFW) couldn't sign on for a popular initiative for school choice in California, because the UFW would risk the annual $200,000 they enjoyed from the American Federation of Teachers.

The idea thus remained largely a specialty of the market enthusiasts for thirty years. My guess is that King could have changed all this, precisely because of his theological focus. The problem has not gone away, and we miss him.

Faith, School Choice, and Moral Foundations
October 1, 2013

If one wishes a profound historical-dialectical account of the fate of religion in our governmental schools—all in 200 pages—make Craig S. Engelhardt's new book, *Education Reform: Confronting the Secular Ideal*, your primer.

Engelhardt's guiding principle is constant and plain. If society wants schools that nourish moral responsibility, it needs a shared premise concerning the source and ground of that responsibility, and this source must stand outside of, and sovereign to, the individual. Duty is not a personal preference; if it is real, that is because it has been instantiated by an authority external to the person. In contemporary theory, the source of such an authentic personal responsibility is often identified in ways comfortable to the secular mind. There is Kant; there is Rawls.

But in the end, the categorical imperative and the notion of an original human bargain are vaporous. We go on inventing these foundations, but, in moments of moral crisis, such devices do not provide that essential, challenging, universal insight that tells each of us he ought to put justice ahead of his own project. Only a recognition of God's authority and beneficence can, in the end, ground our grasp of moral responsibility.

This message is repeated at every turn to support the author's practical and political conviction: that the child cannot mature morally in a pedagogical framework that deliberately evades its own justification. Engelhardt shows in a convincing way that the religious premise was originally at the heart of the public school movement. Americans embraced the government school for a century precisely on the condition that it gave expression to a religious foundation of the good life. When modernism and the Supreme Court gave religion the quietus in public schools, the system serially invented substitutes, including "character education," "progressivism," and "values clarification," each of which in its way assumed but never identified a grounding source. The result: a drifting and intellectual do-it-yourself moral atmosphere, an invitation to the student to invent his own good. And all too many have accepted.

Engelhardt gives fair treatment to all players in the public school morality game. From the start he provides a generous hearing to the century and a half of well-intending and intelligent minds who paradoxically frustrated their own mission of a religious democracy, first by shortchanging the unpromising Catholic immigrant, then — step-by-step — pulling the rug from under that transcendental dimension of education that alone could serve their wholesome purpose of training democrats. In Engelhardt's book, every historical player gets to give an accounting of the good he or she intended and the arguments thought to support it; of course, the rebuttals by Engelhardt are potent and even fun to read.

My first and less basic criticism of the book is its slapdash attention to the legal paraphernalia that will be necessary to school choice if that choice is to serve the families who now enjoy it the least.

Engelhardt makes only a brief pass at describing his ideal of a voucher system. He wants to protect the identity and authority of private schools while serving all families fairly, but seems unaware of the many existing and very specific models that address this real question and strive for a balance. This, I suppose, is my opportunity to commend and recommend the expertise of my hosts in this blog, the American Center for School Choice, and its partner Step Up For Students. In this business, one eventually has to become very specific about both creating and limiting opportunities for choice.

My second criticism is substantive. The author's tight focus is on the specific role of religion in training good Americans. It asserts this goal will be achieved by assuring subsidized choice to parents of privately owned and operated schools. Its profound hope for America simply assumes that parents are the right and proper authority to decide such matters for the child. I accept this, but to leave that assumption so little analyzed seems both an invitation to the enemies of choice and an opportunity missed. There is a literature justifying the superiority of parental authority that goes far beyond the "due process" squibs of *Pierce v. Society of Sisters* (1925). That Supreme Court decision suffices to guarantee the survival of religious schools, but — like Engelhardt's book — it never addresses the substance of the claim that parental empowerment is the best hope for producing the ideal citizen, whether the parent chooses a religious or an atheist school.

For the child to experience the love, responsibility, and hope of the empowered parent is, some of us say, the wellspring of the child's own aspiration for family and for something higher than self-satisfaction. But this conviction holds regardless of the school chosen. And that broader claim deserves notice. In fact, I think Engelhardt believes it but weakens the insight by the implication that most parents will save the day by choosing the religious school.

Now, if parental sovereignty were to be recognized as a discrete source of effective moral learning at school, there could be a logical problem with Engelhardt's religious argument for choice. At least in theory, the superior outcomes he attributes to faith-based education could be simply—or at least partly—a function of the exercise of parental choice quite apart from the chosen school's message about the source of the good. And how could one argue empirically for religion as the true cause of civic devotion when religious schools today are in fact all parentally chosen? Is it not possible that those nonreligious schools that also get chosen are equally effective at producing good citizens?

The relatively few secular schools in the private sector seem to graduate their share of caring types. Meanwhile, even more confounding, in the public sector, the "civic gap" between pupils of inner-city and (chosen) suburban schools is all too evident. I strongly favor choice of faith-based schools, but our supporting policy arguments need to broaden. They must allow, and even emphasize, the real possibility that parental choice itself is the master principle. Parents with no interest in religion—and those schools that they would choose—merit recruitment for this crucial opportunity for the common good.

But, enough, Engelhardt's book deserves a positive send-off. It will be a strong influence for good.

Of Civics and "Sects": Debunking Another School Choice Myth
October 30, 2013

The American Center for School Choice (ACSC) is committed to the empowerment of all families to choose among schools public and private, secular and religious. As in all programs of government subsidy — food stamps are an example — there will be limits on the product that can be chosen; the school preferred by the parent must meet academic standards and respect civic values. Taxpayers will not subsidize the choice of any curriculum encouraging hatred or violence.

Until the 1950s, public schools could, and did, broadly profess a religious foundation for the good society, and both history and serious contemporary research report the powerful contribution of religious private schools to civic unity. Nevertheless, skeptics of parental school choice for lower-income families are inclined to worry: Are faith-based schools perhaps separatist in their influence simply by teaching — in some transcendental sense — the superiority of believers? The critics' principal target is an asserted practice of some religious schools to claim a favored access to eternal salvation for their own adherents.

If this allegation is an issue, it is not one for the lawyer; so long as a school teaches children to respect the civil law and their fellow citizens here on earth, there could be no concern of the state. It is unimaginable under either the free exercise or establishment clauses of the First Amendment (plus the Fourteenth Amendment) that government — federal or state — could undertake to censor the content of teaching simply because it includes the idea that the means of eternal salvation are accessible only to some. The state's domain is this life only, and our governments have so far properly refrained even from asking such an inappropriate question of any school.

The content of religious teaching could become relevant to government concern — and subject to regulation — only insofar as it bore upon matters temporal. Racial distinctions by employers suggest a rough parallel; the school cannot discredit the aptitude of nonbelievers for strictly earthly vocations or civic participation. It may not teach that Catholics tend to make unsatisfactory mathematicians, or that Jews can't cook. It may not warn its children to avoid personal relationships with children of nonbelievers. But note that such a limitation upon temporal stigma is not a restraint unique to religious schools; it is a standard curb on the teaching of the purely secular institution, whether this be Phillips Andover Academy or PS 97. There is really nothing peculiar here to the faith-based school.

Thus, though the opponent of school choice is correct to worry about schools teaching the temporal inferiority of any group, he is bound in sheer logic to broaden his concern to include educators public and private. Just which category of school, by design or choice, most plainly radiates the earthly inferiority of particular groups would be a delicate political issue for the secular critic himself. The obvious candidate for this odious role would be the white suburban public school.

Parents get their children there by a decision to flee the company of particular racial or economic groups whose social limitations appear to make their children unsuitable as fellow students of the worldly arts for the children of the deserter. Paradoxically, the suburban exodus leaves behind the private religious school of the city, whose alumni from all economic levels seem to satisfy anyone's definition of the good citizen. Ask Justice Sotomayor. And, if class defamation be relevant, there is no more invidious contrast than the implicit message emanating from public schools themselves about the temporal inequality of the racial and economic groups avoided. One ponders the paradox that opponents of parental schools choice choose names such as Americans United for Separation—a telling, if unintended, truism.

But, for the moment, let us suppose the critic of religious choice has a point—that distinctions about access to eternal salvation can influence decisions in the temporal world. A hypothetical Catholic shuns the Evangelical stranger because he expects him to harbor an uncivic earthly attitude deriving from some doctrine of exclusivity in salvation. Again, how different is this in temporal terms from the motivation and behavior of the suburban émigré who decided to depart the problems of the city? Call it prejudice or what you like, but the critic should not imagine this escapist attitude to be the specialty of the occasional occult and exclusivist faith-based school. Most of us can find it in the mirror.

Perhaps the ACSC's Commission on Faith-based Schools should consider a declaration regarding the relation of the diverse religious curricula of its members to the civic unity of a democratic society. Even more challenging to the critic of choice would be a declaration of the equality of all in our access to salvation. It is my strong impression that a significant majority of America's many creeds interpret the biblical assurances that "God is love" as the implicit assertion that salvation comes—not by luck—but by doing the best one can, with whatever gifts and luck he has been given, to find and live the truth.

Fear of Words Unspoken
January 3, 2014

"Talk Scheduled at Catholic School in Bronx Promotes Fear of Anti-Gay Message." So read a headline in the *New York Times* back in November 2013. The half-page article sounded an alarm that the scheduled speaker, a priest, just might give parents—and, through them, children—an understanding of good and evil that is plainly unacceptable to the *Times* and probably injurious to the child and society. The article was more an essay than reportage and, perhaps, a prototype of contemporary journalism on issues respecting personal behavior. The relevance of this professional bent for the promoters of school choice deserves a word.

Imagine the mind of the *Times* writers as they blow the cover on this looming mischief. What an exposé—Catholics are conspiring to discourage same-sex relationships! Though this threatening message was to be delivered only to parents, the journalists know that some vulnerable gay child is sure to be injured emotionally in the fallout. Indeed, the particular priest scheduled to speak "has long been involved with the Courage organization, a spiritual support group to encourage men and women to remain celibate." If there were concerns that this organization was pushing further, instead pursuing an unstated strategy of reprograming gay students, the writers provided no clues.

Hence, we were left to imagine this fear: a priest intended to "encourage" chastity. Such a threat. Beware the Inquisition! Happily, the reporters told us to take heart: "More than 200 people" signed a Facebook petition to cancel the meeting. Such a big number, and how many of them parents? It is worth noting that the journalists failed to ask those parents they did interview just what it was they had expected when they freely chose a Catholic high school, or why they did not now simply transfer to PS 209 and save the tuition while getting the message they want.

Flagship journalism frequently feels this obligation either to diminish or dominate public (or, here, even private) discussion of certain moral issues that the editors and writers consider settled. Among these is consensual sex. What one does with his or her own body by choice is, by definition, okay. All opinion to the contrary is irrelevant; hence the threatened expression by this would-be Bronx speaker should be treated like any public nuisance—as a threat to be exposed and denounced. He may have the legal right to speak, but to exercise First Amendment rights in this manner, seeking to discourage same-sex relationships, is at best de trop and, at worst, dangerous to children. It should be hissed from the stage. Bless those 200 Facebookers.

The prevalence of this attitude among these bright minds is suggestive for the politics of parental choice. First, this bent is not likely to diminish soon, partly because it arises from well-intentioned ignorance and long-engrained habits.

These "enlightened" sources appear unaware even of the crucial distinction emphasized in Catholic schools between the goodness or evil of a certain act, on the one hand, and the moral state of the actor himself, on the other. The actor may well intend what he believes to be good, mistaking the error of the objective behavior intended. In most moral theory—whether secular or theological—the actor's good intention is crucial to his own moral state quite apart from the objective evil of his act.

Unaware of this basic distinction between act and actor, the *Times* first informed us that "past Vatican messages . . . included equating homosexuality with evil." But, insist the writers, Pope Francis abandons all this. After all, the pontiff recently declined to judge a gay actor who "searches for the Lord and has a good will." The *Times*—itself apparently in a state of invincible ignorance—allows us to suppose that Francis here has declared the objective innocence of consensual homosexual behavior.

In the design of proposed statutory programs, those of us who pursue school choice may well have to take into account this profound intellectual coma of the press as a fact of life. The *Times* may never grasp that the teaching of celibacy is, in itself, no insult to the gay teenager who may in fact need moral reality and "encouragement" more than the whisper he gets to "do your own thing." From what we are told of how the Courage organization was supposed to structure its message to the school's parents, the message of celibacy to gay children was to be scarcely different in kind from the discouraging of fornication and adultery. Of course, to the *Times*, at least the former can seem merely a medical issue.

Recognition of the endurance of such journalistic miscues about morality could serve a positive public purpose. They stand as a warning to friends of parental choice that, in designing newer, freer, more democratic systems of schooling, one enduring political concern will be the extent, if any, to which the school that is freely chosen by parents will need to forgo teaching some elements of its moral curriculum in order to participate. Like it or not, there will be a voter's concern (I share it) that a school could be simply too outré or, somehow, sinister in its moral teaching to deserve public financial support of its parents. Whatever citizens see as good or evil content in any curriculum will put votes at stake.

There is deep irony in this contemporary misperception of the supposed aberrant and unpredictable content of private compared to public moral schooling, one that seems shared by most professional commentators. Of course, there is no simple metric of what counts as divergence from a mainstream curriculum or even what such a model might contain, but the scene that I seem to behold is rather different from that which terrifies the *Times* and many voters. Historically, and today, private schools have been only modestly diverse in their teaching of the morality of specific behaviors. The Ten Commandments have been a common starting place, distinguished to a degree by various local community and church codes respecting drink, dress, sociality, religious expression, and civic mission. Private high schools do, at the extremes of human behavior, tend to pass judgment upon particular forms of wealth distribution, racial relations, environmental policies, animal rights, sexual behavior, and divine worship. But, in all this, the commonality among them strongly outweighs the diversity. This is bolstered by the greater freedom of the private sector to exclude teachers whose moral message tends to the unusual. Such cases imperil both the school's intended message and the loyalty of its parents. Hence, schools actually prefer to appear centrist, at least in respect of behavior.

As I observe the moral conceptions actually taught and practiced in public schools, they have tended to be a good deal more diverse than the private sector—unpredictable even from room to room. This seeming paradox affecting formally legislated systems should not surprise us. Reigning ideas of free expression and individualism plus local custom, tenure, union protection, and — most of all — the very diverse convictions of individual teachers together make the public school moral curriculum a bit of a bingo game. One must grasp that half a century of John Dewey plus the federal judiciary has made any common moral message to children a difficult enterprise. I won't extend the point with tales of Berkeley and a half dozen other public systems known to me and my own children. The reality is evident enough in the contemporary efforts to create a "core curriculum," an enterprise that seeks to include as little as possible about morality. Insofar as the subject is even tolerated, moral talk is (and must be) diluted in deference to student "self-fulfillment," with perhaps a smuggled and unpredictable subtext of real norms of behavior largely determined, taught, and enforced by individual teachers whose own moral codes are a reality that public school hiring committees and principals can only superficially probe. It is hardly surprising if the codes taught in the private religious sector are in fact more uniform and nearer the center of general opinion.

I will not here revisit the problem of the precise wording of those moral conceptions that would be either required or excluded in a comprehensive legislated system of school choice in the private sector. That thorny business I have addressed elsewhere (several times with Stephen Sugarman). Nor will I let slip my private view of the objective morality of gay sex — the subject that prompted the *Times* essay and, in turn, my own. Let's leave it at this: Pope Francis got it right. The goodness of the person is a separate matter; his moral state cannot be judged.

As a subscriber, I do hope the *Times* begins to recognize the civil ordinariness of parents — rich and poor — who prefer private schooling with its possibly boring and predictable moral message.

Equality, "Created Equality," and the Case for School Choice
August 15, 2014

When words fail the social critic, there always remains some "inequality" to be cursed. Our numberless differences provide the happy hunting ground for those of us seeking either to praise or damn some aspect of American reality. The abstraction that is equality provides the gauge of justice for those differences we lament in the lives of Bill and Sally. Bill owns a plane; Sally takes the bus. Sally is robust; Bill is disabled. Bachelor Bill is a one-percenter; single mother Sally struggles. Bill is a man; Sally isn't. Comes then The Word: any difference in kind or degree can raise an issue of egalitarian injustice. It seldom occurs to us that, were we all to be made equally ill or impoverished, it would be difficult to claim that justice has advanced; the dead world of the classic film *On the Beach* was thoroughly equal.[1] Equality of our objective condition is, in itself, irrelevant.

Of course, early differences can, in fact, alert us to injustice, but not because we are, or should be, equal, but because some particular type and degree of difference merits that special regard that one owes his fellow human. The skeptic, of course, can doubt that one owes anything to anybody, but it is no answer to him that we are unequal. True, almost by definition, any duty to others will ordinarily involve differences of some sort, but nothing is clarified by invoking The Word. Mere difference is an empty moral vessel.

It may not in all cases seem an empty political or legal vessel. The state may act simply to reduce socioeconomic difference, hoping thereby to diminish hostility between groups. But notice that the word "thereby" signals a separate and immediate cause of the state's concern quite distinct from inequality; the group antipathy may well have originated, not from difference, but from some irrelevant historical score. Quite the same holds in private law. A poor man recklessly injures me; our difference in wealth—and, perhaps, his jealousy—are irrelevant to the issue of his responsibility.

Equality, simply as such, has been hard for the critic to defend as a demand of justice. Seeking coherence, some philosophers would substitute "fairness" as the goal; that word may not tell us much, but at least it rejects sheer difference as our favorite object of suspicion. If we could distinctively improve the condition of the most miserable citizen by simultaneously making Bill Gates richer, even John Rawls might be satisfied.

Were the Founders of the United States, then, engaging in mere wordplay when they declared us "created equal" in 1776?

After all, eleven years later, almost the same company of men were to put their names to a document that protected human slavery. Some were themselves slavers who decisively rejected equality of social station. How could this "created" form of equality be taken seriously? Only if the word "equal" in the Declaration refers to some reality of human nature quite apart from differences in our civil status, wealth, and opportunities. The concept must be taken to identify some one crucial and universal human reality, identical in each of us, one that neither shrinks nor grows with time and circumstance—even the condition of bondage. The slave may freely choose to seek the good as he is able to find and engage it, and thereby confirm his own destiny.

Given the Founders' resort to the Creator, it is difficult to ignore the theological dimension. The Declaration is an invocation of the God who apparently created us equal in some particularly crucial sense. Every human knows—he just knows—that he is responsible, and indeed invited, to look for the good, and that is our defining task. But, it is, indeed, only an invitation; we are free to decline and serve ourselves instead of divine authority. We accept the invitation by seeking the objective good and attempting to realize what we find. We make mistakes. But, as Pope Francis seems to think, our honest errors about the good do not corrupt the self that is truly seeking the right way.

Our vocation, then, is to seek the good and realize it as best we can. Anyone can do it. It is a picture of mankind as free and responsible creatures, either seeking the Creator's will or, instead, doing it my way. The choice has consequences here and hereafter. I doubt Dante's version of the latter, but that is not our subject.

Would this transcendental egalitarianism of the Founders bear in any way upon the practical hope for the expansion—the universalization—of school choice?

If we all believed it, I suspect it would. If Baptist, Evangelical, Muslim, Catholic, and Jew all saw a man's best effort as the way to eternal salvation, a politically cohesive union of minds could become a powerful national engine for change. Why is that necessary? Because historically it has seemed to many that access to God was seriously affected by particular creedal commitments. In some quarters, this was a matter of fortune; there was not a bilateral exchange; God did it all. In others, a person was to be judged by his works, and, in still others, simply by his belief. The Founders seemed to assume universal access to God, but I doubt that the free new American of 1776 could have been passive in deserving the relationship. He had to strive to find and serve the good.

A national religious consensus—not necessarily unanimity—on mankind's equality of access to God irrespective of creed (or of no creed) would largely defang the ideological objections to the subsidized choice of religious schools. Much of that ugly discourse insists that religious instruction tends to disunite, even though all the evidence is to the contrary. A solid and well-displayed allegiance of church leaders to the Founders' insight would be a great contribution to both the political side of achieving choice and to the coming and inevitable judicial challenges to the exclusion of religious schools from the widening charter sector in so many states. Is government in this country entitled—in spite of the First Amendment—to help all schools except those who would teach the Founders' belief that it was God who made us equal?

A Tale of Two Turkeys
January 6, 2015

The media report that strongman President Erdogan of Turkey has decided that children whose parents cannot afford private school will soon
be sent to state schools, there to be educated in Erdogan's own new ideal
curriculum. They will be conscripted for his vision of what every young
Turk ought to believe, including the government's version of God and
proper worship. The parents' preference apparently will be irrelevant.

This sounds familiar; henceforth, the primary difference between
the public schools in Istanbul and Kansas City will be found in the ideological curriculum that is served to the poor. In the United States, children are drafted for a school day that is stripped of every reference to
God; their Turkish counterparts—irrespective of the parents' wishes—
will have God thrust upon them. No God versus pro-God, but in both
cases, no choice for the poor.

No doubt Mr. Erdogan's own religious beliefs are intensely important to him. So long as he respects others, he should be entitled to
them. I only wonder how, as a complete stranger to the child and family,
he feels entitled—driven—to decide for his unmoneyed constituents
exactly what shall be taught to their children about God. Has the deity
bestowed upon him the insight—hence the duty—to disempower the
ordinary family, imposing upon little Muhammad the ideas provided
by government strangers who happen to be in a position to enlist him
for their own ideological enterprises?

How does a mind like Erdogan's get returned to office in what
seems at least a proto-democracy? I have no clue. But the spectacle of
Turkey invites a similar query about the Untied States and its many
Kansas Citys. Why haven't millions of parents come to the rescue of
their children by insisting politically upon relocating power in the
family through some system of financial reform? Yes, it is difficult to
organize parents of diverse experience, education, and hopes. But there
is the ballot box. Why haven't more educated parents, especially suburban, insisted upon choice for all? After all, their own choice of residence
was at least partly driven by access to a school they supposed would
transmit their own culture.

I wonder whether we have our own share of Erdogans, either somehow benefiting personally from the continued servility of the poor or/ and confident that whatever public school is teaching is the best ideological message for our less lucky citizens who, left to their own, might not choose it.

As for direct beneficiaries there is, of course, the union, whose members do profit from the servility of the family. And among our individual teachers there are those who repose in the reality that—short of calamity—their job will be secure. They are both protected from discharge and comforted by the predictable enrollment of children whose presence also assures the union its dues. I don't know about Turkey, but the servility of the lower-income urban family is a great comfort to the invertebrate American teacher.

The silence of the American suburbanite is more problematic. He had choice, and he took it. Why does he so seldom emerge as its champion? He imagines, I fear, that choice is a zero-sum game. If everybody has it, it will be self-defeating. Access to his own child's school by diverse sorts of families will subvert the very qualities he paid for when he moved. Nobody talks this way, but I suspect there is no more effective political barrier to school choice. It is a state of mind both understandable and amendable; hope for change will depend upon the insight and determination of legislators for whom many alternative models of choice are available. The basic palliative for suburban fears would be the relative freedom of schools to control admissions. By relative I suggest that, in any system of choice, 10 to 20 percent of admissions be reserved for children of lower-income families—if so many apply.

Having participated in the design of many such legislative models, I feel confident that, over time, with wise and patient politics, the middle-class family could come to appreciate better the wisdom and prudence of well-designed school choice subsidized by government. Convincing the teachers' union and President Erdogan may require stronger medicine. Happily, the awakening of the middle class should be politically sufficient. To witness the fate of Turkish children may convince us to look in the mirror.

On Teaching Human Equality
December 23, 2015

> All animals are created equal, but some animals are more equal than others.
>
> —George Orwell, *Animal Farm*
>
> All men are created equal.
>
> —Declaration of Independence

Teachers in public schools in the United States are expected to affirm the "equality" of all humans. The Founding Fathers saw it as a truth "self-evident." But if human equality were to be considered thus, as something real—a fact not fabrication—what sort of reality would it be? I confess that I have never found the metaphorical identity of equality to be "self-evident." Nonetheless, I do believe in it and will try here to make it a bit more evident here.

For equality to be a reality of our world, of what sort of stuff will it have to consist? What shared property could make me equal to you and to Mother Teresa and to Einstein—and to every baby born with Down syndrome and every vicious criminal? This common element of our being, —if it exists—must be something immune, on the one hand, to any limiting effect of individual ignorance or depravity, and, on the other, to distinctions of genius or virtue.

Happily, the one coherent description of equality has nothing to do with—but asserts the absence of—differences sometimes associated with race or other immutable human characteristics. It is rather the assertion that the specific element of the human self that can qualify all persons for what is often called "salvation" is fully active in us all, namely our freedom to choose or reject the good. This proposition is worth our elaboration for the teacher and the school who face the task of daily asserting the equal worth of every child.

Since 1776, universal equality has been a litany of politicians in the United States, though seldom with definition. As a slogan, the term seems useful to political causes ranging from free markets to socialism.

For example, it is heresy in the liberal academy to doubt that human intelligence is spread evenly among all races. I am in full agreement, but is this even relevant to the question whether equality holds for "all men" as Jefferson wrote? I fear not. Today's academy has made it an issue of the distribution of a certain feature, not of the individuals but of human groups.

So cast, the claim becomes a virtual self-contradiction. If intelligence be the stuff so important to human worth, how does it solve the egalitarian problem to measure it by groups or clusters? And what then is the implication for the dignity of less intelligent individuals in these groups? No one claims that all humans are equal in intelligence; I fear that our well-meaning "egalitarians" have shot themselves (and most of us) in the foot.

This is delicate stuff, and I propose to be understood. The many sciences of the brain are, so far, unable to determine—and thus to compare—the distributions of the genetic intellectual potential of the unborn to perform on Western measures of IQ and the ability to learn in school. Moreover, even if science one day is able to test for the IQ of the early fetus, the problem remains. Human environments are diverse and have very different effects upon the child, even before, but certainly after birth, frustrating scientific comparisons. Hence, I can only assert my unscientific conviction that the genes of children born halfway around the world are statistically indistinguishable in intellectual expectation from those of my own children and the rest of the human mob.

This in no way diminishes my angst over the damage to individuals that is wrought by the IQ fascination of our civilization. The dropout knows that brains are the thing, and necessarily worries that he is short on what the world values. If I only had a brain!

Nor has the ascendance of Darwin done the IQ egalitarians any favors. Gradually becoming the holy scripture of the public school and university, his message seems to leave us humans non-symmetrical, at least if the capacity to "survive" be understood as a personal excellence. In any case, the survival of the "fittest" places an embarrassing burden of explanation on those of Darwin's admirers who would cling to human equality as a fact while teaching children that some of us are born losers.

But this squabble over group "equality" is simply a distraction. To be real and consequential, equality must lodge in us all in some shared capacity that is not subject to the inevitable variations of genetics, material environment, and sheer luck.

My own conviction is this: Equality (if it be real) must involve a universal capacity to choose between apparent good and evil. I emphasize "apparent," because honest mistakes are inevitable, and—for equality's sake—must not diminish the self-perception achieved by the actor. Equality must be understood to consist simply in the universal human ability to honor the good as best one can—or to reject it. This idea that man's perfection lies simply in doing the best he can to find the good, then to do it, can be puzzling. The final good—the perfection of the self—becomes detached from the objective correctness of the ethical decision.

The abiding confusion about the separation is illustrated in the conclusion to Tennyson's *Ulysses*:

> . . . that which we are, we are,
> One equal temper of heroic hearts,
> Made weak by time and fate, but strong in will
> To strive, to seek, to find, and not to yield.

The problem here is "to find." Some of us (all of us) fail on occasion to find. If our honest mistakes about the focus of the good corrupt ourselves, equality is impossible, for we simply don't always get things right. Happily, there is one thing that all minds can always do; that is to strive, to seek the right path, then to act according to one's conviction. Maybe Tennyson meant exactly that. It depends on the comma after "seek"; must one actually "find" or only "seek to find."

Conversely, of course, that same equal self can, instead, freely and rationally, refuse to serve any authority but his own ego. In making decisions, he does not seek beyond it. He pursues nothing but this own apparent advantage. If, unknowingly, he chooses the authentic good, it is to his own corruption.

In this capacity to choose the good—or not—lies the possibility of human equality as something intelligible and real. Doing one's best, first to locate, then to achieve the good is an option for persons of all degrees of intelligence above zero. And, in this view, he who does try his best achieves the enrichment of his own self even as he mistakes the good.

His human opposite (and equal) freely chooses loyalty to himself only, and thereby achieves what? Dante left him in permanent torment. I would rather imagine his self-corruption as painless, inspired, and eternally boring, —just as he was in life. Dante, of course, could be right.

I think this all has practical implications. It is common for the teacher to encourage the student to seek and thereby to "find yourself." Understood as encouraging the child to think seriously about the choices we all have to make 'twixt good and evil, this is plausible pedagogy.

If, however, the teacher means—or is understood to mean—literally, "do your own thing," this is dangerous business, individually and socially. Such amoralism may rarely be the intended message of teacher or school, yet it easily slides into the ambiguous sloppy stew of ethics handed us by John Dewey, the Supreme Court, schools of education, and the acquiescence of too many of the rest of us.

Such dysfunction cries out for a curriculum of ethics more robust and transparent than "follow your own star." Of course, by our free nature, we all must and will do exactly that. But this inevitable personal journey of the human will—toward or away from virtue—will always entail free choice between the authority and invitation of a real good and its replacement and domination by the lure of the ego. The teacher should say exactly this, and offer arguments for choosing the often-hard path of the good.

It is a political curiosity that the only human equality that makes sense cannot be taught, because of the rules governing religious expression and support of education. This may be the historic moment to begin the schools' crawl back to an authoritative ethic. Whether conceived as natural law philosophy or plainspoken religion, the good society does not depend on the state to define the good life, but it rather empowers the parent to be the child's authentic star to honor and follow so long as his or her developing reason and conscience allow. It is thus that government might best honor the reality of the human equality, by giving parents the power to choose schools that reflects the view that all are created equal, and also that all have a creator. This is not the case for most families today. But the rules governing religious expression and support of family choice in education could change before our America's kindergartners are ready for their senior prom.

SCHOOL, SUCH A TRIP
On April 28, 2016

I've written before of an afternoon with Cesar Chavez at UFW head-quarters on the edge of the California desert. The year was 1981, and there was strong hope of putting a school choice initiative on the ballot.

Chavez, his nephew, and I spoke of empowering farmworkers with an educational option. On the one hand, if they wished, they could continue to educate their children in a string of disconnected public schools located in diverse districts along the seasonal harvest path north. On the other, they could choose among public and private schools that traveled in buses, either parked in coordination with the parents' location and/or actually operating in moving buses variously designed for the purpose of schooling.

Chavez was warm, receptive—and frustrated. His impediment was the annual $200,000 he received from Albert Shanker and the American Federation of Teachers (AFT). So he said, and I believed him. I suppose the AFT still protects its monopolies in similar ways. I see no legal impediment except, possibly, the antitrust laws.

Peripatetic schools in buses? I think so.

Most of the mobile schoolhouses would teach only when parked in a location convenient to the parents' current worksite. Whether the bus was equipped actually to provide education en route could be one element of choice for the parents. What would, I think, be the central advantages of either style are two: the convenience of location near the parent, and continuity of atmosphere and substance—the same room, books, teachers—everything about the school itself, plus the settling confidence of the child in the parents' proximity.

To this I would add in the reduction in systemic public costs made possible by liberating school districts from the expense and complexities of providing space and whatever other necessities—a teacher, or several—for a new gang each week or ten days. It could be a relief to all concerned to be able to offer parents a school appropriate to their child's age, and consistent in its milieu and message.

School reformers could seriously consider—as a potential reform to both policy and politics—the convening of well-publicized conferences to consider the question of the most promising forms of itinerant schools for farmworkers' children. So far as I know, they have yet to model and critique the potential variety of such novelties as tools of wise educational policy.

The politically easiest path to such reform at the moment would be various forms of charter schools. Though essentially private, they are labeled "public" and avoid constitutional menace by excluding religion. I see no barrier to the creation of a new such "public" sector by those clever folks who have given us the very successful charters in our major cities. The UFW itself would be eligible to undertake the mission. Let labor sit down with capital; they might learn from one another.

The farm laborers of California—and doubtless elsewhere—would be likely to sense an opportunity to express their religious faith to their children in a coherent curriculum. I can think of no more appealing context in which to raise, in a serious way, the issue of whether charter schools are, indeed, public in any way that forbids public assistance to parents who want religious education.

There is currently very serious thinking and writing in process to address that question—and the even broader one of a constitutional duty of government to allow such schools a practical existence as charters. After all, the power to force the poor into state institutions called "public schools" can seem a rather peculiar way to respect the First Amendment's rejection of laws "prohibiting the free exercise" of one's faith.

NOTES

Foreword by the Editors

1. Terry M. Moe, *Special Interest: Teachers Unions and America's Public Schools* (Washington, DC: Brookings, 2011), 93.

Preface

1. Michel de Montaigne, "Of Anger," in *The Essays of Michel Montaigne*, trans. Charles Cotton (London: George Bell and Sons, 1905), 2:440.

CHAPTER ONE. Intellectual Liberty and the Schools

1. A serious effort in this direction is J. R. Pole, *The Pursuit of Equality in American History* (Berkeley, CA: University of California Press, 1978). Pole's aspiration is, however, frustrated by the problem of giving equality a meaningful definition. John Rawls, *A Theory of Justice* (Cambridge, MA: Belknap Press of Harvard University Press, 1971), may be seen as broadly egalitarian. Michael Walzer, *Spheres of Justice: A Defense of Pluralism and Equality* (New York: Basic Books, 1983) is another prodigious effort to make sense of equality as explanatory. See also Ronald Dworkin, "What Is Equality?," *Philosophy and Public Affairs* 10, no. 3 (1981): 185–245; Kenneth Karst, "Why Equality Matters," *Georgia Law Review* 17, no. 2 (1983): 245–89. For the view that equality is a mere truism, see Peter Westen, "To Lure the Tarantula from Its Hole: A Response," *Columbia Law Review* 83 (1983): 1186–1208, and the series of related articles by Westen and his critics cited therein. Michael Novak, *The Spirit of Democratic Capitalism* (Lanham, MD: Madison Books, 1982); Stephen Arons, *Compelling Belief: The Culture of American Schooling* (New York: McGraw-Hill, 1986); Rogers Smith, "The Constitution and Autonomy," *Texas Law Review* 60, no. 2 (1982): 175–205;

Joel Feinberg, "Autonomy, Sovereignty, and Privacy: Moral Ideals in the Constitution?," *Notre Dame Law Review* 48 (1983): 445–92. There is, of course, an ocean of cognate literature. Even much of the "egalitarian" scholarship can be read as a type of argument for a form of individualism. This includes Rawls, *Theory of Justice,* and, explicitly, David A. J. Richards, *Sex, Drugs, Death and the Law* (Totowa, NJ: Rowman and Littlefield, 1986). Obviously, any historical focus on liberty must come to terms with slavery, but the Civil War Amendments can be read as essentially libertarian. It remains unclear that the equal protection guarantee has anything to do with substantive equality. See Robert N. Bellah, *Beyond Belief* (Berkeley, CA: University of California Press, 1970), especially chap. 9, "Civil Religion in America"; and John Courtney Murray, *We Hold These Truths* (Lanham, MD: Rowman and Littlefield, 1960). The range of interest-group analysts is described and criticized in Theodore J. Lowi, *The End of Liberalism* (New York: Norton & Company Inc. 1969). W. Norton Grubb and Marvin Lazerson, *Broken Promises: How Americans Fail Their Children* (New York: Basic Books, 1982); Samuel Bowles and Herbert Gintis, *Schooling in Capitalist America* (New York: Basic Books, 1976); David Kairys, ed., *The Politics of Law: A Progressive Critique* (New York: Pantheon Books, 1982); Roberto M. Unger, "The Critical Legal Studies Movement," *Harvard Law Review* 96 (1983): 561–675; Adam Przeworski and Michael Wallerstein, "The Structure of Class Conflict in Democratic Capitalist Societies," *American Political Science Review* 76 (1982): 215–38.

2. The Friedmans are a prominent example of the effort to use the welfare of the family unit as proxy for the welfare of individual children. See Milton Friedman and Rose Friedman, *Free to Choose: A Personal Statement* (New York: HarperCollins, 1990), especially chap. 6, "What's Wrong with Our Schools?" It seems to me that Marxism makes a similar mistake in seeing the family as an epiphenomenon of production. On this point, see Brigitte Berger and Peter Berger, *The War over the Family: Capturing the Middle Ground* (Garden City, NY: Anchor Press/Doubleday, 1983).

3. James Madison, *The Federalist,* no. 41, ed. James McClellan (1937), 339.

4. Plyler v. Doe, 457 U.S. 202 (1982). The decision held that undocumented children were entitled to educational benefits on the same terms as other children. The majority opinion is cast within a tradition now established for education cases. See Brown v. Board of Education, 347 U.S. 483 (1954). The Court repeats an encomium to the public school in terms of freedom and independence, advancement on the basis of individual merit, and other aspects of self-determination. The best exegesis of the theme that welfare rights may best be understood as protected instruments of individual political rights is Frank I. Michelman, "Welfare Rights in a Constitutional Democracy," *Wash-*

ington University Law Quarterly 1979, no. 3 (1979): 659–94; and Michelman, "On Protecting the Poor through the Fourteenth Amendment," *Harvard Law Review* 83 (1969): 7–59.

5. E.g., "Economic equality and the familiar individual rights stem from the same fundamental conception of equality as independence"; Bryan Magee, "Interview with Ronald Dworkin," from "Three Concepts of Liberalism," *New Republic* 180, no. 15 (April 14, 1979): 41, 47. See generally Dworkin, "What Is Equality?"; Rawls, *Theory of Justice*, 60. John Stuart Mill, *On Liberty*, R. B. McCallum ed. (Oxford: Oxford University Press, 1964). For Dworkin, it is "the basic liberal idea that justice must be independent of any idea of human excellence or of the good life" (see Magee, "Interview with Ronald Dworkin," 48). John Wilson describes as a "liberal notion" the idea that "we are not entitled to weigh the wills of other men by our own criteria at all"; see Wilson, *Equality* (London: Hutchinson & Co., 1966), 129. Bruce Ackerman adds that "no reason is a good reason if it requires the power holder to assert . . . that his conception of the good is better than that asserted by any of his fellow citizens"; see Ackerman, *Social Justice in the Liberal State* (New Haven, CT: Yale University Press, 1980). See Phillip E. Johnson, "Do You Sincerely Want to be Radical?," *Stanford Law Review* 36, no. 1/2 (1983): 247–92; Arthur Allen Leff, "Unspeakable Ethics, Unnatural Law," *Duke Law Journal* 1979, no. 6 (1979): 1229–50.

6. Walter Lippmann, *Essays in The Public Philosophy* (Boston: Little, Brown, and Co., 1955); Murray, *We Hold These Truths*; Pope Paul VI, *Declaration on Religious Freedom/Dignitatis humanae*, in *Vatican Council II: The Conciliar and Post Conciliar Documents*, ed. Austin Flannery and Laurence Ryan (Collegeville, MN: Liturgical Press, 1975), 799–812, and Paul VI, *On the Development of Peoples/Populorum progressio*, in ibid.

7. Tinker v. Des Moines, 393 U.S. 503 (1969). The popular thesis of a "staged" morality hypothesized by Lawrence Kohlberg (based on Piagetian psychology) may to a degree conflict with this proposition. Kohlberg has committed himself to the gnostic position that "virtue is knowledge of the good," and that "the . . . ethically higher must come later"; Kohlberg, *The Philosophy of Moral Development: Moral Stages and the Idea of Justice* (New York: Harper & Row, 1981), 1:30, 128–34, 184–87. I cannot accept the view that unlettered and intuitive moral choices count less than those of the moral savant; for me, the "ethically higher" is a possibility for all (including children of modest age and sophistication). Hence, even though Kohlberg's data are interesting for some purposes, I reject his thesis as I interpret it. The chaos in the rationalization of a liberty special to children began at least as early as Herbert Spencer, *Social Statics* (London: Chapman, 1851), chapter titled "The

Rights of Children." I recommend it as a hilarious example of nineteenth-century optimism. For cognate modern works of a more sober sort, see Laurence O. Houlgate, *The Child and The State: A Normative Theory of Juvenile Rights* (Baltimore: Johns Hopkins University Press, 1980); Christopher Lasch, *Haven in a Heartless World: The Family Besieged* (New York: Basic Books, 1977); Franklin Zimring, *The Changing Legal World of Adolescence* (New York: Free Press, 1982). In my judgment, none of these effectively analyzes the complex interrelation of the respective liberty interests of parent and child.

The most comprehensive collection of the cases is Robert H. Mnookin, *Child, Family, and State* (Boston: Little, Brown, and Co., 1978). Ginsberg v. New York, 390 U.S. 629 (1968); see also New York v. Ferber, 458 U.S. 747 (1982); People v. Chambers, 66 Ill. 2d 36, 360 N.E. 2d 55 (1976); *Tinker*, 393 U.S. 503; Lacey v. Laird, 166 Ohio St. 12, 139 N.E. 2d 25 (1956); Bellotti v. Baird, 443 U.S. 622 (1979); H. L. v. Matheson, 450 U.S. 398 (1981); Board of Educ., Island Trees Union Free School Dist., No. 26 v. Pico, 457 U.S. 853 (1982).

8. For a romantic example of the problem, see William Golding, *Lord of the Flies* (London: Faber & Faber 1954); for a possible counterexample, see Richard Hughes, *A High Wind in Jamaica* (London: Chatto & Windus, 1929). The argument that follows here is presented in a different form and at length in John E. Coons and Stephen D. Sugarman, *Education by Choice: A Case for Family Control* (Berkeley, CA: University of California Press, 1978). See also John E. Coons, "Law and the Sovereigns of Childhood," *Phi Delta Kappan* 58 (1976): 19–24.

9. There is, of course, an ocean of literature on the family and bureaucracy, but there seems to be none that directly responds empirically or even with serious analysis to the peculiar question of proxy liberty for the child. Part of the problem is the absence of common definitions for basic terms, such as autonomy. Two very thoughtful philosophical and relevant analyses of parental rights and duties are David Bridges, "Non-Paternalistic Arguments in Support of Parents' Rights," *Journal of Philosophy of Education* 18, no. 1 (1984): 55–61; and Amy Gutmann, "Children, Paternalism, and Education," *Philosophy and Public Affairs* 9 (1980): 338–58.

10. The quotation marks signal the familiar and well-regarded work of Albert O. Hirschman, *Exit, Voice, and Loyalty: Responses to Decline in Firm, Organizations and States* (Cambridge, MA: Harvard University Press, 1970).

11. The problem is dramatically represented by Parham v. J. R., 422 U.S. 584 (1979). And see *In re* Roger S., 569 P.2d 1286 (Cal. 1977). The saddest example I know is recounted in Phillip B., 139 Cal. App. 3d 188 (App. 1983). A fourteen-year-old boy with Down syndrome placed in a state institution by his parents needed heart surgery. The parents resisted, apparently on the para-

doxical ground that they feared for the child's welfare if he outlived them. The court approved a guardianship petition and ordered the operation.

12. David Bridges strikes about the right note: "Human love or altruism is rarely perfect and rarely untinged by self-interest or by that complexity of motives which arises when one finds pleasure or joy in giving to others. An account of familial relationships which is devoid of reference to love seems to me to be an impoverished one; but an account which fails to recognize that they also involve a distribution of power is unrealistic. The relationship between love and power in the family is perhaps better the subject of the literary than the philosophical imagination" (Bridges, "Non-Paternalistic Arguments," 60).

13. The contrary position is asserted in Ackerman, *Social Justice*, 139–67. The parental role is viewed as frequently hostile to autonomy, at least by comparison to the role of the liberal state as Ackerman would define it.

14. Though his own concern is broader, Bridges's view of the parental interest is certainly relevant to the liberty element: "Though this sort of parental authority is commonly justified in terms of what is in children's interest (i.e., paternalistically) it is quite reasonably and more convincingly justified in terms of mature judgement as to what is a fair balance of the interests of adults and children (i.e., to some extent nonpaternalistically). In short, parents have the right to protect themselves from what could be the overwhelming egocentrism of children" (Bridges, "Non-Paternalistic Arguments," 58).

15. See cases collected in Mnookin, *Child, Family, and State*, 277–341.

16. Prince v. Massachusetts, 321 U.S. 158 (1944). *Ferber*, 458 U.S. 747.

17. *Ginsberg*, 390 U.S. 629.

18. Carey v. Population Services International, 431 U.S. 678 (1977).

19. Meyer v. Nebraska, 262 U.S. 390 (1923). Pierce v. Society of Sisters, 268 U.S. 510 (1925). That the ordinary family experiences the public school assignment as coercive is plain from its expressed desire to exist. See generally John E. Coons, "Making Schools Public," in *Private Schools and the Public Good: Policy Alternatives for the Eighties*, ed. Edward Gaffney, ed. (Notre Dame, IN: Notre Dame University Press, 1981).

20. See, generally, David B. Tyack, *The One Best System: A History of American Urban Education* (Cambridge, MA: Harvard University Press, 1974).

21. Bridges, "Non-Paternalistic Arguments," 56.

22. On the intellectual quality of the coming generation of teachers, see W. Timothy Weaver, "In Search of Quality: The Need for Talent in Teaching," *Phi Delta Kappan* 61 (1979): 29–32. See generally C. Emily Feistritzer, *The Condition of Teaching: Report to the Carnegie Foundation for the Advancement of Teaching* (Princeton, NJ: The Carnegie Foundation for the Advancement of Teaching, 1983).

23. M. Bowler, quoted in *Monthly Memo of the Institute for Educational Leadership*, no. 25 (October 1976): 7. The most comprehensive and scholarly treatment of the current upset over book selection for schools and libraries is Robert M. O'Neil, *Classrooms in the Crossfire* (Bloomington: Indiana University Press, 1981). See also Joseph E. Bryson and Elizabeth W. Detty, *The Legal Aspect of Censorship of Public School Library and Instructional Materials* (Charlottesville, VA: Michie Publishing Co., 1982); Joseph Nocera, "The Big Book-Banning Brawl," in *New Republic*, September 13, 1982, 20. For an insightful "inside" view of the pressures constricting teachers in American high schools, see Theodore R. Sizer, *Horace's Compromise: The Dilemma of the American High School* (New York: Houghton Mifflin, 1984).

24. See Dinah Shelton, "Legislative Control over Public School Curriculum," *Willamette Law Review* 15 no. 3 (1979): 473–506. See Sizer, *Horace's Compromise*, 210. See generally O'Neil, *Classrooms in the Crossfire*. If each public schoolroom could in practice represent a true marketplace of ideas, the First Amendment criticism of the system might be blunted. The contribution of family-chosen expression would in that case remain frustrated by coercive assignment, but, if each child experienced the marketplace in his own education, arguably this could match in its benign effects the different kind of marketplace that would emerge in a system of family-chosen schools, each with its specific style and message. Realistically, however, only under special conditions can public schools become anything approaching a neutral broker of ideas. Further, at least in an era of mass media, it is the ideologically distinctive school that is most likely to contribute to the system of liberty. Of course, this holds only if it is freely chosen.

25. Robert A. Burt, "Developing Constitutional Rights of, in, and for Children," *Law & Contemporary Problems* 39, no. 3 (1975): 124. And see generally Gutmann, "Children, Paternalism, and Education"; Bridges, "Non-Paternalistic Arguments."

26. Ackerman, *Social Justice*, 159.

27. Ibid., 160n10.

28. Burt, "Developing Constitutional Rights," 124.

29. See, e.g., John Dewey, *Democracy and Education* (New York: Macmillan Co., 1916), 26; Newton Edwards and Herman G. Richey, *The School in the American Social Order*, 2nd ed. (Boston: Houghton Mifflin Co., 1963), 524–75; Joseph Tussman, *Government and the Mind* (New York: Oxford University Press, 1977). And see Mark G. Yudof, "When Governments Speak: Toward a Theory of Government Expression and the First Amendment," *Texas Law Review* 57, no. 6 (1979): 878, where the author argues, in what seems a non sequitur, that "it is precisely because public school teachers are charged with instilling values to a captive audience that the protections of academic freedom should be extended to them."

30. "Argument (Affirmative) on Official Ballot for Initiative to Amend Section 5259 Oregon Laws," reprinted in *Oregon School Cases: Complete Record* (Baltimore: Belvedere Press, 1925), 732–34. A. B. Cain, *The Oregon School Fight* (Portland, OR: A. B. Cain, 1925), 7.

31. See Plato, *Republic*, trans. B. Jowett (Cleveland, OH: World Publishing Co., 1946). As argued at length in Coons and Sugarman, *Education by Choice*.

32. *Pico,* 457 U.S. 853. *Meyer,* 262 U.S. 390. *Pierce,* 268 U.S. 510. West Virginia State Board of Education v. Barnette, 319 U.S. 624 (1943). Wisconsin v. Yoder, 406 U.S. 205 (1972). *Tinker,* 393 U.S. 503.

33. Epperson v. Arkansas, 393 U.S. 97 (1968).

34. See Engel v. Vitale, 370 U.S. 421 (1962); School Dist. of Abington Twp. v. Schempp, 374 U.S. 203 (1963). *Pico,* 457 U.S. 853.

35. *Pico,* 457 U.S. at 866–67. For detailed analysis, see Note, "The Supreme Court, 1981 Term," *Harvard Law Review* 96 (1982): 62–150.

36. In a narrower context, Laurence Tribe has described such intellectual regimen as "the special place of public schools in American life. Nothing could be more expressive of our society's commitment to a particular . . . practice than our willingness to use, as a forum for that [practice], the facilities through which basic norms are transmitted to our young"; see Tribe, *American Constitutional Law* (Mineola, NY: Foundation Press, 1978), 825.

37. Van Geel would apparently approve such a solution. See Tyll Van Geel, "The Search for Constitutional Limits on Governmental Authority to Inculcate Youth," *Texas Law Review* 62 (1983): 197–297.

38. *Pico,* 457 U.S. at 869. See, e.g., United States v. Robel, 389 U.S. 258 (1967).

39. *Pico,* 457 U.S. at 864.

40. Ibid., 914.

41. Goss v. Lopez, 419 U.S. 565 (1975); Wood v. Strickland, 420 U.S. 308 (1975); *Tinker,* 393 U.S. 503; Ingraham v. Wright, 430 U.S. 651 (1977). And see New Jersey v. T.L.O., 469 U.S. 325 (1985). Note should also be taken of the rash of cases that reached the U.S. Courts of Appeals involving such relevant matters as hair length and student newspapers. These are collected in David L. Kirp and Mark G. Yudof, *Educational Policy and the Law,* 2nd ed. (Berkeley, CA: McCutchan, 1982), 168–72, 187–93, 201–6, 210–18. The excitement over these issues appears to be spent, the old practices are unabated, and "remarkably little judicial intervention has actually occurred"; see David L. Kirp, "Pupil Control: How Innocents Get Caught in the Classroom Dragnet," *Times Educational Supplement,* August 10, 1984.

42. *Barnette,* 319 U.S. 624. See Arons, *Compelling Belief*; see also Stephen Arons, "The Separation of School and State: Pierce Reconsidered," *Harvard*

Educational Review 46 (1976): 76–104; Stephen Arons and Charles Lawrence III, "The Manipulation of Consciousness: A First Amendment Critique of Schooling," *Harvard Civil Rights Civil Liberties Review* 15, no. 2 (1980): 309–61.

CHAPTER TWO.   Making Schools Public

1. Editors' Note: See Timothy Weaver, "In Search of Quality: The Need for Talent in Teaching," *Phi Delta Kappan* (September 1979): 29–32, 46. Weaver also addressed this theme in his keynote address, "The Tragedy of the Commons: The Effect of Supply and Demand on the Education Talent Pool," before the February 1981 meeting of the American Association of Colleges of Teacher Education in Detroit, Michigan.

CHAPTER THREE.   School Choice as Simple Justice

1. Karl Barth, *The Word of God and the Word of Man*, trans. Douglas Horton (New York: Harper & Row, 1957), 228.

CHAPTER SEVEN.   Education

1. To "obtend" is "to put forward as a reason." By a scant extension, I apply the word to the actor's subjective presentation to himself of a justifying external purpose. The "ob-" and the "-ten-" crudely suggest the outside/inside aspects of this moral quest that perfects even the actor who mistakes the behavioral good of the particular circumstances. According to the *Oxford English Dictionary*, the noun form appears in Samuel Johnson's *Dictionary* of 1755. Some such term is needed to distinguish this version of moral self-perfection from that of the gnostics; other candidates are welcome.

2. John Coons and Patrick Brennan, "Nature and Human Equality," *American Journal of Jurisprudence* 40 (1995): 287–334.

3. Aristotle, *Politics* 1.2 (1252a31–34); 1.5 (1254b20–23); 1.13 (1260a12); 3.9 (1280a33–34). Aquinas, *Summa theologiae* Ia, q. 19, a. 2, ad 3. And see Jean Porter, "The Subversion of Virtue," *Annual of the Society of Christian Ethics* 23 (1992): 19–41, 25–26. See essays by Nagel and Williams in Daniel Statman, ed., *Moral Luck* (New York: SUNY Press, 1992). Each bears the same title as the collection, that is, "Moral Luck": Nagel is at 57; Williams at 35.

4. See, e.g., Hannah Arendt, *On Revolution* (London: Pelican Books, 1977), 190. See Coons and Brennan, "Nature and Human Equality," 306–12, where the sources of the Suarezian quotes are specified.

5. Coons and Brennan, "Nature and Human Equality," 312–19. John Finnis, "Natural Law and Legal Reasoning," *Cleveland State Law Review* 38 (1990): 3.

6. John Finnis, *Fundamentals of Ethics* (Washington, DC: Georgetown University Press, 1987), 72. See Russell Rittinger, *A Critique of the New Natural Law Theory* (Notre Dame, IN: University of Notre Dame Press, 1987), 93–154.

7. Our views of Lonergan appear along with the documentation in Coons and Brennan, "Nature and Human Equality," 319–32. See also John Coons and Patrick Brennan, "The Idea of a Descriptive Equality: Lonergan Explains Jefferson," *Lonergan Workshop Journal* 12 (1996): 45–76.

8. Bernard Lonergan, *Understanding and Being: The Halifax Lectures on Insight*, 2nd. ed., in *The Collected Works of Bernard Lonergan* (Toronto: University of Toronto Press, 1990), 5:172.

9. Bernard Lonergan, *Insight: A Study of Human Understanding*, 4th ed. (San Francisco: Harper and Row, 1958), 691–92.

10. Richard Herrnstein and Charles Murray, *The Bell Curve: Intelligence and Class Structure in American Life* (New York: The Free Press, 1994).

11. "Be robbers and conquerors, as long as you cannot be rulers and owners, you lovers of knowledge! Soon the age will be past when you could be satisfied to live like shy deer hidden in the woods. At long last the pursuit of knowledge will reach out for its due: it will want to *rule* and *own*, and you with it"; Friedrich Nietzsche, *The Gay Science*, in *The Portable Nietzsche*, ed. Walter Kaufmann (New York: Viking Penguin, 1984), 97–98 (emphasis in original).

12. Among the other ideological victims of natural gnosticism is the idea of servant leadership. No doubt we barbarians need direction from the intellectuals, but not for any superior capacity of theirs to be good persons. It is, rather, for their ability to illuminate for us the empirical choices that face the society and to help us evaluate them in reasoned dialogue about the common good, a conversation in which all rational persons are obliged by their nature to participate. It is Everyman's responsibility to deploy the insights of the gifted as he participates in social life, seeking, with Lonergan, to become authentic by dedication to the task. The smart people are merely working for and with the rest of us as we search together for the natural moral good of the extended world.

Still another victim is the idea of human greatness. Centuries of enlightenment have taught us to identify the great person in the manner of Carlyle's hero. He—or the very occasional she—is the one whose (good?) deeds of statecraft or intellect have altered the visible course of history. I am prepared to join the gnostics in the celebration of good deeds, but I think it a dreadful corruption to teach school children that there is some special connection between large enterprises and large souls. What they ought to learn is that we have insufficient evidence for any natural hagiography of good persons. Moral prodigies may lurk in the least visible quarters. To admire persons simply for their deeds would be a non sequitur.

13. Milton posed the problem for Adam: "Among unequals what... harmony or true delight . . . which must be mutual"; John Milton, *Paradise Lost* (New York: Viking Press, 1949), 425–26 (8.384–88). See Joseph Telushkin, *Jewish Literacy* (New York: William Morrow Co., 1991), 214–18; Stephen Wylen, *Settings of Silver: An Introduction to Judaism* (Mahwah, NJ: Paulist Press, 1991), 250–57 and 378 (bibliography). The reader may wish to consult "The Responsive Communitarian Platform," *The Responsive Community* 2 (Winter 1991–92): 4–20.

14. Pope John Paul II, in his critiques of errant theologians, repeatedly emphasized that good intentions do not transmute bad acts into good. However, nothing in *Veritatis splendor* or the new *Catechism* requires Catholics to suppose that mistakes about content prevent the diligent but mistaken actor from advancing his own moral perfection by his choices. The pope's restraint on this point reaffirms the theme of Vatican II that the invincibly ignorant conscience is to be followed "without thereby losing its dignity" (*Gaudium et spes*, sec. 16). This does not *prove* a Catholic commitment to descriptive equality, but it is hard to find explicit rejections of the concept.

15. I am wholly content in this respect with the views of J. Budziszewski, *True Tolerance* (New Brunswick, NJ: Transaction, 1992).

16. The most accessible version of my views on schools may be John Coons, "School Choice as Simple Justice," *First Things*, April 1992, 193–200. Editor's note: reproduced in full as chapter 3 of this book.

17. An obtensional argument for the child's right is elaborated in John Coons, "The Religious Rights of Children," in *Religious Human Rights in Global Perspective*, Vol. 2, *Religious Perspectives*, ed. John Witte Jr. (The Hague: Martinus Nijhoff, 1996), 157.

18. For a full-dress technical description, see John Coons and Stephen Sugarman, *Scholarships for Children* (Berkeley, CA: Institute of Government Studies, 1992).

19. Andrew Greeley and Peter Rossi, *The Education of Catholic Americans* (Chicago: Aldine Publishing Co., 1966); Andrew Greeley, William McCready, and Kathleen McCourt, *Catholic Schools in a Declining Church* (Kansas City, KS: Sheed and Ward, 1976); James Coleman and Thomas Hof-

fer, *Public and Private High Schools* (New York: Basic Books Inc., 1987); Anthony Bryk, Valerie Lee, and Peter Holland, *Catholic Schools and the Common Good* (Cambridge, MA: Harvard University Press, 1993).

CHAPTER EIGHT.   Magna Charter

1. Stephen D. Sugarman, "Is It Unconstitutional to Prohibit Faith-Based Schools from Becoming Charter Schools?" *Journal of Law and Religion* 32, no. 2 (2017) 227–62.

CHAPTER NINE.   Luck, Obedience, and the Vocation of the Child

1. Deitrich Bonhoeffer, *The Cost of Discipleship* (New York: Macmillian, 1959), 63.

2. Jacques Maritain, *An Introduction to the Basic Problems of Moral Philosophy* (Albany, NY: Magi Books, 1990), 141.

3. See, e.g., John Finnis, *Natural Law and Natural Rights* (New York: Oxford University Press, 1980), 64–99. John E. Coons, "A Grammar of the Self," *First Things*, January 2003, 37.

4. Coons, "Grammar of the Self," 41–42. Regarding this usage, I risk one suggestive scriptural reference: "What will a man gain by winning the whole world, at the cost of his true self?" (Matt. 9:25; *The New English Bible*, 1967).

5. For the origin of this usage, see John E. Coons and Patrick McKinley Brennan, *By Nature Equal: The Anatomy of a Western Insight* (Princeton, NJ: Princeton University Press, 1999), 14.

6. Christina L. H. Traina, "A Person in the Making: Thomas Aquinas on Children and Childhood," in *The Child in Christian Thought*, ed. Marcia J. Bunge (Grand Rapids, MI: Eerdmans, 2001), 103.

7. On the interpretation of baptism, I warmly recommend Anthony J. Kelly, C.Ss.R., "Hope for Unbaptized Infants: Holy Innocents after All?" in *The Vocation of the Child*, ed. Patrick M. Brennan (Grand Rapids, MI: Wm. B. Eerdmans, 2008), 215–39.

8. C. S. Lewis, *The Great Divorce* (New York: Macmillan, 1946).

9. John Ferguson, *Pelagius: A Historical and Theological Study* (Cambridge: Heffer and Sons, 1956), gives the old heretic rounded treatment.

10. "Vocation" is variously used, but I confine the term to the constant consciousness of obligation to seek the specification and actualization of second good. This sounds Kantian, but any serious pedigree would require more elaboration; my chief aim here is to be clear.

11. Phyllis McGinley, "The Giveaway," in *Love Letters of Phyllis Mc-Ginley* (New York: Viking Press, 1954), 50–52.

12. Note well that in certain cases of ignorance, the actor may be *excused* without *improving* his own moral state. See Coons and Brennan, *By Nature Equal*, 195–97. So could it be with children. Finnis does not focus upon the specific effect of being excused. Nor is this my subject, except to observe that the distinction I would draw between self and persona would probably entail separate interpretations of the function of excuse. That is, if perfection of the self depends only upon best effort, the concept of excuse is, for that purpose, redundant or even tautological. By contrast, in respect to the effect of mistake upon the persona, excuse might be understood to preserve some important innocence in the contingent elements of the blundering seeker of the good. My assumption that Bridget's acts were unjustified is, of course, an interpretation of the poet's meaning, hence vulnerable and heuristic. See John Finnis, *Aquinas* (New York: Oxford University Press, 1998), 41. If the injury to the character of the blunderer is automatic, it is hard to grasp the benign aspect of being "excused." Note that, in effect, the gnostic view collapses the distinction between first and second good. Goodness ceases to be a separate and unique quality of the self; instead the self takes on moral impress of whichever second goods happen to get accomplished or are left undone by the persona. I think we are allowed to hope that one day natural law theory will find coherence in its embrace of the two basic distinctions: that is, between self and persona and between first and second goods. At present it continues to merge these discrete elements of the moral person in ever-more complex forms of gnosis. See, e.g., Darlene Fozard Weaver, "Take Sin Seriously," *Journal of Religious Ethics* 31 (2003), 45–74.

13. Finnis, *Aquinas*, 41n68. For my part, on the role of free will I could leave it as summarized by Joseph Flanagan: "Our identity as choosers subsumes . . . our identity as knowers"; see Flanagan, *The Quest for Self Knowledge: An Essay in Lonergan's Philosophy* (Toronto: University of Toronto Press, 1997), 9–10.

14. I thank Patrick Brennan for spotting this passage and add that he (Brennan) finds Maritain equivocal on the point. Barth is extremely difficult to locate on the underlying question of freedom and election. But the forty-five pages of his essay "Parents and Children" are consistent with a responsibility for obedience by the child under the commandment, an obedience that seems disconnected from correct outcomes and hence free of gnostic baggage: "The nerve of the whole is always this willingness to learn. This is the honour which is required of children in relation to their parents." Barth, of course, stresses throughout that the primary obedience is to God alone. See Karl Barth, *Church Dogmatics* III/4 (Edinburgh: T&T Clark, 1961), 245. The reference is to Bernard Lonergan, SJ; Brennan and I do some of the necessary

teasing of his work in John Coons and Patrick Brennan, "Created Equal: Lonergan Explains Jefferson," in *Lonergan Workshop Journal* 12 (1996): 45–76. For St. Alphonsus Liguori (1698–1787), it is precisely in seeking the good that any person acts from reason and thereby "probably acquires merit" in spite of honest errors. He "ought to be meritorious on account of the good end by which he acts"; see Liguori, *Theologia Moralis*, 1.1.6, in *Liguori Opera* (Turin: Marietti, 1846), 5:2. Hans Urs von Balthasar, *Dare We Hope "That All Men Be Saved"?* (San Francisco: Ignatius, 1988). See Coons and Brennan, *By Nature Equal*, 145–215, part III, "Could the Christians Believe in Human Equality?" Summarizing roughly, we see many a difficulty among traditional Calvinist confessions in their official theology, but at the same time probable acceptance among their lay adherents. Catholics seem comfortable with the antignostic view both in the pulpit and the pew. The Koran's strong focus on correct acts gives Islam a resolutely gnostic air, and there is no obvious clue to a different implication in the case of children, but here I would play the obedient child and accept correction. See John E. Coons, "Good Selves and Just Wars," *Notre Dame Journal of Law Ethics and Public Policy* 19 (2005): 71–90. Belief in many of its forms could invite analogy between (1) the relation of first to second good and (2) the relation of faith to works. Faith becomes salvific in its free acceptance, which entails a dedication to rectitude; goodness emerges in the self's free commitment to its calling to seek second good. The analogy could at first seem limited; not all are offered the gift of faith, while all receive the vocation to seek. But if full salvific effect attaches to a positive answer to either invitation, the practical difference would be narrowed; it would consist in the specifically religious duties incumbent upon the believer.

15. Coons and Brennan, *By Nature Equal*, 88–89. The *Oxford English Dictionary* seems to imply that the obtender acts for a reason he supposes to be justifying of the action. The most vivid example: "Origenes . . . did gelde hymselfe . . . for the obtente and will of chasitity."

16. See John Finnis, "The Illicit Inference from Facts to Norms," in *Natural Law and Natural Rights*, 33–48. So far as I know, psychology has never attempted empirical assessment of the claim that moral consciousness originates in all children independently of environment. That inquiry would be challenging—but in theory possible—and far closer to authentic science than visions drawn post hoc from psychoanalysis of middle-age patients or the needs of radical evolutionary theory.

17. In any case, most children appear conscious of their condition of responsibility long before reaching traditional versions of the "age of reason." I note that the encyclical *Deus caritas est* refers to the human consciousness of vocation in terms (and in tone) that might encourage empirical inquiry into the initial appearance of consciousness of an obligation to seek as a

phenomenon. For example, "the command of love of neighbor is inscribed by the Creator in man's very nature"; Pope Benedict XVI, *Deus caritas est* (2005), pt. 2, no. 31.

18. On this aspect of Finnis's work I am indebted to James V. Schall, "On the Most Mysterious of the Virtues: The Political and Philosophical Meaning of Obedience in St. Thomas, Rousseau and Yves Simon," *Gregorianum* 79, no. 4 (1998): 755–56. Karl Barth would have them "ambassadors of God"; see Barth, *Church Dogmatics* III/4, 256.

19. See generally Bunge, ed., *The Child in Christian Thought.* The January 2003 issue of *Theology Today* comprises a dozen essays, many quite useful. I especially recommend it as an enthusiastic counter to my own conclusion here about the role of government schools. See, in particular, John Wall, "Animals and Innocents: Theological Reflections on the Meaning and Purpose of Child-Rearing," *Theology Today* 59, no. 4 (2003): 559–82.

20. See virtually all the essays in Bunge, ed., *The Child in Christian Thought*; see, especially, Mary Ann Hinsdale, "'Infinite Openness to the Infinite': Karl Rahner's Contribution to Modern Catholic Thought on the Child," 406. Karl Rahner, "Ideas for a Theology of Childhood," in *Theological Investigations*, Vol. 8, trans. David Bourke (London: Darton, Longman and Todd, 1971), 33–50, amounts to a celebration of the mystery of childhood that delicately (and typically) skirts the question here. My own take on Mark 10:14 would be this: Jesus made *these* children the type "of the kingdom of heaven" because they *chose* to come to him. Suffer them, he told the disciples; allow them to do what they willed to do. These children were answering a vocation. Were there others who turned away? We don't know.

21. I read the Lord's Prayer as (1) a submission to the divine will, but also (2) our embrace of the vocation to cooperate by seeking an optimal moral state of contingent reality.

22. Yves R. Simon, *Philosophy of Democratic Government* (Chicago: University of Chicago Press, 1951), 7–19; Simon, *A General Theory of Authority* (Notre Dame, IN: University of Notre Dame Press, 1962), 133–34.

23. See, e.g., James Dwyer, "Parents' Religion and Children's Welfare: Debunking the Doctrine of Parents' Rights," *California Law Review* 82 (1994): 1371, 1375. Meira Levinson adopts Dwyer's replacement of right with "privilege" in Levinson, *The Demands of Liberal Education* (New York: Oxford University Press, 1999), 50; see also 183, n35. I have no objection to the general idea of treating children instead of parents as the focus. But the ultimate gesture of respect for children is to recognize not merely their *rights* but also their *responsibility*, and then ask where authority over them is to be located. For some big person will inevitably have it. See Bruce Fuller and Richard Elmore, eds., *Who Chooses? Who Loses?* (New York: Teachers College Press, 1996). The book gives voice to a collection of educators generally

devoted to keeping things in the hands of the professionals, at least for children from families too poor to escape by moving or paying tuition.

24. See John E. Coons, "Law and the Sovereigns of Childhood," *Phi Delta Kappan*, September 1976; John E. Coons and Stephen Sugarman, *Education by Choice* (Berkeley: University of California Press, 1978).

25. See John E. Coons, "The Religious Rights of Children," in *Religious Human Rights in Global Perspective: Religious Perspectives*, ed. John Witte Jr. and Johan van der Vyver (The Hague: Martinus Nijhoff, 1996), 157. Consider here Matthew 7:11: "You, evil as you are, know well enough how to give your children what is good for them"; trans. Ronald Knox (New York: Sheed and Ward, 1944). Among the possible constructions of this passage is that in my text.

26. See, e.g., Richard D. Kahlenberg, *All Together Now* (Washington, DC: Brookings Institution Press, 2001).

27. No doubt the Amish secondary system of education could be deemed an exception. *See* Wisconsin v. Yoder, 406 US 205 (1972); Michael S. Ariens and Robert A. Destro, *Religious Liberty in a Pluralist Society* (Durham, NC: Carolina Academic Press, 2002); see 434–38 regarding legal "uniformity" of curriculum requirements.

28. Rosemary C. Salomone, *Visions of Schooling: Conscience, Community, and Common Education* (New Haven, CT: Yale University Press, 2000). The current celebrations of "multicultural" pedagogy are earnest both of the fashion and the curricular fact. "Teachers, like parents, regularly share with students what they see as indisputable wisdom and guidance with regard to moral and existential issues. And when sharing wisdom, they do not typically present 'the other side'"; Katherine G. Simon, *Moral Questions in the Classroom* (New Haven, CT: Yale University Press, 2001), 192. Christopher Barnes, "What Do Teachers Teach? A Survey of America's Fourth and Eighth Grade Teachers," *Civic Report* 28 (New York: Center for Civic Innovation, 2003); Kenneth Karst, "Law, Cultural Conflict, and the Socialization of Children," *California Law Review* 91 (2003): 967.

29. There may somewhere be a public school course on the philosophy of Aristotle, but woe to the teacher who would "baptize" him with Scholastic refinements.

30. Simon, *General Theory of Authority*, 23–80.

31. The authority reserved to the family can be variously understood. It can, for example, be seen as an independent system of law in the sense of law that is common to American lawyers—it makes and enforces rules. It is a jurisprudential reality that lacks nothing but a literature. And that may come.

32. The relevant works of James S. Coleman and those scholars who later secured the ground he took are all cited and vetted in Joseph P. Viteritti, *Choosing Equality* (Washington, DC: Brookings Institution Press, 1999).

33. See John Coons, review of *The Education Gap*, by William Howell and Paul E. Peterson, *Education Next* (Fall 2002): 84. That our systems of school assignment might corrupt the family that lacks choice is a rare theme among academics. Education writers have preferred to assume the opposite course of causation, at least since Coleman reported that family and class greatly affect school performance. See *Equality of Educational Opportunity (Coleman) Study (EEOS)* (Washington, DC: U.S. Government Printing Office, 1966). This intellectual habit may be traceable to the "Moynihan Report," in *The Negro Family: The Case for National Action* (Washington, DC: U.S. Government Printing Office, 1965).

Appendix

1. Editors' note: Film year is 1959, remade in 2000, and a "classic serial" released in 2008 by BBC. The original film was based on a novel: Nevil Schute, *On the Beach* (London: Heinemann, 1957).

BIBLIOGRAPHICAL ESSAY
An Informal Bibliography of Parental Choice

As a law professor with the limitations this vocation suggests, I have, never-theless, dared to publish certain philosophical and religious ideas of my own, such as the groping *By Nature Equal: The Anatomy of a Western Insight* (with Patrick Brennan) (Princeton University Press, 1999). To be fair, however, I am no encyclopedia of the protean thoughts relevant to school choice, a subject that deserves multiprofessional insight. For example, I have scanned too little of ancient Asian and other materials—Confucian, Buddhist, Hindu, Incan—to even point to a literature suggesting who, in those societies, decided which members of the community would teach the child the specifics of language, ethics, religion, and the arts of sociability. Maybe it doesn't exist.

The very term "school" seems in ancient times, as in ours, to have been used in connection with very different loci of authority over children. All that seems clear is that the ancient world, like our own, limited any systematic education largely to favored social classes; for the most part, the child of the common man learned agriculture from the father, home economics from the mother, and prayer from both. On occasion, perhaps, a child would hear from a guru or priest who might encourage him to learn. But the conception of one particular locus of authority to choose wasn't there, with the possible excep-tion of the Jews. Is there in pre-Christian scripture—or, for that matter, the New Testament—a revelation of just who rules the child's intellectual diet?

Anno Domini, first the Romans, then the Muslims, were perhaps better organized in their systems of authority to choose and were to set a fair ex-ample. But the general illiteracy, the absence of printing, the scattering geog-raphies of both agricultural and nomadic societies, and the poverty of so many kept any organized system of choice off society's agenda.

Today, the law reviews, the educational school journals, books, maga-zines, and dailies swarm with opinion for and against government's subsidiz-ing impoverished families to choose private, including religious, schools. All of this modern expression is available on the internet and easy for the younger maven to find. I don't keep up, because I cannot. But, in any case, the many issues about schools (besides money) and the various certified but opposing

253

paths to their solution seem sufficiently clear, and their representation in our media for and against choice is rampant. What is more needed now is perspective and distance. I will here suggest sources that I feel will be with us for the long run.

To that end, rather than assemble a comprehensive index, the aim will be first to praise and then criticize a few of those that I consider the best among ideologies and authors that were already locked in my own mind before I ever heard of vouchers. They reflected the human wisdom I retained from the classics of my college days when, in 1962, I undertook the first of several studies of racial separation in Chicago and Evanston public schools. I was then on the Northwestern Law faculty and contracted for these probes with two federal agencies. I knew little about public schools: except for a year in junior high, I had been a Catholic schoolboy.

I witnessed the misery of most inner-city Chicago children, especially Black kids, but not all were Black. I had read various theories of how to ameliorate the human condition, but I could not imagine this public school "system" among them. My preference for family choice was stimulated, of course, by direct personal experience, but also by some of that old literature I knew, albeit sometimes negatively, such as my recollection of Plato's *Republic*. The old Greek recommended—parents being generally incompetent and damaging to young citizens—that the state should, at birth, seize the babe, who would then be raised by professional strangers. Chicago, it seemed, had embraced Plato's solution, at least for the lower-income child during the prime hours of the day. One should read the *Republic* for the historical context of this mindset that remains alive and well. For example, see Carmen Green, "Educational Empowerment: A Child's Right to Attend Public School," *Georgetown Law Journal* 103, no. 4 (2015): 1089–1134. For the opposite view that schools should be abandoned altogether in favor of a family-and-village culture and mode of education, try Ivan Illich's *Deschooling Society* (Marion Boyers Publishers, 2000). Sugarman and I got to know Illich rather well, first in Cuernavaca, then in Berkeley. If he was radical, he was also coherent and helped set the intellectual boundary opposite that of Plato. Even in its own day, Plato's statist—some would say totalitarian—vision was rivaled by that of Aristotle. Aristotle's notions of the ideal society and of serious thought rejected Plato's for a more empirically based ideal. Indeed, the clash between the two visions is still unresolved and continues to reverberate throughout society. Directly on point is Arthur Herman's superb *The Cave and the Light: Plato versus Aristotle, and the Struggle for the Soul of Western Civilization* (Random House, 2013).

Oregon was to take Plato seriously in the 1920s; all children were compelled to attend state schools. Period. Read again *Pierce v. Society of Sisters* (1925); it is short and to the point, the Supreme Court announcing the "due process" rule of parental authority to choose. What the Court did not do (nor was it asked to do) was make the state fund tuition. So school remains semi-Platonic for those families in want of the necessary cash.

Plato's vision of schooling failed to move Athens, and for nearly two millennia—except for educating clergy in the Catholic Church—the issue of education by choice remained rather less visible to the historians I have read. In Greece and Rome, "schools," it seems, had flourished but generally for the solid citizen only; even then, education was often a private affair of tutors.

Early on, the churches in New England and around the colonies had made the effort to assemble believers once a week, mostly to hear their duties toward each other and to God. Gradually, in pre-Revolutionary times, some had begun to morph into semi-full-time schools open to all children. Reread Washington Irving, *The Legend of Sleepy Hollow* (New York: Harper & Brothers, 1897), but more seriously, peruse John Demos, *A Little Commonwealth* (Oxford, 1970).

Before and about the mid-nineteenth century, as the movement for compulsory public schooling began to appear and flourish, some city governments (New York City most visibly) for a time began to subsidize in part the emergent Catholic schools serving immigrants. This brief gesture to choice was soon snuffed out by anti-Roman responses across the country, culminating for many states in the "Blaine" amendments to state constitutions forbidding public aid to religion. Here, read Stephen D. Sugarman's recent and excellent "Is It Unconstitutional to Prohibit Faith-Based Schools from Becoming Charter Schools?," *Journal of Law and Religion* 32, no. 2 (2017): 227–62.

A rich scholarship has chronicled the birth and careers of our new public school systems; the books began with Horace Mann and steadily multiplied to the academic avalanche of our own time. David Tyack's classic *The One Best System* (Cambridge, MA: Harvard University Press, 1974) is an excellent history of the political and ideological combat over the first century of public education—sans universal choice.

Charles Glenn has for decades delivered masterful studies of school systems, their histories, and their habits, across both Europe and the United States. Once an Episcopal priest, still a Christian cleric, and ever a powerful religious and political voice, Glenn has been the director of desegregation for Massachusetts and long a professor at Boston University. He is, without exception, the most prolific academic I have known. All of his immense product is well worth reading. Don't miss Glenn's *The Myth of the Common School* (Amherst: University of Massachusetts Press, 1988), or his later work, *The Ambiguous Embrace: Government and Faith* (Princeton, NJ: Princeton University Press, 2002). Glenn is curiously practical; his down-to-earth but illuminating testimony has helped inform the decision of more than one court in school choice litigation. To this day, the school politicians of Europe augment his air miles.

Joseph Viteritti of Hunter College and the CUNY Graduate Center might come closest to my own policy ideal in the technical design of a working system of family choice. He sees the crucial need for a system designed to expand the sophistication of parents and provide assurance of reasonable access for a cadre of less promising students to participating schools, all the while protecting the integrity of each school's message. See *Choosing Equality* (Brookings, 1999). Read also the works of his spouse, Rosemary Salomone, particularly her book *Visions of Schooling* (Yale University Press, 2000). In 1990, John Chubb and Terry Moe of Stanford published their influential volume *Politics, Markets, and American Schools* (Washington, DC: The Brookings Institution, 1990). Moe continues his exposés of the teachers' unions. It is deserving of all the broad coverage it has received. See *Special Interest: Teachers Unions and American Public Schools* (Brookings, 2011).

Read Stephen Arons's 1983 book, *Compelling Belief: The Culture of American Schools* (New York: McGraw-Hill, 1983); turn then to Arons, *Short Route to Chaos: Conscience, Community, and the Re-Constitution of American Schools* (Amherst: University of Massachusetts Press, 1997). Arons, of the University of Massachusetts at Amherst, does an exposé of the unpredictable morass that I call the "bingo" curriculum of the public schools. He is most readable.

Eventually (inevitably) this bibliography acknowledges ourselves. William Clune, Stephen Sugarman, and I first addressed family choice briefly in a 1969 essay on school finance: John E. Coons, William H. Clune III, and Stephen D. Sugarman, "Educational Opportunity: A Workable Constitutional Test for State Financial Structures," *California Law Review* 57, no. 2 (1969): 305–421; and again in *Private Wealth and Public Education* (Harvard University Press, 1970). Steve and I, beginning in 1971, managed four more volumes—our last coming in 1999. I recommend our *Education by Choice: The Case for Family Control* (University of California Press, 1978). That's enough of us.

Of course, long prior to our earliest efforts stand Milton Friedman and his *Capitalism and Freedom* (1962). This book—and others of his that touch upon school choice—are all well-executed efforts to imagine schooling as a free market commodity; hence, like food, it is a proper object of state-subsidized consumer choice, almost barren of regulation. Steve and I see the market metaphor as a proper medium of healthy competition, but overstated; the child, not the parent, is the critical consumer. And we think that some regulation is necessary to protect those families most disempowered. Of course, read Friedman; he is the Old Testament of choice and deserves the status of scripture.

A report of 1965 from a public servant whom I knew and admired deserves a place here. This report was not specifically about school choice, but its author later, as a U.S. senator, was, for a brief space, to propose a federal voucher scheme. I refer, of course, to Daniel Patrick Moynihan. His report, *The Negro Family: The Case for National Action* (Office of Policy Planning and Research, United States Department of Labor, 1965), remains an indelible writing on the wall of our society. School choice is about individual (parental) responsibility. Moynihan recognized the diminishing role of family responsibility in a sector of "we the people" that is especially vulnerable to civic desuetude. If the parent has none of this responsibility . . . well, you finish the thought after reading Moynihan.

I got to know James Coleman early in the 1960s. He was the overall director of a second round of studies of segregation in northern cities in 1965. I reported again on Chicago, and then Evanston. Jim was for subsidized choice, but he recognized the unpredictability of individual families and the need for at least a thin veil of regulation. He wrote introductions to both our *Private Wealth and Public Education* and *Education by Choice*. His words are encouraging, if discrete. Jim also introduced us to Fr. Andrew Greeley, his colleague at the University of Chicago. Greeley became a friend of ours. His several books on schooling are also well worth the time.

Lost Classroom, Lost Community by Margaret Brinig and Nicole Stelle Garnett (University of Chicago Press, 2014) is a probing empirical description of the near disappearance of Catholic schools serving the poor, which reminds me that the rich wisdom of Garnett's husband, Rick, on our subject is also must reading. Rick and Nicole are both law professors at Notre Dame and heroes of school choice.

From here on I will, for most authors, offer only names and titles, divided into three rough and very overlapping categories that seem to make up the principal ideas about school choice. The first batch is general and historical, tracing the basic ideological conflict between state and parent from classical Greece forward to our own time. The second will display ideal roles assigned to the family by today's combatants, with justifications offered by these philosophers, economists, political scientists, and sociologists. The third is a glance into the forest of comment and conflict over the social and civil effects of family choice for the not so well-off parent. The overlapping of sections two and three is unavoidable; most of these volumes address both issues.

In the second and third sections, I will include a couple of volumes by Stephen Sugarman and me; we have batted this subject about since the mid-1960s.

THE HISTORICAL OVERVIEW

Here, then, are a few dozen writers and citations of their works identifying the deeper issues of the ideal relationship of parent to government. Some of these authors are metaphysicians with a particular view of the source and nature of the human sense of responsibility. All are trying to view the calling of the parent from an objective distance. Their words will disagree as sharply as those of Plato's *Republic* and Rousseau's *Emile*.

Abbot, Grace, ed. *The Child and the State.* 3 vols. Chicago: University of Chicago Press, 1938.

Adler, Mortimer J. *The Great Ideas: A Lexicon of Western Thought.* New York: Macmillan, 1992.

Bailyn, Bernard. *Education in the Forming of American Society.* New York: W. W. Norton, 1960.

Bane, Mary Jo. *Here to Stay: American Families in the Twentieth Century.* New York: Basic Books, 1976.

Barzun, Jacques. *Teacher in America.* Garden City, NY: Doubleday, 1944.

Bengston, Vern L., Timothy J. Biblarz, and Robert E. L. Roberts. *How Families Still Matter.* Cambridge: Cambridge University Press, 2002.

Berdyaev, Nicholas. *The Meaning of History.* London: Geoffrey Bles, 1936.

Berger, Brigitte, and Peter L. Berger. *The War over the Family.* New York: Anchor Press, 1984.

Boyd, William, and Edmund King. *The History of Western Education.* Lanham, MD: Rowman & Littlefield, 1994.

Brennan, Patrick M., ed. *The Vocation of the Child.* Grand Rapids, MI: William B. Eerdmans, 2008.

Bunge, Marcia J., ed. *The Child in Christian Thought.* Grand Rapids, MI: William B. Eerdmans, 2001.

Carlson, Allan. *The American Way: Family and Community in the Shaping of the American Identity.* Wilmington, DE: Intercollegiate Studies Institute Books, 2003.

Carter, Stephen L. *The Culture of Disbelief: How American Law and Politics Trivialize Religious Devotion.* New York: Basic Books, 1993.

Childs, John L. *Education and Morals: An Experimentalist Philosophy of Education.* Whitefish, MT: Literary Licensing, 1950.

Coles, Robert. *The Secular Mind.* Princeton, NJ: Princeton University Press, 1999.

Coulson, Andrew J. *Market Education: The Unknown History.* New Brunswick, NJ: Transaction, 1999.

Deneen, Patrick J. *Why Liberalism Failed.* New Haven, CT: Yale University Press, 2018.

Encyclopedia Britannica. *History of Education.* Chicago: Encyclopedia Britannica, 1986.

———. *The Great Ideas: A Syntopicon* (including a 54-volume set of original works). Chicago: Encyclopedia Britannica, 1988. Included therein are the following:

Aquinas, Thomas. *Summa Theologica.*
Aristotle. *Politics; Nicomachean Ethics.*
Augustine. *On Christian Doctrine; City of God; Confessions.*
Hobbes, Thomas. *Leviathan.*
Hume, David. *A Treatise of Human Nature.*
Locke, John. *A Letter Concerning Toleration.*
Mill, John Stuart. *On Liberty.*
Montaigne, Michel Eyquem de. *Essays.*
Plato. *Crito* and *Republic.*
Plutarch. *Lives of the Noble Grecians and Romans.*
Rousseau, Jean-Jacques. *A Discourse on Political Economy; A Dissertation on the Origin and Foundation of the Inequality of Mankind; Emile.*
Smith, Adam. *An Inquiry into the Nature and Causes of the Wealth of Nations.*

Frost, S. E. *Basic Teachings of the Great Philosophers.* New York: Doubleday, 1942.
———. *Historical and Philosophical Foundations of Western Education.* 1st ed. New York: Charles E. Merrill, 1966.
Heraclitus. *Fragments.* New York: Penguin, 2003.
Herman, Arthur. *The Cave and the Light: Plato versus Aristotle, and the Struggle for the Soul of Western Civilization.* New York: Random House, 2014.
Hirschmann, Albert O. *Exit, Voice, and Loyalty: Response to Decline in Firms, Organizations and States.* Cambridge, MA: Harvard University Press, 1970.
Jencks, Christopher. *Inequality.* New York: Basic Books, 1972.
Keim, Albert, ed. *Compulsory Education and the Amish.* Boston: Beacon Press, 1975.
Levering, Matthew, ed. *On Marriage and the Family.* Lanham, MD: Rowman & Littlefield, 2005.
Magee, Bryan. *The Story of Thought: The Essential Guide to the History of Western Philosophy.* London: DK Publishing, 1998.
Moustakas, Clark. *The Child's Discovery of Himself.* New York: Ballantine, 1966.
Paine, Thomas. *Rights of Man. Being an Answer to Mr. Burke's Attack on the French Revolution.* New York, E. P. Dutton, 1915.
Piaget, Jean. *The Moral Judgment of the Child.* New York: Free Press Paperbacks, 1997.
Ross, Jacob, and Joshua Ross. *The Virtues of the Family.* New York: Free Press, 1994.

Salomone, Rosemary C. *Visions of Schooling: Conscience, Community, and Common Education*. New Haven, CT: Yale University Press, 2000.

Simon, Katherine G. *Moral Questions in the Classroom*. New Haven, CT: Yale University Press, 2001.

Tocqueville, Alexis de. *Democracy in America*. New York: Vintage Books, 1961.

Tooley, James. *The Beautiful Tree: A Personal Journey into How the World's Poorest People Are Educating Themselves*. Washington, DC: Cato Institute, 2009.

Viteritti, Joseph P. *Choosing Equality: School Choice, the Constitution, and Civil Society*. Washington, DC: Bookings Institution, 1999.

———. *The Last Freedom: Religion from the Public School to the Public Square*. Princeton, NJ: Princeton University Press, 2007.

West, Edwin G. *Education and the State*. 2nd ed. London: Institute of Economic Affairs, 1971.

West, John G. *Darwin Day in America: How Our Politics and Culture Have Been Dehumanized in the Name of Science*. Wilmington, DE: Intercollegiate Studies Institute Books, 2007.

Yudof, Mark, Betsy Levine, Rachel F. Moran, James E. Ryan, and Kristi L. Bowman. *Educational Policy and the Law*. 5th ed. Berkeley, CA: McCutchan, 2011.

THE MODERN-ERA DEBATE OF PARENT, SCHOOL, AND GOD

This second section aims to identify the work of social scientists and others whose work is theoretical but closer to the American political realities of pursuing choice for all. Many of these could qualify for the more historical and philosophical of the first section or the more immediately political works in the third section, below.

Abbot, Grace. *The Child and the State*. 2 vols. Chicago: University of Chicago Press, 1938.

Aries, Philippe. *Centuries of Childhood*. New York: Random House, 1962.

Bailyn, Bernard. *Education in the Forming of American Society*. New York: W. W. Norton, 1960.

Bane, Mary Jo. *Here to Stay: American Families in the Twentieth Century*. New York: Basic Books, 1976.

Banfield, Edward. *The Unheavenly City*. Boston: Little, Brown, 1970.

Bell, Daniel, ed. *The Radical Right*. Garden City, NY: Doubleday Anchor Books, 1964.

Bell, Daniel, and Winfred Bell. *Aid to Dependent Children*. New York: Columbia University Press, 1965.

Berger, Peter, and Richard Neuhaus. *To Empower People: The Role of Mediating Structures in Public Policy*. Washington DC: American Enterprise Institute, 1977.

Blankenhorn, David. *Fatherless America: Confronting Our Most Urgent Social Problem*. New York: Basic Books, 1995.

———. *The Future of Marriage*. New York: Encounter Books, 2007.

Blum, Virgil. *Freedom of Choice in Education*. New York: Macmillan, 1963.

Bonhoeffer, Dietrich. *The Cost of Discipleship*. New York: Macmillan, 1963.

Bowles, Samuel, and Herbert Gintis. *Schooling in Capitalist America: Educational Reform and the Contradictions of Economic Life*. New York: Basic Books, 1976.

Bremner, Robert, ed. *Children and Youth in America: A Documentary History*. 3 vols. Cambridge, MA: Harvard University Press, 1974.

Bronfenbrenner, Urie. *The Two Worlds of Childhood: USA and USSR*. New York: Russell Sage Foundation, 1970.

Browder, Lesley. *Who's Afraid of Educational Accountability?* Denver, CO: Cooperative Accountability Project, 1975.

Burleigh, Anne, ed. *Education in a Free Society*. Indianapolis: Liberty Fund, 1973.

Carlson, Allan C. *Family Questions: Reflection on the American Social Crisis*. New Brunswick, NJ: Transaction Publishers, 1988.

Carnot, Martin, and Henry Levin, eds. *The Limits of Educational Reform*. New York: D. McKay, 1976.

Castle, E. B. *A Parent's Guide to Education*. Baltimore: Penguin, 1968.

Chall, Jeanne. *Learning to Read: The Great Debate*. New York, McGraw-Hill, 1967.

Chapman, John, and Roland Pennock, eds. *Equality*. New York: Atherton Press, 1967.

Chesterton, G. K. *What's Wrong with the World*. New York: Sheed & Ward, 1956.

Childs, John. *Education and Morals*. New York: Appleton-Century Crofts, 1950.

Cicourel, Aaron, and John Kitsuse. *The Educational Decision-makers*. Indianapolis: Bobbs-Merrill, 1963.

Client, Remi. *Liberty and Equality in the Educational Process*. New York: John Wiley, 1974.

Coons, John, William Clune III, and Stephen Sugarman. *Private Wealth and Public Education*. Cambridge, MA: Harvard University Press, 1970.

Coons, John, and Stephen Sugarman. *Family Choice in Education: A Model State System of Vouchers.* Berkeley, CA: Institute of Governmental Studies, 1971.

Coser, Lewis A. *The Functions of Social Conflict.* Glencoe, IL: Free Press, 1956.

Cox, C. B., and E. E. Dyson, eds. *The Black Papers on Education.* London: David-Poynter, 1971.

Cremin, Lawrence. *The Transformation of the School.* New York: Random House, 1964.

Dahl, Robert. *Who Governs? Democracy and Power in an American City.* New Haven, CT: Yale University Press, 1961.

deMause, Lloyd, ed. *The History of Childhood.* New York: Psychohistory Press, 1974.

Demos, John. *A Little Commonwealth.* London: Oxford University Press, 1970.

Deutsch, Karl. *Politics and Government.* Boston: Houghton Mifflin, 1970.

Dewey, John. *Liberalism and Social Action.* New York: Capricorn Books, 1935.

Douglas, J. W. B. *The Home and the School.* Manchester: Philips Park Press, 1964.

Erickson, Donald, ed. *Public Controls for Non-Public Schools.* Chicago: University of Chicago Press, 1969.

Erikson, Erik. *Childhood and Society.* New York: W. W. Norton, 1950.

Fantini, Mario D. *Public Schools of Choice.* New York: Simon and Schuster, 1973.

Fesler, James, ed. *The Fifty States and Their Local Governments.* New York: Knopf, 1967.

Freud, Anna, Joseph Goldstein, and Albert Solnit. *Beyond the Best Interests of the Child.* Glencoe, IL: Free Press, 1973.

Friedman, Milton. *Capitalism and Freedom.* Chicago: University of Chicago Press, 1962.

Furnivall, Frederick. *Early English Meals and Manners.* London: Moran Press, 2008.

Galbraith, John Kenneth. *The New Industrial State.* New York: Signet Books, 1967.

Garfinkel, Irwin, and Edward Gramlich. *A Statistical Analysis of the OEO Experiment in Educational Performance Contracting.* Washington, DC: Brookings Institution, Technical Service Reprint T-002, 1972.

George, Robert P., and Jean Bethke Elshtain, eds. *The Meaning of Marriage: Family, State, Market, and Morals.* Princeton, NJ: Witherspoon Institute, 2006.

Goldstein, Joseph, and Jay Katz. *The Family and the Law*. Glencoe, IL: Free Press, 1965.

Goodman, Paul. *Compulsory Miseducation*. New York: Horizon Press, 1964.

———. *Growing Up Absurd*. New York: Random House, 1956.

Goodman, Paul, Paul Adams. and Leila Berg. *Children's Rights*. New York: Praeger, 1971.

Grams, Walter, James Guthrie, and Lawrence Pierce. *School Finance: The Economics and Politics of Public Schools*. Englewood Cliffs, NJ: Prentice Hall, 1977.

Greeley, Andrew, William McCready, and Kathleen McCourt. *Catholic Schools in a Declining Church*. Kansas City: Viking Press, 1972.

Greer, Colin. *The Great School Legend*. New York: Viking Press, 1972.

Gross, Ronald, and Beatrice Gross, eds. *Radical School Reform*. New York: Simon and Schuster, 1971.

Grubb, W. Norton, and Stephan Michelson. *States and Schools*. Lexington, MA: Lexington Books, 1974.

Haar, Charles, and Demetrios Iatrides. *Housing the Poor in Suburbia: Public Policy at the Grass Roots*. Cambridge, MA: Ballinger, 1974.

Habermas, Jürgen. *Knowledge and Human Interest*. Boston: Beacon Press, 1968.

Handler, Joel, and Ellen Hollingsworth. *The "Deserving" Poor*. Chicago: Marham, 1971.

Handlin, Oscar. *The Uprooted*. Boston: Little, Brown, 1952.

Hanushek, Eric. *Making Schools Work: Improving Performance and Controlling Costs*. Washington, DC: Brookings Institution Press, 1996.

Hartman, Robert W., and Robert D. Reischauer. *Reforming School Finance*. Washington, DC: The Brookings Institution, 1973.

Heilbroner, Robert L. *An Inquiry into the Human Prospect*. New York: W. W. Norton, 1974.

Hofstadter, Richard. *The American Political Tradition*. New York: Random House Vintage, 1948.

Holt, John. *How Children Fail*. New York: Dell, 1964.

———. *The Underachieving School*. New York: Dell, 1969.

Hutchins, Robert M. *Two Faces of Federalism: An Outline of an Argument about Pluralism, Unity, and Law*. Santa Barbara, CA: Center for the Study of Democratic Institutions, 1961.

Illich, Ivan. *Deschooling Society*. New York: Harper and Row, 1971.

Jefferson, Thomas. *Notes on the State of Virginia* (Query 17). Boston: David Carlisle, 1801.

Jencks, Christopher. *Inequality*. New York: Basic Books, 1972.

John Paul II. *The Role of the Christian Family in the Modern World*. Boston: Pauline Books, 2015.

Keim, Albert N., ed. *Compulsory Education and the Amish: The Right Not to Be Modern*. Boston: Beacon Press, 1975.

Kirst, Michael W., and Frederick M. Wirt. *The Political and Social Foundations of Education*. Berkeley, CA: McCutchan, 1976.

Kohl, Herbert. *The Open Classroom*. New York: Random House Vintage, 1970.

Kozol, Jonathan. *Free Schools*. Boston: Houghton Mifflin, 1972.

Lambert, William W., and Leigh Minturn. *Mothers of Six Cultures: Antecedents of Child Rearing*. New York: John Wiley, 1964.

Laqueur, Walter, and George L. Mosse, eds. *Education and Social Structure*. New York: Harper and Row, 1967.

Levin, Henry, ed. *Community Control of Schools*. Washington, DC: The Brookings Institution, 1970.

Levin, Joel. *Final Report on the Implementation of the Second Year of the Alum Rock Voucher Project*. Alum Rock, CA: Alum Rock Sequoia Institute, n.d.

Levinson, Eliot. *The Alum Rock Voucher Demonstration: Three Years of Implementation*. Santa Monica, CA: Rand Paper Series P-5631, April 1976.

Macedo, Stephen, and Yael Tamir, eds. *Moral and Political Education*. New York: New York University Press, 2002.

Macedo, Stephen, and Iris Marion Young, eds. *Child, Family, and State: NOMOS XLIV*. New York: New York University Press, 2003.

Mayer, Martin. *The Teachers Strike: New York 1968*. New York: Harper and Row, 1969.

McCoy, Raymond F. *American School Administration, Public and Catholic*. New York: McGraw-Hill, 1961.

McDermott, John, ed. *Indeterminacy in Education*. Berkeley, CA: McCutchan, 1976.

Mill, John Stuart. *On Liberty*. Great Books Edition. Chicago: Encyclopedia Britannica, 1952.

Montessori, Maria. *The Secret of Childhood*. Notre Dame, IN: Tides Publishers, 1966.

Moschella, Melissa, *To Whom Do Children Belong? Parental Rights Civil Education and Children's Autonomy*. Cambridge: Cambridge University Press, 2016.

Mosteller, Frederick, and Daniel P. Moynihan, eds. *On Equality of Educational Opportunity*. New York: Random House, 1972.

Moustakas, Clark, ed. *The Child's Discovery of Himself*. New York: Ballantine Books, 1966.

Murray, Charles. *Real Education: Four Simple Truths for Bringing America's Schools Back to Reality*. New York: Three Rivers Press, 2008.

Novak, Michael. *The Rise of the Unmeltable Ethnics*. Toronto: Macmillan, 1971.

Olson, Mancur. *The Logic of Collective Action*. Cambridge, MA: Harvard University Press, 1965.

Paine, Thomas. *Rights of Man. Being an Answer to Mr. Burke's Attack on the French Revolution*. New York: E. P. Dutton, 1915.

Pellegrini, Angelo M. *Americans by Choice*. New York: Macmillan, 1956.

Phelps, Edmund S., ed. *Private Wants and Public Needs*. New York: W. W. Norton, 1965.

Piaget, Jean. *The Construction of Reality in the Child*. New York: Ballantine Books, 1954.

Pincus, John, ed. *School Finance in Transition*. Cambridge, MA: Ballinger, 1974.

Rabb, Theodore K., and Robert I. Rotberg, eds. *The Family in History: Interdisciplinary Essays*. New York: Harper and Row, 1971.

Ravitch, Diane. *The Revisionists Revised: Studies in the Historiography of American Education*. Proceedings of the National Academy of Education, Vol. 4, 1977.

Rawls, John. *A Theory of Justice*. Cambridge, MA: Harvard University Press, 1971.

Reimer, Everett. *School Is Dead: An Essay on Alternatives in Education*. Cuernavaca, Mexico: CIDOC, 1979.

Rubinstein, David, and Colin Stoneman, eds. *Education for Democracy*. Baltimore: Penguin, 1970.

Russell, Bertrand. *Education and the Good Life*. New York: Boni and Liveright, 1926.

Santayana, George. *The Sense of Beauty*. New York: Modern Library, 1955.

Schumacher, E. F. *Small Is Beautiful: Economics as If People Mattered*. New York: Harper and Row, 1973.

Skinner, B. F. *Beyond Freedom and Dignity*. New York: Knopf, 1971.

Skolnick, Arlene S., and Jerome H. Skolnick, eds. *Family in Transition*. Boston: Little, Brown, 1971.

Smith, Adam. *An Inquiry Into the Nature and Causes of the Wealth of Nations*. Great Books Edition. Chicago: Encyclopedia Britannica, 1952.

Sonnenfeld, David. *Family Choice in Schooling: A Case Study*. Working Paper 3. Eugene: University of Oregon, 1972.

Spencer, Herbert. *Social Statics: The Conditions Essential to Human Happiness*. London: John Chapman, 1851.

Steiner, Gilbert. *The Children's Cause*. Washington, DC: The Brookings Institution, 1976.

St. John, Nancy. *School Desegregation: Outcomes for Children.* New York: John Wiley, 1975.

Taft, Robert. *Welfare Alternatives.* Washington, DC: Government Printing Office, August 1976.

Talbot, Nathan B. *Raising Children in Modern America: Problems and Prospective Solutions.* Boston: Little, Brown, 1976.

Tyack, David B. *The One Best System: A History of American Urban Education.* Cambridge, MA: Harvard University Press, 1974.

Unger, Roberto. *Knowledge and Politics.* Glencoe, IL: Free Press, 1974.

Weil, Simone. *The Need for Roots.* New York: G. P. Putnam, 1952.

Weiler, Daniel. *A Public School Voucher Demonstration: The First Year at Alum Rock.* Santa Monica, CA: Rand Corporation, 1974.

Weintraub, Sidney, ed. *Income Inequality.* Philadelphia: American Academy of Political and Social Science, 1973.

Wertheimer, Jack, ed. *Family Matters: Jewish Education in an Age of Choice.* Waltham, MA: Brandeis University Press, 2007.

Whitehead, Alfred North. *The Aims of Education and Other Essays.* Glencoe, IL: Free Press, 1929.

———. *Science and the Modern World.* New York: Mentor, New American Library, 1954.

Wilms, Wellford W. *Public and Proprietary Vocational Training: A Study of Effectiveness.* Berkeley, CA: Center for Research and Development in Higher Education, 1974.

Wilson, Edmund. *To the Finland Station.* Garden City, NY: Doubleday, 1949.

Wise, Michael B., ed. *Desegregation in Education: A Directory of Reported Federal Decisions.* Notre Dame, IN: Center for Civil Rights, 1977.

Wolfe, Alan, ed. *School Choice: The Moral Debate.* Princeton, NJ: Princeton University Press, 2003.

Wolff, Robert Paul. *The Poverty of Liberalism.* Boston: Beacon Press, 1968.

Is Choice or Government Conscription Better at Educating and Socializing the Poor?

Here are authors whose work is scholarly but more intensely relevant to the political issues of achieving choice for the not-so-rich. Some would prefer to include choice of private religious schools, some would limit choice to religiously barren "charter" schools designated "public." Some see all choice as the enemy of our society.

Brinig, Margaret F., and Nicole Stelle Garnett. *Lost Classroom, Lost Community: Catholic Schools' Importance in Urban America.* Chicago: University of Chicago Press, 2014.

Carnoy, Martin, and Henry M. Levin, eds. *The Limits of Educational Reform*. New York: D. McKay, 1976.

Carpenter, Dick M., Rebecca Keith, and Andrew D. Catt. "The Private School Landscape: The Effects of School Choice on Student Capacity and Composition." 3rd ed. EdChoice, November 2016. https://www.edchoice.org/wp-content/uploads/2016/11/2016-11_The-Private-School-Landscape_Update-18.pdf.

Catt, Andrew D., and Evan Rhinesmith. "Why Parents Choose: A Survey of Private School and School Choice Parents in Indiana." EdChoice, June 2016. https://www.edchoice.org/wp-content/uploads/2017/03/Why-Parents-Choose-A-Survey-of-Private-School-and-School-Choice-Parents-in-Indiana-by-Andrew-D.-Catt-and-Evan-Rhinesmith.pdf.

Chavis, Ben, and Carey Blakely. *Crazy Like a Fox: One Principal's Triumph in the Inner City*. New York: New American Library, 2010.

Chingos, Matthew, and Paul E. Peterson. "The Impact of School Vouchers on College Enrollment." Education Next (Hoover Institute), April 2012. https://www.educationnext.org/the-impact-of-school-vouchers-on-college-enrollment/.

Cicourel, Aaron, and John Kitsuse. *The Educational Decision-makers*. Indianapolis: Bobbs-Merrill, 1963.

Crittenden, Brian. *Parents, the State, and the Right to Educate*. Melbourne, Australia: Melbourne University Press, 1988.

Fantini, Mario D. *Public Schools of Choice*. New York: Simon and Schuster, 1973.

Ford, Virginia Walden. "Back to School: The Transformational Impact of School Vouchers." *The Daily Signal* (Heritage Foundation), April 26, 2014. https://www.dailysignal.com/2014/08/26/back-school-transformational-impact-school-vouchers/.

Forster, Greg. "Segregation Levels in Milwaukee Public Schools and the Milwaukee Voucher Program." EdChoice, August 2008. http://www.edchoice.org/wp-content/uploads/2015/09/Segregation-Levels-in-Milwaukee-Public-Schools-and-the-Milwaukee-Voucher-Program.pdf.

———. "A Win-Win Solution: The Empirical Evidence on School Choice." EdChoice, May 2016. http://www.edchoice.org/wp-content/uploads/2016/05/A-Win-Win-Solution-The-Empirical-Evidence-on-School-Choice.pdf.

Forster, Greg, and Matthew Carr. "Disruptive Behavior: An Empirical Evaluation of School Misconduct and Market Accountability." EdChoice, June 2007. http://www.edchoice.org/wp-content/uploads/2015/09/Disruptive-Behavior-School-Misconduct-and-Market-Accountability.pdf.

Galston, William A. *Liberal Pluralism: The Implications of Value Pluralism for Political Theory and Practice*. Cambridge: Cambridge University Press, 2002.

Greene, Jay P. "Vouchers in Charlotte." Education Next, Summer 2001. https://www.educationnext.org/vouchersincharlotte/.

Heft, James L. *Catholic High Schools: Facing the New Realities*. New York: Oxford University Press, 2011.

Hill, Paul T., ed. *Choice with Equity: An Assessment by the Koret Task Force on K–12 Education*. Stanford, CA: Hoover Institution Press, 2002.

Kahlenberg, Richard D. *All Together Now: Creating Middle Class Schools through Public Choice*. Washington, DC: Brookings, 2001.

Kelly, James P., III, and Benjamin Scafidi. "More Than Scores: An Analysis of Why and How Parents Choose Private Schools." EdChoice, November 2013. https://www.edchoice.org/wp-content/uploads/2015/07/More-Than-Scores.pdf.

Kozol, Jonathan. *Free Schools*. Boston: Houghton Mifflin, 1972.

Lieberman, Myron. *Public Education: An Autopsy*. Cambridge, MA: Harvard University Press, 1993.

McDermott, John E., ed. *Indeterminacy in Education*. Berkeley, CA: McCutchan, 1976.

McGarry, Daniel D., and Leo Ward. *Educational Freedom and the Case for Government Aid to Students in Independent Schools*. Milwaukee: Bruce Publishing, 1966.

McShane, Michael Q. "What Research Tells Us about School Vouchers." Statement before the Maryland House of Delegates Ways and Means Committee, February 27, 2013. https://www.aei.org/research-products/testimony/what-research-tells-us-about-school-vouchers/.

Moe, Terry M., ed. *Private Vouchers*. Stanford, CA: Hoover Institution Press, 1995.

Peterson, Paul E. *Saving Schools: From Horace Mann to Virtual Learning*. Boston: Harvard University Press, 2010.

Peterson, Paul E., and William G. Howell. *The Education Gap: Vouchers and Urban Schools*. Washington, DC: Brookings Institution Press, 2002.

Rouse, Cecilia Elena. "Private School Vouchers and Student Achievement." *Quarterly Journal of Economics* 113, no. 2 (1998): 553–603.

Salomone, Rosemary C. *Visions of Schooling: Conscience, Community, and Common Education*. New Haven, CT: Yale University Press, 2000.

Stewart, Thomas, and Patrick J. Wolf. *The School Choice Journey: School Vouchers and the Empowerment of Urban Families*. New York: Palgrave Macmillan, 2014.

Sugarman, Stephen D., and Frank R. Kemerer, eds. *School Choice and Social Controversy: Politics, Policy, and Law*. Washington, DC: Brookings, 1999.

Tooley, James. *The Beautiful Tree: A Personal Journey into How the World's Poorest People Are Educating Themselves*. Washington, DC: Cato Institute, 2009.

Walberg, Herbert J., *School Choice: The Findings*. Washington, DC: Cato Institute, 2007.

Watkins, Shanea. "Are Public or Private Schools Doing Better? How the NCES Study Is Being Misinterpreted." *Backgrounder*, no. 1968, Heritage Foundation, September 1, 2006.

Wolf, Patrick J., and Anna J. Egalite. "Pursuing Innovation: How Can Educational Choice Transform K–12 Education in the U.S.?" EdChoice, April 2006. https://www.edchoice.org/wp-content/uploads/2016/04/2016-4-Pursuing-Innovation-WEB-2.pdf.

Zimmerman, Jonathan. *Whose America? Culture Wars in the Public Schools*. Cambridge, MA: Harvard University Press, 2002.

Aquinas. *See* Thomas Aquinas, St.
Aquinas (Finnis), 156
Aristotle
  dignity and, 123
  equality and, 107
  gnosticism and, 153, 156
  goodness and, 107, 131, 150
  natural law theory and, 118–19,
    121, 131, 156
  obedience and, 150
  self-perfection and, 106, 121
Arons, Stephen, 72
Augustine of Hippo, St.
  goodness and, 107
  obedience and, 161, 176
  self-perfection and, 179
authority. *See* obedience; parental
    authority; sovereignty
autonomy
  academy and, 90
  accountability and, 13
  caring and, 13–14
  children's liberty and, 8–15, 17,
    33–34, 60–61, 187, 208–9
  civic education and, 4
  compulsory education and, 30,
    33, 79
  dignity and, 58
  diversity and, 25, 79
  First Amendment and, 22, 25
  historical development of, 5–7
  intellectual liberty, as core of,
    4–7, 23, 34
  lack of consensus on model for,
    24–25, 240n9
  liberal education and, 6, 23–24,
    74–75, 77
  love and, 13
  low-income students and, 61, 68
  moral autonomy, 177, 180
  nature of, 24–26
  neutral education and, 24–25

parental authority and, 9, 12, 171,
    177, 180, 187, 209, 241n13
  parental choice and, 15, 58, 64
  parental liberty and, 11–16, 61–62
  private education and, 69
  professional educators and, 61
  public education and, 21, 83, 210
  regulation and, 5–6
  religious rights of children and,
    175–76, 180
  school choice and, 54–55, 60–62,
    75, 82–83
  Supreme Court and, 6, 22, 27–28
  tolerance and, 25
  values and, 4–7, 24–25, 90, 178
  wealthy students and, 61, 64, 83

Barnes, Christopher, 169
Barth, Karl, 64, 157, 248n14
Beautiful Mind, A (film), 98
Bedford high school, 78–79
Bell Curve, The (Herrnstein and
    Murray), 124
Benedict XVI, 249n17
Blaine, James, 63, 143, 145, 195
Blaine Amendments, 143, 145, 195
*Board of Education, Island Trees
    Union Free School District No.
    26 v. Pico* (1981), 28–30, 32
Bonhoeffer, Dietrich, 149
Bowler, Mike, 20
Brennan, Patrick, 118–21, 158,
    248n14
Brennan, William, 29–32
Bridges, David, 19, 240n9, 241n12,
    241n14
Burt, Robert, 21–23

C. S. Lewis Foundation, 86
California Plan
  accessibility of education and, 41
  accreditation and, 43

New Schools and, 41, 43, 67
obedience and, 171–74
parental choice and, 61, 71,
  138–39
poverty as disabling circumstance
  and, 68
private education and, 68–70,
  113, 207, 213
public education and, 55–56,
  58–60, 63–64, 191–92, 195–96,
  229
regulation and, 73
religious education and,
  197–98
school choice and, 55–56, 58,
  63–64, 67–70, 72, 218, 229
sovereignty and, 191
teachers' unions and, 196
vouchers and, 72
luck, 98–99, 119, 167–69

Macedo, Stephen, 75–78
Madison, James, 5
Maine, Henry, 182
Mann, Horace, 63
Maritain, Jacques, 149, 157
Marx, Karl, 95, 238n2
materialism, 87–91, 100, 150,
  153
Meyer v. Nebraska (1923), 18,
  27–28
middle-class students, 67, 79,
  170–71, 229
Mill, J. S., 7
Moe, Terry, 54–55, 62, 69
moral development, 64, 71, 120,
  135, 140, 206, 223–24,
  249n16
moral luck, 98–99, 119
moral responsibility, 109, 176, 202,
  215–17
Moynihan, Daniel P., 72

*Mozert v. Hawkins County Board
  of Education* (1987), 76
multiculturalism, 169, 251n28

Nagel, Thomas, 119
National Education Association,
  72
natural gnosticism, 118–20, 132,
  245n12
natural law theory
  authenticity and, 121
  bell curve and, 124–25
  Catholicism and, 127, 156
  common sense tradition in,
    118–19, 121
  community and, 84, 125–28
  curriculum and, 84, 125
  dignity and, 107, 123–25
  diversity and, 132, 136
  equality and, 122–25
  fallibility and, 117, 121
  gnosticism and, 118–20, 124–25,
    129–33, 138, 156–57, 245n12
  God and, 119
  goodness and, 117–20, 123,
    129–40, 150–53, 156–59,
    162–63, 167–68
  inner self and, 120–22
  Integration tradition in, 119–20
  lessons for education and, 122–40
  moral luck and, 119
  obtension and, 118, 129–34,
    136–40
  organizing schools for, 131–32
  parental authority and, 135–36
  parental choice and, 136–40
  pluralism and, 132–40
  reason and, 120
  self-perfection and, 117–23,
    129–30, 132–36
  sovereignty and, 183–84
  Supreme Court and, 92–93

natural law theory (*cont.*)
  teachers and, 130, 133
  tolerance and, 129–31
  values and, 117, 121–22, 132–36
neutral education, 22–25, 56, 59–60,
    78, 104, 140
New Schools
  accessibility of education and, 41,
    67
  articles of incorporation and, 42
  cost saving measures of, 48
  curriculum and, 48, 50–51
  disabled students and, 41
  dismissals from, 44
  entrepreneurialism and, 46
  formation of, 46
  funding of education and, 41–44,
    46, 48, 52, 67
  initiative for, 50–53
  low-income students and, 41, 43,
    67
  management consultants and, 46
  middle-class students and, 67
  New Private Schools, 41–42, 48,
    50, 52
  New Public Schools, 41–42, 46,
    48, 50–51, 66–67
  overview of, 40–41
  regulation limited for, 42
  school boards and, 41
  structure of, 41–42
  teachers and, 46, 50
  teachers' unions and, 46
  traditional schooling distin-
    guished from, 41, 44, 46, 48
  values and, 51
  See also California Plan
New York v. Ferber (1982), 17
Nietzsche, Friedrich, 124, 131,
    245n11
Novak, Michael, 95
Nussbaum, Martha, 124

obedience
  accountability and, 166
  caring and, 166
  children's liberty and, 154–55
  Christianity and, 150
  civic education and, 169–70
  community and, 168
  conscience and, 160
  curriculum and, 168–74
  freedom and, 154–55
  gnosticism and, 153, 156–57,
    159–60, 162, 174
  God and, 154, 167
  goodness and, 150–53, 156–59,
    162–68
  holy innocents and, 161–62
  human nature and, 150
  knowledge and, 166
  low-income students and, 171–74
  luck and, 167–69
  materialism and, 150, 153
  middle-class students and, 170–71
  obtension and, 153, 157–59,
    162–63
  overview of, 149–50
  parental authority and, 164–71
  persona and, 152–53
  persons and, 152
  pluralism and, 178
  practice of, 164–66
  primary obedience, 155, 159–61,
    163–64
  public education and, 168–69, 173
  reason and, 150–53, 157–61
  relativism and, 150
  secondary obedience, 159–61,
    163–64
  selfhood and, 151–52
  self-perfection and, 150–53, 159,
    161
  theology of childhood and,
    161–62

parental liberty (*cont.*)
  First Amendment and, 16–17, 19,
    56–59
  knowledge and, 14–15, 62, 166,
    177
  limits of, 15–18
  professional educators and,
    61–62
  reasons for primacy of, 12–16,
    61–62
  school choice and, 56–57, 61–63,
    207–11, 217
  self-interest and, 12–15
  Supreme Court and, 16–18,
    26–27, 192
Pierce v. Society of Sisters (1925), 18,
  26–28, 75, 187–88, 190, 192–93,
  204, 216
Plato, 132, 165–66, 168, 178, 187
pluralism
  curriculum and, 113
  goodness and, 178
  natural law theory and, 132–40
  obedience and, 178
  obtension and, 133
  public education and, 208
  self-perfection and, 132–36
  tolerance and, 112
  See also values
Plyler v. Doe (1982), 6
*Politics, Markets, and America's
  Schools* (Chubb and Moe),
  54–55
Prince v. Massachusetts (1944),
  16
private education
  autonomy and, 69
  California Plan and, 40–43, 45
  caring and, 217
  civic education and, 217
  curriculum and, 24, 42, 66, 68, 70,
    79, 81, 113–14, 201, 223, 228

  equality and, 114
  funding of education and, 46–49,
    69
  God and, 195
  integration and, 65, 213
  liberal education and, 75
  low-income students and, 68–70,
    113, 207, 213
  New Private Schools, 41–42, 48,
    50, 52
  parental choice and, 195
  regulation and, 28, 66
  school choice and, 55, 64, 66,
    68–69
  Supreme Court and, 27–28
  tolerance and, 64, 112–14
  values and, 223
  vouchers and, 113, 216
  wealthy students and, 24, 56
professional educators, 12–14,
  61–62, 72, 210. *See also* teachers
professionalism, 40, 45, 81
Protestantism, 55–56, 76, 80, 94, 98,
  116, 141, 194, 207
public education
  accessibility of education and,
    36–37, 56, 83–84, 195
  autonomy and, 21, 83, 210
  California Plan and, 40
  caring and, 217
  censorship and, 60
  charter schools and, 143–45, 235
  children's liberty and, 37–40
  civic education and, 132, 191–92
  community and, 111–16
  compulsory education and, 18,
    32, 34
  conscience and, 191
  curriculum and, 24, 28, 59–60, 83,
    135, 168–69, 205–8, 228
  deliverance defense of, 21–27
  democratic mythology of, 37–38

JOHN E. COONS is the Robert L. Bridges Professor of Law (Emeritus) at Berkeley Law, University of California, Berkeley.

NICOLE STELLE GARNETT is the John P. Murphy Foundation Professor of Law at the Law School, University of Notre Dame.

RICHARD W. GARNETT is the Paul J. Schierl/Fort Howard Corporation Professor of Law, concurrent professor of political science, and the director of the Program on Church, State, and Society at the Law School, University of Notre Dame.

ERNEST MORRELL is the Coyle Professor in Literary Education, professor of English, professor of Africana studies, and director of the Notre Dame Center for Literary Education at the University of Notre Dame.

CPSIA information can be obtained
at www.ICGtesting.com
Printed in the USA
LVHW081507260123
738002LV00004B/208

9 780268 204846